T0367379

Chopping
the Onion

DUSANA MICHAELS

BALBOA.
PRESS

A DIVISION OF HAY HOUSE

Balboa Press books may be ordered through booksellers or by contacting:

Balboa Press
A Division of Hay House
1663 Liberty Drive
Bloomington, IN 47403
www.balboapress.com
1 (877) 407-4847

Because of the dynamic nature of the Internet, any web addresses or
links contained in this book may have changed since publication and
may no longer be valid. The views expressed in this work are solely those
of the author and do not necessarily reflect the views of the publisher,
and the publisher hereby disclaims any responsibility for them.

The author of this book does not dispense medical advice or prescribe the use
of any technique as a form of treatment for physical, emotional, or medical
problems without the advice of a physician, either directly or indirectly. The
intent of the author is only to offer information of a general nature to help
you in your quest for emotional and spiritual well-being. In the event you use
any of the information in this book for yourself, which is your constitutional
right, the author and the publisher assume no responsibility for your actions.

Any people depicted in stock imagery provided by Thinkstock are models,
and such images are being used for illustrative purposes only.
Certain stock imagery © Thinkstock.

Printed in the United States of America.

ISBN: 978-1-4525-8485-0 (sc)
ISBN: 978-1-4525-8487-4 (hc)
ISBN: 978-1-4525-8486-7 (e)

Library of Congress Control Number: 2013919077

Balboa Press rev. date: 11/06/2013

TABLE OF CONTENTS

DEDICATION

Ah Lois, he had said, there is in life a suffering so unspeakable, a vulnerability so extreme that it goes far beyond words, beyond explanations and even beyond healing. In the face of such suffering all we can do is bear witness so no one need suffer alone. (Remen, 2000 p. 105)

To the survivors braving this path and the witnesses of our journey.

PREFACE

Once upon a time there was a beautiful little girl who lived in the village of Evil. She was a perfect child with eyes as blue as the sea. She had a smile for everyone she met and was love itself. When she walked into a room it was like a breath of fresh air had entered. Everyone noticed her for she was like the sun shedding light onto everything she touched. The world vibrated just because she was in it. Exceptional was the only word to describe such a child.

Unfortunately in this village there lived a monster that came at night. During the day the monster was as sweet a man as could be found and he gave her whatever she wanted. But the monster hated all the love she had to give. What kind of life could such a beautiful person have? She was bound to get hurt so he decided to kill her. He had to destroy the little girl for her own good.

The monster would come and do things to the little girl that he could never imagine doing during the day. He made sure she felt dirty, ugly and bad. It had to be her fault that the sweet man turned into such a monster. She was the one forcing him to perform disgusting acts and she enjoyed it. She wasn't the beautiful child that everyone thought she was—she was evil. Why else would he treat her so inhumanely? The monster hit her and told her she was a wicked child for coercing him to behave so horrendously.

It didn't take long for clouds to cover the village. The sunshine went away as the little girl died. Her smile was lost as her world slowly crumbled. Gloom and misery spread through the village as the once beautiful child evolved into a plastic doll who did everything right. The child who had been a joy to be around grew into a cold void. She was going through the motions but the life in her was gone.

The sweet man walked around like a peacock for what the monster had accomplished. Now the child was just a doll and nothing could hurt her. He was unable to understand that the monster did more harm to her than the entire world ever could. Believing his love for the child killed her, he felt she was finally safe.

However, the beautiful child never did fully die. She hid deep inside the doll until she could escape and start her own life. Incredible things happened to her and she came out to brighten up the world.

One day the doll will be entirely gone and only the little girl will remain. Her love will shine down once more and nothing will destroy her ever again.

INTRODUCTION

For the first 23 years of my life I thought I had a happy childhood. It has taken another 23 years for me to appreciate that part of my life again. The time in between has been a heart-wrenching journey that I have not been sure I ever wanted to write down. Even as I write this, I'm still not sure. Will the world understand what my story is and why I feel compelled to share it?

The contention between the person who had ingrained into her the effects of abuse and the beautiful person I was born to be has been waged within my soul and documented in my journals. Somewhere within me I knew there was a part that had never been touched. Then there was the body that has been ravaged with doubt and pain: emotional, mental, physical and spiritual. The incessant question of a human being dealing with earthly problems versus the spirit able to transcend it all—which one was truly me? I have seen this struggle repeated from one end of the spectrum to the other as I healed through the years.

How does one heal from incest? Slowly, gently and very carefully. It's a precarious tightrope walk to confront the demons ever ready to raise their heads and take you down. The mental anguish of self-destructive beliefs incorporated to make sense of the unimaginable. Emotions that have torn me apart from the inside, sometimes to the point of retching. The embodiment of physical ailments as the emotions and thoughts attempted to find a form of expression that could be heard. And the ensuing spiritual crisis resulting from searching for answers to the questions: where was God when I needed Him, how do I learn to love and trust again and what does it mean to forgive?

Incest has never been anything I would wish upon my worst enemy. I am still trying to make sense of it all. I've needed this time to gain distance and perspective in order to gleam a new wisdom from the experience. My attitude has been able to change from being burdened and put upon by the actions of others to it being a part of my life that occasionally needs attention. Accepting the process as on-going recovery instead of the proverbial mountain that needs to be climbed and conquered. It never goes away and triggers provide a chance to heal pieces of myself that once had a function for survival, but were now hindering my growth toward wholeness. New situations and stages in life bring opportunities for the continuous healing that accompanies recovery from trauma. I've found a deeper understanding regarding the effects of the abuse as I've healed my unhealthy coping skills. In each situation, I've lived my way to what was empowering and freeing as surviving evolved into thriving.

The day I found my sense of humor about what I had been through was the day grace entered my life. I was finally able to ask, seriously, you expect me to go along with and believe what? I don't think so. I often chuckle at the absurdity of the human condition and all its incarnations. It's what keeps me sane.

In order to answer the question, *why write this down now*, I need to take a step back. I've always known I've needed to write a book about my experience. I have started it countless times. I've been writing it in my head for years. I had a title for it and felt a pang when other people talked about writing a book that accompanied my inner voice saying, but I have a book.

When I was in college, a friend of my sister's talked about spirit or an inner knowing that would wake you up at a specific time without setting an alarm clock. This information appealed to my desire to use the 90% of the brain's capacity that most humans never access. It spoke to a level of trust in the unseen I didn't currently have. It meant giving up a little bit of my belief in the tangible world around me. It started my journey of listening to this other voice.

The voice speaks to me in many different ways. Sometimes it's a vision or intuition, other times it's auditory. The voice came through the loudest after I had been to a family weekend at a treatment center. My brother was starting recovery for drug and alcohol abuse and I decided to have an assessment while I was there. I didn't think there was a problem with my alcohol use but I was learning to live with integrity so I met with a counselor. I told her my drug of choice was sugar. She didn't want to do the assessment on sugar so the next drug was alcohol. After she was done she asked me if I would be surprised if it showed I was an alcoholic. I replied, yes. She let me know it did.

I left the office and admitted it to my parents, my sister and my brother. When I got home I let my friends know. They laughed. They informed me I was the one they were least concerned about.

One specifically told me, of all the people in her life, I was the most responsible drinker she knew. Based on the criteria of the counselor, everyone I knew was an alcoholic. I was processing the different sides of this issue when I heard the voice say, forgive yourself. In the decades that have passed, it was the loudest and clearest I ever heard this other voice.

During my 20s I learned to listen to this voice more and more. I asked for its guidance with remembering little things I needed to do. It gave warnings of events that were about to take place. It introduced people, books and ideas into my life that offered new and different perspectives. I didn't always listen to it and would regret when I ignored it. I learned to heed and trust what it had to tell me.

The year of 2009 became a turning point in my life. Everything was falling apart. I lost my job, the counseling center I opened was proving to be a failed business venture, sustaining relationships had not developed and the economy was tanking. Finally, the main reasons I had been staying where I lived weren't as pressing anymore.

I needed to make a dramatic change and was resisting the guidance being offered from the voice. I know how fast my life changes when I finally surrender to it and I wasn't sure I had the energy to make it happen. My usual kicking and screaming period wasn't making the prompting go away so at last I agreed, okay I'll do it.

Once I stopped fighting the flow wanting to happen in my life, I was able to tackle each problem set before me. I knew I needed to physically move and each step I took brought me closer to that reality. I left only the essentials as I packed up my house. I re-painted and fixed and gave away and cleaned. I envisioned and dreamt of living in Denver. Energetically I was already gone, now to get my body there. I put my house on the market in January of 2010. Two weeks later it was under contract. Within three months of willingly surrendering my life towards moving in a new direction, I was living in Denver.

As part of my process I made a vision board with things that spoke to me instead of my life looking a specific way. Most were obscure images I have spent the past three years of my life living my way to the answers. I'd put it away for a time and then would bring it back out. Each time it made more sense as situations presented themselves to bring clarity from the obscure. Two prominent features on the vision board were a typewriter and a keyboard. Since making it I've been joking with friends, whatever could they mean? Though the signs were clear, I wasn't ready to write. I went down my own path.

I took temporary work as a Census Enumerator and spent the rest of my time looking for a job while ignoring the writing message. In July I took the first one I was offered. It had taken a few months longer than expected and I was feeling desperate. Still it was something I could do or learn to do. I knew it offered skills I'd wanted to learn and an opportunity for growth in areas where I felt insecure and unsure of myself.

I started teaching English as a Second Language for a Family Literacy Program within an elementary school in the Aurora Public School District. My students were the adult parents of the children within the school. Family Literacy offers the opportunity for parents to understand the United States school system, learn the teaching techniques used in the classroom, practice helping their children with homework and learning the English language to become independent contributing members of society. The majority of my co-workers and students responded well to my overtures but all it takes is one who doesn't.

Going down my own path ended up presenting situations in my work life that allowed me to hear messages planted long ago in my mind. Interpersonal dynamics with people played themselves out and the little triggers I was experiencing grew to a point I could no longer ignore.

I was reminded of how I had been treated as a child and it hurt to the core. I felt incredibly intense emotions—they hadn't been this bad in years. The questions repeated in my head of 'How do people know? What is it about me that they can disrespect me as a person and disregard my boundaries? What is it about me that makes it okay to treat me like this?' All the times it has happened to me as an adult came rushing back and flooded me mentally and emotionally.

I have worked so hard through the years with healing the wound. It has been my goal to feel my feelings in such a complete way that the issue gets resolved. That every hurt I experienced as a child gets the attention it needs to fully heal. Yet here it is once again. Why? What haven't I looked at?

During the spring of 2012, a close friend was diagnosed with terminal cancer. I spent a lot of time with him as his health deteriorated until his death in July. I was close to his daughter as well and, having lost her mother seven years before, I knew she had a lot of challenges ahead of her. I wanted to do what I could for his family. I asked him questions which I wrote down the answers for in a journal so she would still have a part of him when she's older. It was a poignant time for me and one I will cherish for the rest of my life.

My journey continued with making changes for a more fulfilling life and answering the question, how do I want to be living? I spent the summer looking for a job back in the counseling field thinking it would bring me to the path my soul needed to continue growing. The school year was looming closer as I waited to find out the results of interviews. No offer came and I went back to the teaching job I was ready to move on from.

I was still working in Aurora, CO as the fall semester started in August of 2012. Our community had been hit hard with the shootings at the movie theater and I felt I knew why the school needed me there. I was a familiar and consistent face for the children and their parents. I helped to stabilize the fears and concerns as we tried to get things back to normal.

The tension in the school became unbearable as the fall semester progressed. Interpersonal dynamics continued to trigger my incest issues as I felt blamed for things I didn't do and unsupported with my struggles. As others were trying to control everything happening within the building, I saw the parallels with the dynamics from my family of origin. Thoughts of what my dad had done to me ran through my head. I still didn't understand how a father could do that to his daughter. I thought of how my dad dealt with his stress. I kept hearing *shut up and take it.* There was no support; no one sided with me. I was being massively triggered. Friends were worried about me and I felt like I was hanging on by a thread. I wanted out of there. I needed a new job.

I gave notice and quit without having anything lined up. I trusted if I heeded the message from the voice, I would be taken care of. I knew what I needed to do. I needed to write. It had been coming for a long time. Subsequently, two checks arrived with money owed to me and I was financially set for several months.

I found all the journals I've kept through the years and started to read them. I looked for a place to start—print it out and answer the questions. They were repetitive—so let's add more and answer those too. If I write it out will it finally be put to rest? Even that question had been asked before.

I was amazed at the brilliance I displayed at a young age and the vast insecurity. One makes me wonder where it came from while the other makes me cringe. I want to hold that young woman and let her know it'll all be okay. The other makes sense as the foundation that would support the journey I was about to embark on. I had to feel my way through the lowest lows in order to experience the highest highs. Though I've found the journals include more of the lows than the highs.

I was never heard. I was never seen. These can still be two triggers for me that cause anxiety. I have been silenced. I have been taught not to talk. Not to speak up. Not to be. I go along with what is expected of me. I have gone along with the masses. Show up, shut up, and smile. It is the tip of the iceberg interacting with the world.

What has happened to me? I've made it too convenient for them to blame me for what others did. I live out this scenario over and over in my life. It's funny how much of a trigger that has become for me. I can't stand to be blamed for something that I didn't do. Will writing this bring the needed peace that has averted me all these years?

I see my strength when I started this journey and wonder how I ever let it be taken away again. This is what is hurting now. I feel I've let myself down. I feel I haven't been there for the young girl that lives inside me who was hurt so badly by others. Has my silence been any different from my family's?

I understand how it became easier and safer to stop talking. Secondary wounding,* acceptance of what is and hope for what could be all played a part in it. But I can't do this anymore. Once more I embark on a journey that needs to be done. I am listening to the inner voice that is telling me it is time.

The 2013 entries interspersed within earlier entries are my current reflection back on my experiences. I've intentionally kept the journal entries, for the most part, as I wrote them at the time. They were my process and I was not concerned with using correct grammar or punctuation. Here and there I changed a word for clarity but, by keeping them intact, I hope the experience of my healing is clearer. Within paragraphs the verb tense changes as I wrestle the past from the present. I have not always included the entire passage under a specific date and names have been changed. It can be seen through the months and years the repetitive unconscious beliefs running through my head. This time was needed to admit the horrors of incest to myself and

---

* Discussed later.

challenge them with new beliefs and perceptions. I learned to live in the present without being haunted by the past.

I know mine is not a typical journey for someone who has lived through incest. There are many factors involved in its effects upon someone's life. How long it happened, how many abusers, whether help or support was given and whether the survivor was believed all play a role in recovery. This is my story and experience and is not indicative of every survivor nor does it advise how healing and recovery should proceed.

What lies behind us and what lies before us are tiny matters compared to what lies within us.

~Ralph Waldo Emerson

INKLINGS

2013

I'm older now, 16 or 17. Though I know it's not what woke me up, I become aware of my father leaving my bedroom. He runs into my oldest brother. As I hear them exchange greetings I have the thought, that hasn't happened in a long time. What *that* entailed I was uncertain but I remember thinking, that's an odd thought...

4/7/84

I've decided that I've got to start living my own life. No one else can make life easier for me than me...

9/12/88

Once again I've decided to get my life in order. I must learn a self-love and realize I'm only human. A lot of people don't understand it but I feel a need to finally come to terms with myself. Maybe deep down it really is a copout, but I don't think so. I need to realize the inner strength other people see in me. I've made a lot of choices in my life that I must now learn from. I am self-sufficient. My true colors must come out. The next year is my time to grow from within. This self-search does feel right for me and whatever anyone else says about it doesn't make it wrong. By getting to know myself, I can help mankind. I must love myself in order to love others. Maybe my little help can open the eyes of my friends and spread the word of love.

I've had a lot of other people get to know and love me. Now I must get to know and love me. It's not my place to judge others nor should I worry about their judgments of me. It's what I feel that matters. I can't please everyone so I'd better learn to please myself. What I'm doing is not wrong just because other people follow *tradition*. In learning about myself, I'll learn what to do. How to affect the world. I must start from myself and grow in order to grow outwards. Maybe my sole reason for this life is self-knowledge so I can guide others to the same self-knowledge.

6/6/90

I need to change and I'm hoping by writing it down it'll become easier. I didn't realize it but I do have low self-worth. I love myself but don't think I'm worthy of people's respect. I have a hard time standing up for myself and getting what I need. I really need to change and I know it'll be slow so I have to be patient. I have a hard time getting what I need out of my friends and family. I have to figure out why I'm afraid to hurt people's feelings. I think I'm afraid of them abandoning me. But that's a risk I have to take in order for the relationship to grow. I do deserve to get what I need out of relationships.

I keep on feeling I need to do things for my family.* I think I do it to get the family together and close. I also do it to be

---

* I am the youngest of five children.

important and the center of attention. But I can't make the entire family better, just myself. I can't stop the alcoholism. No matter how good I am, I can't make anyone stop drinking. I can't fix the family's dysfunction. I can only stop my own.

7/10/90

My family is really fucked up. Steven is crazy. The alcoholism is making him insane. I don't think he's in touch with reality at all. Steven and Charlie* are so obnoxious. Steven's got to mellow out. I can't do anything about their craziness.

I'm feeling sad about my whole family. And I can't help them. I need to stay away from them. I can handle them one-on-one but forget all of them together. Is it me? Is it them? It's too much for me to handle when they're all together. It's them. I'm learning to take care of me.

I am not the caretaker of the family. My family isn't right and I don't know if they ever will be. But this doesn't mean I have to put up with it.

I think I've got to break away from them. I can't be around them. It hurts too much. Or I can be around them in small doses. Just because they can't change doesn't mean I have to accept it or figure they are all I have so I'd better put up with it.

First, let's think of what I wish we were like:

- I'd like us all to relate and talk to one another differently
- I wish we were all on the same level of communication

---

* Out of the five children, Steven is the middle child and Charlie is second youngest.

- I don't think that any of us really appreciate each other. Is it a TV fantasy I want?
- I wish it would be more relaxing when we're together
- I wish we could talk to one another

We talk but does anyone listen? The one thing we do talk about is the family business. There is no way any monetary value is worth the price paid by all the family. No amount of money can make up for the trouble that damn company has cost. It makes me sick.

I need some sanity in my life. Help me be a better person. I haven't been patient lately. I can only save me, no one else. I'm the sane one. I'm the one who can get me out of it. I LOVE ME!

2011 about the fall of 1990

I was standing behind the bar on a quiet autumn afternoon. It wasn't time for the after work crowd to commence and the lunch crowd had long gone. The bar was stocked and the glasses washed. As I gazed out over the lake I once again thought, is this all there is? It seemed to be the focus of my life, to be unsatisfied with work and friends and family. I had the odd feeling that I was missing something. There was something hidden below the surface. On some level, I was aware of two things: it involved sex and it involved my father. It would take another six months for the memories to start coming forth from my body.

I could feel the long-forgotten rumblings of terror pushing their way slowly to the surface. I had been putting on a smiling face for so long at this point that I had no way of knowing

4

my happy childhood would soon crumble like a building being demolished by dynamite. What once stood strong and tall would be wiped out with the slightest push of a button.

I can laugh now at my cluelessness as decades cushion the event. The horrors of incest were not something that entered my mind. I couldn't fathom having an experience where I could feel the paws of madness grabbing me. The mental attention I needed to stay present and not descend into the webs of insanity-provoking confusion threatening to entangle me as things were done to my body that were incomprehensible to a ten year old. What was it that could possess my beloved father to hurt me so? What was he doing? What is that? What did I do and how do I get him to stop? The stifled screams burn in my chest and throat to this very day. My defenses eventually took over as I learned to leave the moment and repress what I could not understand.

My body feels thin like a piece of paper as I lay flat on the ground looking up. I hope for a slight breeze to come along and take me where it wants to go. Anywhere but here. Get me away from this situation. How many times will this plea be thought throughout my life? Flattened by the enormity of it all and unable to gather the wherewithal to change it. Hoping someone would find the piece of paper and pick it up to fold it away in a pocket. Tucking it away where no one can find and hurt it again.

9/14/90

I'm mad at Dad and I need to figure out why and put it past me. I don't like the way he treats my mom, yet she allows herself to be treated that way. He's such a selfish bastard who doesn't have anything to give. It's always him, him, him. I guess it just hurts because he can't give of himself. Does Dad know what to do in a crisis? Dad cannot give of himself. Mom deserves better. What I have to do is not expect anything from him. Poor Mom, she has needs too. It's only his life that is important. Dad is like a spoiled child who expects everyone around him to bow down to him. I don't want or need that in a man. My life will be equally important. I will not bow down to him for I am a human being and my life is just as important as his.

11/29/90

Help me find the way Jesus. I'm lost. I've let the incredible giving part of me go. It's such a good feeling to give. I like to be good, I love giving to others. I love loving others. Thank you for not expecting us to like everyone. I feel it back now, thank you. I feel so lost when I lose the love. I forget that all I have to do is ask. You never leave, I do.

12/15/90

Core-self is shame-based:

I have a hard time asking people for help or their time because I don't feel important enough for others to waste their time on me. I am special and others are better off knowing me. I'm not used to any time being spent on me. Others lives have always felt more important than mine. Other people's time was always worth more than my time. Damn it, I am not worthless. If people can't make time for me then fuck them. I am very much worth other people's time. It is my right as a human being to ask for the time

I need from others. If they can't give it to me it's their loss. I am worth it.

I am also worth my own time. I am a very incredible person! I am not worthless and I will not let myself think I am.

Other-ation:

I put too much emphasis on my looks and I don't put enough attention on the strong, beautiful person I am on the inside. Yet I hate it when others only do pay attention to my looks. I kind of hide behind my glasses so I am not just another pretty face. I don't come across to others as the strong person that I am.

I am the lost child. I am a life spectator. If I'm not comfortable with people, I don't join in. I sit on the sidelines. It is only with people I am comfortable with that I am able to join in the fun. I disappear or I blend in when I am in a crowd. I don't know how to act in crowds. I never know what it is I should be doing. I don't have my true self. I am acting my way through life. I don't know how to have fun in a group of strangers.

Extremes:

I either have no sexual encounters or I let men have my body when I don't want them to.

I give of myself so others will like me. I don't listen to my inner voice enough. This has got to stop. I am worth it. I want to know my true self and quit living this lie. God help me find me. I've got to stop living for others. It's my life that's important. I don't want to live for anyone else anymore. I want to live for me. I am here. This is my life. It's my life and I have a right to live it the way that's right for me. It's my life, it's my life. I can't help you, only you can. I can only help me. I'm not here for anyone else but me.

12/31/90

This past year has been wonderful. I've definitely become a better, more whole person. That is what I want to continue doing into 1991. I truly love myself now. I'm getting to know myself and I like what I know. Life really is amazing.

What I want for 1991:

- To appreciate life
- To enjoy the moment
- Passion for living
- Increased confidence in myself
- Become a whole person
- Know myself even better
- Recognize my needs and get them met
- Develop more intimate, deeper relationships with healthy people
- Appreciate the friends I have
- Be less critical of my family members
- Give more of myself to others in need without jeopardizing myself
- Set boundaries between myself and others
- The ability to receive gifts from others
- Let others know me better
- Recognize my feelings and let them out in a healthy manner

- Develop a stronger, more flexible: body, mind, and soul
- Ability to forgive past hurts
- Honesty with myself and others
- More healthy eating habits
- Trust myself that I am not going to let anything happen to me
- Trust appropriate people
- Listen to my intuition
- Become closer to nature
- Be more Christ-like
- Love all my brothers and sisters
- Generate love
- Be at peace with myself
- Accept myself just as I am
- Every man to love himself
- Mankind to respect himself and others
- Peace on this planet and in the universe
- Mankind to respect and follow nature's example
- Get a job I enjoy
- Treat others as I want to be treated
- Get into an intimate, healthy relationship with a man
- Learn my full capabilities
- Know that I can attain what I want
- Get rid of the junk I don't need
- Let go of things I have no control of
- Be more direct with people
- Have fun
- Let little Dusana play

- Give up some of my responsibility to others
- Walk 15-20 miles a week
- Start dance lessons when my body is ready
- Go someplace I've always wanted to go
- Develop my own interests and likes
- Let the world be my playground
- Keep it simple
- Lower my percentage of body fat
- Be open to others
- Surround myself with love
- Be happy
- Surround myself with good things
- Treat myself with TLC
- Ability to ask for what I need from others who can give it to me
- Stand up for my rights
- Not allow others to violate my rights
- Directly confront those who have violated my rights
- Respect I deserve

2/2/91

It's very interesting what I'm going through right now. I have a slightly inflamed hip that's making it a little difficult to get around. It's really not that limiting but it's bringing back some issues from having arthritis* when I was young. My world doesn't

---

* After a misdiagnosis at age eight, I was diagnosed with Juvenile Rheumatoid Arthritis at twelve.

stop because of this ailment. It's frustrating but I haven't slipped back into self-pity. The world does keep on spinning.

It's fine to have this and it doesn't make me any less of a person. I'm still the same person and that is great, all of me is great the way it is. No matter what I look like, I am still the same special person. I'm perfect the way I am.

I've just got to figure out why this happened.

It's slowed me down. It's made me less mobile. It's forced me to sit and spend time on me. It's inflamed. Part of my life isn't moving smoothly or working for me. Alright, this will be painful but let's go through it.*

I haven't been moving toward wholeness as quickly. I've started to treat people not as good as they should be treated. I've gotten to be more immature also. I'm a bird that needs to be set free to soar to new heights. I need my passion for life back.

Help me Jesus. Help me get it back. Open me up to others again. Let me feel the peace, love, and understanding again. Or more appropriately, don't let me lose it again.

It's always there, people just don't always take it. Especially now we need a kinder, gentler world and people. There are over 5 billion of us on this planet, we'd better start learning to live with each other. I love myself and accept myself unconditionally. I love myself unconditionally and I accept myself unconditionally. I love others and I accept others unconditionally.

---

* Unfortunately no sign popped up stating, beware what you wish for.

2/13/91

Why am I sad? I feel something's wrong with me. I feel like a mistake or unworthy. I deserve love and attention. I have to open myself up to it.

Does anyone really care? I care what happens to me. I'm the only one who can change it. I'm never going to get the world's approval. My life is not a joke. It's mine.

I'd better find happiness within or I'm never going to find it outside. I want to feel love. I've been outside it too long. I am a very beautiful person. I want pure love to enter my life. I'm sick of all the hate and pain. I just want love and acceptance. Help me discover the love around me.

Open up, feel it, let it flow through my veins. I want every cell to feel love. Quit holding it in. Let it flow. Let go and let God. I am a being very capable of giving and receiving love. Let it flow in and back out of me. I just want love in my life. Help me start seeing the love all around me. Open me up.

SURFACING

3/9/91

I'm feeling down today. I have to get to the root of this so I can parent the child that is crying out. I am not that child but I am the survivor of that child and I am here to give that child what it needs.

I hated the way I was treated by my family. My family had no right to treat me that way. They robbed me of my spirit and my childhood. I was kept down and I wasn't able to grow the way I needed to. I need a break from my family for a while. It's something from childhood because I'm sitting on the floor. I need people on my side right now.

3/12/91

I'm doing very positive things for myself right now. I'm giving me time, goals, permission to have fun, patience, and respect.

I'm cleaning out my apartment. Getting rid of the clutter. I'm doing that in my life too, keeping what I need and trying to get rid of the rest.

I love the person I've become. I am very independent and keep my power in more situations. When I give it away, I recognize it faster and am able to change or realize that's not how I want to be.

I've been mourning the loss of my childhood family and my spirit. It really is hard not having the supportive family I need.

I'm thankful I've done the work and had the courage to become more healthy. I am alive and that's enough. There is so much to discover in this world, I must never think I know it all. There is so much to experience. I must break down more of my walls and bring it in. It never ends, there's always more to do. Let's open this body and soul up to receive life.

4/8/91

Things are still going well. I don't feel a need to write but I wanted to so I could catch up on some important things that have happened in the last month. I started in a support group and will be starting in therapy to deal with the sexual abuse I had as a child from Kevin* and as an adult from Charlie. The first few days were hard because of the intensity of the anger. But it is very positive to get this out and get on with my life. And because of it I am able to value my friends better. I know whom I can trust and rely on and whom I am not ready to. I'm also dealing with my family better and finding a balance between getting what I want and giving what I can to them. I feel I have actually achieved some healthy adult relationships.

Boy I've come a long way. I really love my life and who I have become. I'm keeping my power more and more and talking about things when they aren't quite right. I don't let people walk all over

---

* Kevin is the second oldest child.

me either. I really am getting what I need from others and giving what I can to them.

4/18/91

Self-esteem and personal power:

My self-esteem is very good and I know I have the power to choose. I know that there is always something that I can do. Rarely do I want to be someone else. I know that I am human and will make mistakes but I am trying to be a better person. I also know that I am responsible for my actions.

Feelings:

This is a hard one for me. I don't always recognize my feelings and, when I do, I don't know what to do with them. I usually eat them away. I don't always feel that I am worth it to tell someone when they've done me wrong. Or I feel that they won't like me. I usually react physically instead of verbally when someone's done me wrong. I need to start speaking up. I'll start by expressing myself, if even a little bit, the next time I feel like slapping someone*. Or when I get an uncomfortable feeling when someone's talking to me. I need to verbalize when someone is stepping on me.

Body:

I have a good body image when I have my clothes on. I am critical of it in the nude and I am insecure about men seeing it. I think I have arthritis because of the abuse. I started to get symptoms within six months of the abuse. I have tried to commit

---

* Internal impulse of wanting to slap someone.

suicide but I could never do that now. I know my body is one incredible machine. I love being physical with my body. I feel present in my body most of the time. I'm concerned about any drug I put in my body be it aspirin, alcohol, caffeine, sugar, etc. I'm aware of messages my body sends me but I don't always listen to it. I need to respect this friend of mine.

4/24/91

I'm sick of people thinking they have power over someone else. I have power and control over every aspect of my life and I'm going to act on that. This is my life. No one is going to overpower me again. I'm going to exercise my power and control over my actions. That is all I'm responsible for in this life. I'm sick of men who are so afraid of women that they have the need to overpower them. It is so damn disrespectful. There isn't enough respect on this planet. People should exercise their own power instead of trying to take it away from someone else to make them feel important. Everyone has power.

I want a man who likes to be around both sexes. I was overpowered by grandpa* and my brothers and other men all these years but they can have it back. It's their own inferiority feelings that made them act that way but I can't heal them. I cannot think of one male that I know of that respects both sexes equally.

I want and need my own power instead of taking someone else's in order for me to feel that power. Thank you Lord for

---

* I had repressed the sexual abuse from my grandpa and had started to recover the memories.

giving me the gift of strength. I want my power. I own my power. It's mine, no one can take that away from me. It's mine!

I have free choice and I can do and act as I want. I just want to be. I'm Dusana. I AM. I was not put here so others could overpower me so they can feel better about themselves. I'm giving them back their inferiority. I don't want it anymore. I've had too much taken away from me. No one will take from me though I may choose to give. I give everyone their responsibility and control back to them. It's not mine and I don't want it anymore. I have me to worry about.

I give everyone their actions back. I'm not responsible for anyone else's actions nor do I want them. I give everyone their lives and freedom of choice back, it's not my responsibility and I don't want it. I don't want or need anyone else's junk. It's theirs, they can have it all back. It's not mine, it's not mine. Take it back, I don't want it anymore.

I am not responsible for your life. Leave now, get it out of here, it's not mine. I want whatever isn't mine out of this body and mind. It's not mine. It's yours, take it back, I don't want it. I want me. I AM! I AM! I AM! I don't want it anymore. It's yours to keep forever. It's not my responsibility anymore! Everyone just take it all back! This is my life. I won't take it anymore. It's yours and not mine and I won't take it anymore.

4/26/91

I want to feel. I am sad over something but I'm not sure what. I keep picking assholes to go out with. I could be mourning the end of a relationship. I'm also changing so I am mourning my old self. A close friendship is changing and I need to let go.

Why is it always us and them? This planet is a we. Why can't people be accepting of each other? People are so disrespectful. We are a sad group of animals. Sometimes I really hate being human. We turn and beat each other up whenever we can.

I just want to be. Look at how I judge people. We've all got problems. I'm as far as I can be right now. I'll change but this is where I currently am. I can't face it. I just am.

This is what is right for me now. I just want to be. It's all in the acceptance of myself and others. Things are going to change but this is where I am. No wonder I felt a split, I wasn't being. It always comes back to I am-ness. I feel much better. Thanks.

5/25/91

All right, so I'm sad again. It's a good emotion. Any emotion is good. I am currently sad.

Life and its changes. We can't fight it, change just happens. What's going on in my life? Something is changing but I don't know what. I'm growing and attempting to become whole. On that endless process to wholeness. Keep it short and simple. Letting go of the old and welcoming the new. Why have I been so deep lately? I'm eating a lot and putting on weight. Why? I want to get away. Life and its changes, I can't run from me. I'm here. I have to face me. Let's look in the mirror. What's happening? What's changing? I've been mellow and deep in thought. With an underlying emotion of sadness.

I need to give up my old life but what does that mean? What do I need to give up right now? What do I need to change? I'm right here, I can't leave, there's no escaping me. What do I need to do? What is it? Why is it so hard to live with others?

Life is ever changing. Nothing remains the same. Life goes on. I'm here. I can never leave me. I'm the one person I can never leave.

What do I want? What am I after? Let's not be afraid to love.

When I project I fight and scream and use more energy "against" the other person. I'm selfish and like things my way. I'm close-minded about doing things just for the sake of doing something. I also make excuses for not doing things. I can be negative about trying new things. I need to expand my horizons and venture out of my little safe area. I'm trying. I need to be willing to hear other's suggestions and be open to them. There's more than Dusana's way to do things. It's all a give and take. An expansion and contraction. I need to remember that there are others around me.

Others can't get over my fears for me. They can offer support but I must do the work. I'm the one who has to stop being so selfish and negative. I guess I can admit to not always being right.

It can't be that everyone around me doesn't want to do things, they just don't want to do my things. I must be open and enter other people's world. And even though someone doesn't want to do what I want, it doesn't mean I can't. That's why I have so many different people in my life, so I can try everything I want to.

I must respect other people's limitations. We all have some sort of limitation. I guess I'm not the only one in the world and

I have to start thinking of others too. It's a great big world out there and there are many people to do many things with. I'm willing to try things in other people's world so I can expand my own.

I must make conscious when I am ranting and raving in my head and figure out who has the problem and the needs to change.* How come this integrating never ends? Because I am alive.

6/4/91

What am I feeling? Where am I? How am I going through life? Now what's going on? I'm okay.

6/11/91

What are my beliefs about relationships and men?

Relationships should be trusting with each person getting their needs met. My beliefs of relationships are healthy but not of men. I believe that men want sex right away from women. I believe that men don't want to take time or make the effort to work at a relationship. I believe men deserve more respect than me. I believe that men are right and you shouldn't stand up to them. I believe that men find my friends more attractive than me. I believe that men will be interested in my friends before me. I believe that I am bad in bed. I believe that others won't be interested in my life. I believe that no man wants me.

I believe myself to be sexy. I believe myself to be attractive.

---

* Projections I made on other people that I needed to own as my issue and not theirs.

6/13/91

Why do I feel that I am never enough? I am me! I never feel that I am good enough the way that I am. No matter how much someone loves me there always seems to be someone better. I'm trying to be the best I can. Why can't I find someone to love me for me? I always feel I'm being compared to someone else. Why do I always pick men that I feel just don't hit the mark? What/ who am I angry at? Help me God. I need help. Why am I never enough? I'm all I have. I'm not bad!

Victim:
- Ugly
- Powerless
- Bad
- Worthless
- Evil

Survivor:
- Beautiful
- Powerful
- Precious
- Valued
- Loving
- Trustful

7/16/91

I need more, I deserve more. I want more from this life. I want fun, adventure, different things. I want to know I'm alive. I'm here, it's my life. I can't hold me back for others. Either they come with or I leave them behind. I can't wait, I need to move on. Let it go.

I don't need to change for anyone. I'm fine the way I am. I'm perfect. I don't want someone who undermines me. I'm fine the way I am. I don't need to change. I'm fine. I can have all my thoughts and they're okay. They're mine. No one can undermine me, I'm fine, I'm perfect.

If something isn't right for me, that's great. You can't change me. I'm not perfect and that's perfect. I'm perfect the way I am. Everything changes but I'm fine today the way I am. I need a man to think I'm fine and perfect the way I am. I don't need to change but I will.

I don't need to explain myself. No one else has to, why do I? I don't have to do what others say. I'm right for me. I know what's right for me and I don't need to explain myself. I want people that accept my decision about my life without my need to explain my actions. What's right for me is my decision. I don't have to go with the flow.[*]

I can change. I need to change. No one can stop me, I'm changing. I know what's right for me. No one can tell me how to live. It's my life. Fully my life. You can't tell me what to do. I know what's right. No one can tell me what to do. Understand and accept me or leave. I need support. I know what I can and cannot do. What I need to do.

Don't force me to do anything I don't want to do. If you can't accept my decisions, that's your problem not mine. It's my life. I

---

[*] Gerbil-wheel thoughts/questions as it was very difficult and scary for me to challenge the status quo and move into my own vision for life.

know how to live it. I'm free to do what I want. I don't have to do what everyone else does. Has it gotten them anywhere? No. I know what's right for my life right now. You can't change me to fit your image. I have my own. Leave me alone. Let me go. You won't let me go. You won't let me change. I need to grow. I need good men in my life. I don't want your limited world.

My world is expanding. I'm going to change and you can't stop me. I'm moving on. I don't need it anymore. I'm done with that. I want more. I'm mad that you try to stop me. I'm going to change and you either come with or stay behind.

It's my turn. I'm choosing life. It's my turn to live, to thrive, to find me and you can't stop me. No one can.

Women hold the power. The power that counts. We hold this world together. Quit undermining my intelligence. Women aren't stupid. We aren't silly. We're great. We hold the power and you can't take it away. It's ours. I don't need you to think for me. I travel through this world just fine. The world is my playground. It's mine to discover. I need to show me the world before I can show it to someone else.

I feel I need a man to tell me I'm okay. I don't think I'm okay. I need outside affirmation of me. What others think is more important than what I think. I don't value myself. I can't have a limited image of myself when I am still discovering myself. I put others before myself. I have a higher value on men than on women. I get my value by being important in a man's life.

I put too much value on others, especially men, and not enough on myself. I don't feel I'm okay.

Worthless, bad, evil, ugly.

2013

As I read through my journals, I realized that I didn't write anything about what it was like to get a memory. I started the healing process only remembering what had happened with my brothers. When I opened this wound to look at it, memories of what my grandfather and father had also done came forth. During this time, I was too busy learning how to tolerate and regulate the emotions and images that were surfacing to write about it. I needed to learn how to gain control of them so they didn't take over the moments of my life. The emotions were seeping out of me uncontrollably at times.

My friends and I would often go and see a blues band. Blues music has been an accompaniment to my healing over the years as it touches my soul with a truth and understanding of despair and redemption. One particular Friday night, in the midst of accessing my past, I was sitting on a bar stool and another regular was sitting next to me. He was in front of me as we were both facing the band with the bar being to our right. At one point he turned around and asked me to stop it. He said he could feel the pain radiating off of me. If I remember correctly, he was a psychotherapist or counselor. I replied with something like, I wish I could. The next week he brought me a rose quartz which I still have to this day.

I'm not sure I can access the anxiety or exact emotions which proceed a memory nor do I really want to try. I've learned how to control them and shut them off as needed when they do pop up. The movie *The Fisher King* with Robin Williams accurately portrays the experience when the Red Knight is noticed on the periphery of life and starts chasing him. I knew it was coming and the "crazies" invaded my thinking. There was an anxiety and repetitive scattered-ness to my thinking as I tried in vain to keep the memory from surfacing.

I remember as I got one specifically horrifying memory I literally walked on the edge of insanity. And it was an edge. It took everything I had not to fall into what felt like an abyss because I knew I might not ever come back out. I held on moment-by-moment until I could get in to see my counselor who was able to walk through it with me. In the safety of her office, I was able to tell what I heard, saw and what I was doing. When it was done, all I could do was wonder: how do I incorporate this one into my life? What do I do with it?' Time answered the questions as more pieces of a puzzle I had to put together. It's still a disturbing memory in that it's so insane. It is so messed up.

I'm not including all of my obsessive thinking during these internal ranting and ravings. I'm chalking some of it up to the drama of being in my twenties. I learned how to work through the projections onto my friends and loved ones and draw out the nugget of truth I needed in order to grow. I am including the beliefs I was working through at the time as I assume I'm not the only person on the planet who has experienced them.

While I went through life as a functionally "normal" person, I had to learn how to interact in relationships in new ways. My quest was for a more genuine and healthy connection with other people and my life. I had to bring to light what I was doing, learn a healthier way to do things and then change my behavior accordingly.

There is no manual for healing that will answer all the questions about how you learn to proceed through your recovery. I used *The Courage to Heal* by Ellen Bass and Laura Davis for guidance on how to begin. Through the years I've learned that how it shows up in survivor's lives will be unique to the healing that needs to occur for that person. How often and how intense the lessons are presented in life cannot be predicted. Everyone's situation will be different and that needs to be respected.

For myself, I knew I had lived through the worst thing I could ever go through. It has given a freedom in its own way. I knew no one would ever hurt me as bad as I had been during my childhood. If I could survive that, I could survive anything. It didn't mean I wasn't overly cautious in some areas and I know for sure I hesitated from taking risks in other areas. I know how completely the world can be fooled by outward appearances versus what is actually happening behind closed doors. But that turned into another area of growth for me. On a whole different level, I feel safe in the world because no one can ever hurt me as bad.

I have never felt a need to get a gun for protection. I didn't want my protection to be something that could be taken away from me. I also knew, with the arthritis, that a gun would be hard for me to handle. I remember how shocked I was the day I realized I could kill someone. I had always thought of myself as a peaceful person. Then one day I found the cold-blooded killer inside. At that point I knew I should never own a gun *because* of the damage I could do with it. I know if I am ever physically attacked, this wound will get hit. I will either freeze or you will unleash a rage and psycho-ness that will bask in making you suffer. One of us is going down and it's not going to be me.

PICKING APART

8/1/91

What will happen to my family once I tell about the incest? Doesn't matter when you tell it, if you're young or old, you still destroy the family. Who will be on my side and who won't? Who will talk and who won't? What will happen to Mom and Dad's marriage? And why should I care?

I have to worry about myself but I also realize with these questions in the back of my head, they can be a hindrance to my healing. I can only worry about myself and not the people around me.

I feel the need to tell Charlie and Monica[*] since they are the first ones with children. Really the only family members I am worried about are Mom and Dad. Steven will want to deny it.

It really shatters a family. It's not fair that as the victim or survivor I'm the one who has to worry. I didn't do anything wrong. I'm not the one shattering the family, Dad did that a long time ago. I just can't ignore it anymore. I am not the one to blame. I am not going to be destroying the family, as a matter of fact I

---

[*]   Charlie's first wife.

may be bringing us closer together. There will definitely be that possibility but most importantly, another generation is at risk.

2013

The above thoughts still run through my head. I have lived my way to the answers for most of them but I am still concerned with how this will affect my family. It has always been my intention to live my life in such a way as to be helpful to the most people. Writing is an extension of that intention. What I am struggling with is 'will writing this potentially help more people than it hurts?'

8/13/91

What are the major issues I'm facing with the incest? I haven't trusted myself because "the what" I perceived in childhood was pretended not to be happening. My world around me and other's perceptions of it didn't match. I also couldn't trust myself because I thought I was a bad little child who had the power to make nice people do evil things. I also haven't thought I deserved any good in my life because I was an evil little girl. I don't accept the good things that happen to me because I am a good person. I have been afraid of opening up and letting people have the chance to get to know me because I was afraid they'd find out how bad I was.

I also don't trust others because I could never count on others to behave the way I thought they should. I don't trust men because they are only nice to you in order to get what they want. They were also two-faced and you never knew how they were going to act. I feel the need to give myself up and take care of others. This is because my needs were pushed aside for those around me. This also made me feel unimportant and not worthy of other people's time.

My sexuality has been blown out the window because I never did anything but I still provoked a sexual response out of men. Therefore I was never sure what it was exactly that I was doing that made men react to me that way. I am now afraid of men and the response I get out of them because I feel I am bad that I can get a man to respond to me that way. I also didn't have any power over what was done to me by men and I still feel that whatever they want is all that matters.

It was never let known that I mattered to anyone as a child. My needs were unimportant. I was just an object and I never knew that I was a person.

I am not an object to be abused! I am a human being and I have needs and wants just like the rest of the world. I do have a value as a human being! There are people that value me and meet my needs when I express them. I am not ignored anymore. My friends appreciate me and love me for who I am. I am a valuable and worthwhile person. I have value as a human being. I matter to the people around me. It would matter if I wasn't around. I am a good person. I'm worth it. I'm not here to kick around. I have my space on this planet and you can't invade it. I AM a somebody. I'm worthwhile knowing and I have a lot to offer. People are lucky to know me. I am worthwhile. I AM worth it. I'm worth the time and energy I'm putting into my healing. And I will heal. There's hope in sight. This won't last forever. I'll get through this just fine. I am worth it. I can spend my time around people who value me because I am worth it.

I never did anything wrong. I did not have power over other people's actions. I'm worth the pain. My wholeness is worth the pain. I deserve the good things that happen to me. I don't do bad things. I'm too good of a person. I'm worth my time. When men find me attractive, it isn't to abuse me. Men find me attractive because they see the value in me. I have a lot to offer. I deserve all the goodness around me. I am not damaged goods. I have a value as a human being. I am a beautiful person. I can take care of others without losing me. I am a good person who had bad things happen to her. It wasn't my fault and I deserve better. I can surround myself with people who value me because I am worth it. I value me. I deserve my life, all my life. I am worth it to get through my pain and suffering. I am worth it. I don't have to abuse me anymore. I can surround myself with people who value themselves too. I don't have to put up with anymore crap.

I AM WORTH IT!

8/29/91

I'm moving. I feel real good about moving, it's almost a ritual for the work I have been doing with the incest. I am able to leave the comfortable and go to the unknown. I'm confident that I'll find the "other side" better also. I get too settled into old routines without venturing out into the unknown. It's scary to move but I don't think I'm making a mistake. I'm working on this grasping life concept. I know I'll get to the point where I can fully reach out and embrace life. Rome wasn't built in a day. I had a lot of damage done to me and it'll take a long time to change, but change I will.

I haven't spent any time on myself lately. It's all been work and moving. I haven't stopped and talked about me. It wasn't others company I was missing, it was my own. Sorry I haven't been here for me.

Life is getting better. I don't have to be afraid of men noticing me. I'm something to look at and I'm someone worthwhile to spend time with. God I'm worth it. I should make a victory banner. That's something I can do, go through old magazines and cut out celebration phrases. That's fun, that's a great celebration for all I've accomplished.

I've set out to do what a lot of people can't do in a lifetime. I don't have to feel guilty for moving on. It's a choice that everyone has and I've made mine just like they've made theirs. Other people can do this too. It's all a choice and my life has been better. I'm much more calm and I don't feel as pulled by extremes. I know what to do. I know what to do.

9/2/91

I don't think I deserve a nice guy in my life. All I've ever known from men is abuse and that is so hard to change. I have a repeating fantasy going through my head that a man will think I'm okay. God, I have to stop this. I'm the only one who can determine that I am okay. It can't come from the outside. It's in me. I am a loving, giving, compassionate, beautiful person. I deserve all the goodness around me.

It will never come from the outside. No one else can tell me I'm okay. I want to break this pattern damn it. I'm okay. I know I am a strong, incredible person who has been through hell but I survived it. I never did anything wrong. What is the purpose of this obsessing that I can get validation from "out there"? Why do I do it?

I need to recognize my value before someone else can. I'm needed and loved on this planet. I am me and that is all I can offer.

10/7/91*

My body has forced me to stop and give it some attention. I've felt a cold coming one so I took the day to rest and meditate. Why don't I meditate more often? It feels so good. I feel love and goodness in and around me and I deserve it. I am a beautiful and worthwhile person to know. I am perfect the way I am. I deserve all the goodness and happiness around. I can receive love in my life. I can give love to others. Love makes the world go around. I feel so peaceful and light right now.

Once upon a time there was a beautiful little girl who was forced to live in the village of evil. She was a perfect child with eyes as blue as the sea. She had a smile for everyone she met and was love itself. She was fun and a joy to be around. When she walked into a room it was like a breath of fresh air and everyone noticed her for she was like the sun shedding light onto

---

* This is the original journal entry that was re-written for the preface.

33

everything she touched. Beautiful is the only word to describe such an exceptional child. The world vibrated just because she was there.

Unfortunately the little girl lived in a village that had a monster that came at night. During the day the monster was as sweet a man as could be and gave the little girl whatever she wanted. He saw how beautiful she was and he hated it. He couldn't stand all the love the little girl had to give. He decided he had to destroy the little girl for her own good. What kind of life could such a beautiful person have? She was bound to get hurt so he had to kill her.

He let the monster come out at night and do things to the little girl that he would never do during the day. He made sure she felt dirty, ugly and bad. It had to be her fault that the sweet man turned into such a monster. She made him do disgusting things to her and she enjoyed it. She found pleasure in making him a monster. She wasn't the beautiful child that everyone thought she was, she was evil. Why else would he do such things to her if she wasn't evil? The monster hit her and told her she was an evil child for making him do such things.

It didn't take long for clouds to cover the village of evil. The sunshine went away as the beautiful little girl died. The little girl lost her smile as her world was destroyed. A light was blown out in the world and gloom and misery were apparent to all in the town of evil. Cold and darkness spread through the town as the once beautiful child was destroyed. In her place evolved a plastic doll who did everything perfectly for the world to see. She did everything right and could not make a mistake. The world saw a perfect child but felt something was lacking in this child. Everyone noticed that the child that was once a joy to be around was now a cold void. She was present but it really didn't matter because the life in her was gone. She was just a doll going through the motions of a life.

The sweet man was very proud of what the monster accomplished. Now the child was just a doll and nothing could hurt her. He was unable to understand that the monster hurt the child more than the entire world could. The man walked around as proud as a peacock for what he had done. His love for the child killed her and now she was safe.

However, the beautiful little child never did fully die. She hid deep inside the doll until she could escape from the town of evil. The doll stole away from evil and started her own life. Beautiful things happened to the doll and slowly the little girl knew she was safe to come out and brighten up the world once more.

One day the doll will be gone and the little girl will shine her love down on the earth once more and nothing will destroy her ever again.

10/14/91

'I'm a sucker for abuse'. I've noticed this phrase going around in my head the last couple of days. I've been saying it to myself for as long as I can remember but I've finally *heard* myself say it. I want it to stop. I deserve better than abuse. I deserve to be treated well and fairly. I am a beautiful person. No one deserves any kind of abuse, least of all me. I never did anything to deserve the treatment I received as a child.

I want and can receive love. I can and want to be close to a man. I want and can trust men. I don't want any more abuse. No more. I deserve to be treated well. I deserve consideration. I can freely give and receive love. I can trust my perceptions of life. I am not a sucker for abuse. I will not take it anymore. I don't need to relive the abuse anymore. I can fully live my life. I don't need sorrow anymore. I love my life. I like who I am. I'm so lucky. I don't need abuse in my life anymore. I was not an evil kid who asked for the abuse. I am not evil. I don't need to prove that I am evil anymore.

The abuse served the purpose of showing the world how evil I was and how that was all I deserved. I never was, never will be evil. I want and deserve better. I want someone to appreciate me for me. I don't have to prove anything to anyone. I am fine by myself.

11/17/91- A technique I learned from *The Courage to Heal*, written with my non-dominant hand to access my inner child:

> Dear Dad,
>
> You never loved me. No matter what I did, you couldn't love me. But I loved you anyhow. I am never going to earn your love. I can now stop going out with men who don't love me. I can stop repeating my trying to get you to love me by trying to get men to love me. I can be loved just the way I am. I am perfect. I can receive love from a man. I can give you up now. I love myself

and I can let others love me too. I don't need your
love. I can be loved for who I am. I am ready to
receive love from a man. I am letting you go.

Love,

Dusana

11/19/91

Why did Sarah* have to die? Why couldn't she make it?
Another victim falls in the incest war. How many lives will be
taken? How long will all this last?

God I hate mom and dad. The bitch let it happen. How
could she not know? She didn't love me enough to protect me.
The world could see what dad was doing and she just turned the
other cheek. He had to get out of their bed every night to come
and abuse me. How could she not know? She let it happen. The
spineless bitch. What a wench.

She used me to give something to dad that she couldn't. What
a fucking bitch. No wonder I need so much love now. I am not
an unlovable person. It's my parents who are incapable of love.
They have nothing to give to anything. They are just selfish jerks.
What a couple of assholes. It was always me, me, me. They had no
consideration at all for us kids. We weren't unlovable; they were
just incapable of love.

God, I was dad's special girl. He didn't love me, he manipulated
me. He used my love and goodness for his own benefit.

---

* Family friend who was also an incest survivor and completed death by
suicide

Who are these people who are my parents? What is the matter with them? I won't carry their shame any longer. It's costing me too much. I am giving them back their shame. I don't have to hate them either. I can let them stay in their world but I need to move on. There is more waiting for me out there. There is love. I can receive love from others. Real love in which people care about me. They aren't out to use or abuse me. I can be me. I don't have to fall back on that fake personality. It's okay to be me and I am beautiful.

There is love all around me and I can let it touch me. I love life and I can be alive. I am free to be alive.

Good-bye mom and dad.

11/24/91

My Dad:

My dad is kind with gentle eyes and hands. He would not harm me. He loves me for who I am and accepts me totally. He doesn't want to change me but thinks I am perfect. He loves my beauty and my smile. He is wise and friendly. People love to be around him and listen to his funny stories. I am proud of my dad. Children and animals love my dad and feel safe around him. He has friends wherever he goes, whether he knows them or not. My dad has a smile for everyone. He wouldn't hurt anyone.

My dad helps others just for the pleasure it brings him. My dad wants only respect and honesty from others because that is what he offers them. My dad has power because he is himself. My dad wouldn't take advantage of anyone. My dad loves for the sake of love. My dad is giving and uses his experiences to help others with their problems. My dad is patient and always has an ear to offer. My dad wants the best for others and loves unconditionally. My dad loves life and lives it fully.

People are safe around my dad and can be themselves. My dad is real and can be trusted. My dad is truly a beautiful person. My dad is happy and always has time for others. My dad hates the injustices in the world and does something about it. He fights for the underdog and believes that good will overcome evil.

My dad believes in brotherhood and mother earth. My dad is one with nature and all that is good.

My dad is proud and strong. Nothing hurts my dad but he shares other's pain. He carries other's pain when they can't. My dad heals other people and they always leave him feeling better than when they came to him.

Goodness clings to my dad like dew on a flower and just as easily runs off. My dad is funny but can't tell a joke. My dad is lucky and good things naturally happen for him. My dad has wealth beyond measure in his friends and the things he loves. My dad greets everyday with wonder and joy. My dad knows what it means to be alive and won't waste this precious life. My dad enjoys a good fight but most of all he tries.

My dad will always believe in the goodness of mankind. My dad can bring out the best in others and knows the importance of touch. My dad's true love is life.

My dad[*] is me, now who is my father?

---

[*] My animus, Carl Jung's term for the inner male within a female. The anima is his term for the inner female within a male.

12/1/91

When does this finish? Do you ever end? I don't want to be in therapy for the rest of my life. Do I expect this incest stuff to be over when I stop therapy? No, I just want it to be less of an issue in my life. It is not the only factor in my life. I have many different areas of me. I don't want to have to fight my entire life. Fighting is just surviving. I want to move on to thriving. I can't fight for the world, I can only fight for me. That's enough for now.

Everyone has their own choices. It isn't up to me to save the world. Saving the world won't save me. I need to be saved right now. I can't save my family, I can't save my friends and I can't save strangers.

The only reason I want to save the world is because no one saved me. I need to save me. I am my knight in shining armor. My male side is very safe and he loves me.

I am asking you, old wise one to save the little girl in me. Can we please keep her safe together? You are her dad and I am her mom. I need you to help me parent her. I can't do it alone. I need help. She needs her dad. I can't think of a nicer dad for her. She will be safe with us. We can give her all she needs. We will keep her safe and do our best to protect her from harm.

But we are human and I will fail her. I will promise, little Dusana, that I will apologize when I do.

What do you need to be saved? I will love you and care for you the best I can right now. I can't take care of others. I need to stop caring for others.

What is life? What are relationships? What is love? When do you find it? Can I take a week off and just live? Not do anything whatsoever involving incest? Can I take a week off and not even speak of it?

I can just live. Can I just pretend it didn't happen? Is it denial? Not if it's a conscious choice. Not everything in my life is because of incest. This doesn't have to depress me forever.

I need to learn to live. I don't need to ignore the little girl in me either by doing this. I can still listen to her and get her needs met. She has other needs, not just those involving incest. She can have fun. I won't be denying her by not thinking of incest.

True she was a child that was abused by incest but she was so much more. She loved to dance, sing, and finger paint. She loved to dream and play and wonder about the world. This is the best Christmas present I could give myself. It's living well as the best revenge. I don't want this always to be such a big influence on my life. There is so much more that I've also done this year. There is so much more to me than just an abused incest survivor. It really is a depressing subject. I can move on. It'll never go away but it can lessen.

12/4/91

Once upon a time there was a little girl who was loved for her incredible beauty. She was allowed to grow at her own pace and could make mistakes without harsh judgment. It was understood that the mistakes she made were not life threatening. She was free to learn from her mistakes instead of being castrated for them. It was okay not to be perfect. Everything always came out fine in the end.

She was allowed to live in the present and not the 'could have been' world which creates crisis. Nothing bad happened and that was fine. She was okay the way she was and she did the best she could at the moment. It was understood that she was trying and she was loved for it. She was trying to do a good job and work hard. She didn't have to be perfect because her parents knew that no one was perfect. She didn't have to worry about how she would be judged if she did do something wrong. She was fine and loved the way she was at the moment. She gave so much and wasn't belittled for the mistakes she made. Her strengths were nurtured to grow in a safe environment. She knew there were areas in which she needed to grow and was given the support and guidance to do so. She was able to listen to herself and not what others told her to do.

12/6/91

I hate having to admit that my parents don't love me. They don't care for me. They do not love me unconditionally and that's what I want from them. They are not able to let me be. They can't let me go even if it's in my best interest. Or is it that I can't let them go for my best interest? A part of me is still longing and grasping for their love. No matter what I do they are not capable of loving me the way I want. They do have some feelings for me but it's not love. I'm not sure what it is. They are both incapable of love. Smothering is more what they do to another person. Love is just not something that radiates from my parents. Even with Eric*, it's not love.

They have concern for other people but lack the feelings that they want what's best for others. I really cannot be around

---

* My nephew, Charlie and Monica's oldest son.

them because I want their love but I'll never get it. They can't and it hurts me too much because I keep wanting their love. I keep setting myself up for disappointment. I can't have the relationship I want with my parents. It will not do me any good to have any relationship with them right now. I can't take care of them, I can only take care of me. I need to move on and I can't if I still feel tied to them. I need to cut the cord. My parents need to die for me. I have to give up my fantasy parents and look at the stark reality of what I got for parents. They don't care about me and they never will. Unrequited love. I love them and that's the burden I have to carry. They will never be what I want or deserve.

It would really be painful to do a face-to-face confrontation with them because I will be facing a void. There will be nothing there. They will never do anything and I don't have to put myself through that.

Do I think I'll avoid the pain another way? Do I want or need that slap in the face? There is nothing there. They don't care.

It really doesn't matter how I confront them because their reaction will be the same. I need to do it the easiest way for me. It comes down to the fact that they don't love me and they never will. There will never be anything there for me.

2013

It's been hard to read the past few entries. After all these years it still hurts. It continues to be a wound that can 'get hit', as I think of it. Once in a while the scab gets totally ripped off through my interactions with others but luckily that's few and far between. I deal with the rawness and vulnerability of emotions.

I tend to myself with loving care and prepare myself to face the world again. I have been slain to the core and go forth carefully and cautiously. Not even able to muster a proper defense except avoidance.

I gravitate toward the people who will treat me with respect and away from those who can do further harm. I need quiet and avoid crowded, noisy places. My senses are so open they take in way too much stimuli. I get overloaded quickly. But, again, this only happens every couple years. I recognized the last time was when my boundaries were repeatedly ignored over several months.

This is why it is imperative for me to write. I don't know what I will do with this but I need to write. I need to get it down. I need to channel the inner turmoil into something that doesn't involve destruction of myself or others. Not the physical destruction as in a mass killing spree. Not all survivors go on mass killing sprees. I hate that assumption. Though I think it myself. When I see the killers on TV I can't help but wonder, what happened to them? I know how we can fool each other as we go through life without ever revealing what goes on within a family. I need to channel the fight occurring between the part of me that is private and the part of me that wants change. Will anyone else relate to what I feel? What I think?

I hesitate publishing this because of the next generation. Not Eric and Anton so much. They'll be fine. They were raised farther away from the family. But Briana and Colin. They are so entrenched in it all and I'm worried about how they will get treated. They are innocent. I wonder if Kim and the kids will stand by Kevin's side. Do Charlie's exes know? What is wrong with me that I even care what will happen to them when I haven't seen them display any caring towards me?*

I have the feeling of walking away. What will this do to the relationships, or lack there of, that I have with my siblings? I do remember the choice I made a few years back to betray myself and adhere to their unspoken demands. I'd not mention what dad did to me and they'd still not call when visiting Colorado. I'd diminish myself and not mention how their lack of support has deeply affected my definition of relationships and they'd finally let me be near their children. I'd grovel and play the bad sister who went against the rules and they'd never say they were sorry for the years we lost while I was banished from the family. Or as they see it, the years I needed to be away from them. We'd silently agree that it's okay that they never ask how I really am. They didn't need to ask what losing both sides of our extended family, not to mention childhood friends, did to my self-worth. I thought no one cared. No one has ever asked what's going on with the family and why I have stayed away. I didn't think I mattered enough for others to make the effort. The bad behavior I have put up with in relationships because it's what I've known love to be. What exactly would I be losing by walking away? That answer is becoming a little less clear to me now.

---

* Charlie and Monica's second son is Anton. Charlie is twice divorced and has had other relationships. Briana and Colin are Steven and Diane's son and daughter. Kevin's second wife is Kim and she has four children from a previous marriage. This journal entry is a combination of several written over many years.

12/9/91

Why am I obsessing about Aidan? What is love? I don't love him. I can talk with him easier than I can with anyone I've ever known. I think everyone can talk with him. Why do I feel so safe with him? I am so comfortable with him. We fit together so well.

I think I am projecting my animus on him. I'm always projecting on him. Isn't that how I described "my dad" who was me? My male side is: wise, safe, honest, and fun. He would be comfortable for me to be with since it's me.

What's going on here? Do I love him or am I looking at me? Why don't I want to know? Why can't I look other people in the eye when I talk about him? I'm afraid they'll see something I don't want to face.

What is love anyway? What are relationships and intimacy? Can't I be intimate with a man without thinking it's love? I love him but it's useless. I don't know. Yes I do, now what's going on here? I promised myself no more going after men who don't love me. I promised.

We are a great couple. Aidan and I or animus and I? Why do I feel it is so right? Am I being smart or stupid? Why don't I want to know? God I am so comfortable with him.

Does he feel the same? Is that what it's about or are we just friends?

I'm afraid; I don't want to do this to my inner child. I must protect her. I made a promise to her and I won't go back on it.

Why do I feel so comfortable with Aidan? So I can talk with him and I feel so comfortable, does that make it love? No! Why can't I be friends with a man? Okay, so I can be friends with a man who is gay.

What is it about Aidan? Just because I have never been so intimate with anyone else doesn't make it love. I don't want to love him. Why? What do I feel? I am not going to find the answer because I don't want to know. I can't love him. I won't put little Dusana through that again. She needs love, real love. Oh, that feels better. Quit testing me.

Aidan is just helping me pave the way for the real one. I am so afraid of relationships. I don't know how to have one. I can't move from friends to lovers. It scares me too much. I get all weirded out. I can't and won't play games with myself anymore.

I deserve better. I want the fairy tale. I want love and friendship. I want my best friend. I want the whole enchilada.

12/11/91

What is love? How do you know? Do you truly love the person or is it just a projection? How do you know? How do you know it'll last? How am I going through the world?

What are my beliefs and values about love? Love involves deep respect and honesty. Honesty with yourself and the other person. Love is wanting the other person to be happy. But not taking responsibility for that happiness. Love is being able to be yourself and that is perfect. Love is the comfortableness of a flannel shirt. Love is peaceful and quiet. Love is dawn's hush, the serenity of a snowy night. Love is the clear and crisp winter's night. Love is majestic like the mountains and flows like the streams. Love takes your breath away and gives you strength.

Love never sits still and is as expansive as the horizon. Love never needs an explanation, it just is.

Love exists in everything. Love makes the sun shine and the birds sing. Love is a wave lapping at the shore, there's always more coming. Love never goes away.

Love is forgiving but it also brings justice. Love is as warm as a fire and as refreshing as a mountain spring. Love is as strong as the wind and as quiet as the forest. Love is a circle. Love is always at hand yet can be out of reach. Love is so easy that it's hard. It's too simple for man to understand.

Do I analyze too much? Maybe you love him and that is why. But is it a good choice?

1/3/92

I want:

- To be more assertive
- To get my needs met in healthy ways
- To be comfortable with my sexuality
- To continue growing as a person
- To be comfortable in my body
- To stay present in my body
- To be awake and aware
- To be in a emotionally and physically intimate relationship with a man
- To be more comfortable with straight men
- To confront my parents
- To work on relationships with my siblings

- To work on relationships with friends
- To continue healing from incest
- A job which I love and I'm valued and respected
- To continue being content with life
- To continue loving life
- To use humor less as a defense
- To use my flippant attitude less as a defense
- To be more real
- To stay focused
- To meditate more
- To continue developing a strong, flexible body and mind
- To work more with my inner world
- To be more accepting of people
- To continue developing healthy relationships
- To trust myself more and to know I'm worth it
- To stay away from people who play mind games

2013

For some strange reason I thought everyone needed to confront their abusers. It would be the ultimate crescendo in the healing process. I wrote out the following and planned on videotaping it and getting the family together to watch it. I had sent a letter to my siblings a few months before about the abuse and what I was going through. I did make a video but didn't end up sending it.

The confrontation with my parents happened in person sometime during January or February of 1992. I am glad I did it though they didn't admit what was done to me. All I know that was said about it was my dad told my brother Steven, it didn't happen. And then Steven told me, this can never get out; it would be bad for business.

Though the following seems a little psycho to me now, I remember at the time it was a way for me to get more of my power back. I had a lot of anger to get through. It was part of my path to reconciling, 'I'm not crazy, what I lived through was crazy.'

1/5/92

Confrontations:

I was not brought into this world to comfort you. You had a wife for that. What you did you know was wrong and you'd hope that I'd forget it forever, but I didn't. You are a sick man and I'll kill you if you ever do that again. You killed that child the first time you came into my room. That was me, dad, that you killed. Take a good look at me dad, I am the same person that you killed. I am the daughter you say you love so much. You don't love anything but money and power.

Welcome to reality dad, you don't have enough power or strength to get help and money will never buy you the power I now have. You are nothing. It takes a weak man to do what you did to me. How much power does it take to physically overtake a ten year old?

Your selfishness and powerlessness cost me many years of my life but I am happy to say my life is mine again. You don't have any control over me anymore. I can choose to do what I want with my life and I've chosen not to include people like yourself in it. There is nothing you can say to make me want to be around sick people like yourselves. I will never be able to forgive what you did dad and since they were your actions, I doubt I will ever be able to forgive you. You disgust me and I don't want you a part of my life.

Mom and Dad, you were the two people in the world that were to love and protect me and you didn't. It took me a long time to get over that but you know what? I'm lovable and I deserve more than you will ever be able to give me. I cannot keep up the charade any longer. We are not the perfect little family and I want to be a real person and not an actress. The incest damaged me physically, mentally, emotionally, and sexually but I am getting all those parts restored. I am overcoming each and every one as I work through the blockages. Overcoming the incest is the greatest gift I, or anyone, could ever give me.

I really loved you dad, and you hurt me bad. Nothing will ever be as painful an experience for me to endure but I have lived through it twice.* As a matter of fact I'd like to thank you dad, this experience has given me a strength and power that I couldn't have gotten anywhere else. I don't like the price I had to pay but I love what I got.

Just for your own knowledge to know exactly what I had to endure, I was also abused as a child by Kevin, as an adult by Charlie, and you also failed to protect me from Grandpa Walter. I have told and warned Sandra**, Kevin, Lucy, Steven, Diane, Charlie and Monica about what you did.

---

* The physical act as a child and feeling the emotions as an adult.

** Sandra is the oldest child. Lucy is Kevin's first wife and Diane is still married to Steven.

I could not stand by and let incest destroy another generation. It is too damaging and there is no guarantee that the next generation would fare as well as mine did. We are the generation that is going to have to change things in order to give the next generation a fighting chance. Each of us has our own truths we have got to come to terms with to change in order for the incest to stop with my generation.

I do love you and wish you well. All I'm asking for is that you don't contact me-not by letter, phone or in person. I truly don't care what you two have to say for yourselves. I also request that you give a $5,000.00 donation to the sexual abuse program at the Women's Center and also a $5,000.00 to The Task Force on Battered Women. Both should be anonymous except that they are from an abuser at the request of a victim.

1/10/92

Blackness—it is all around me.

I reach out to nothingness,

Where did it all go?

I thought I was alive but my heart was torn out years ago.

Let me live in the void, God, the mirror is too clear.

I'm wearing glasses but I can't see.

Help me, someone.

Why must I be so strong?

Someone take it away.

The pain is too intense.

I must get out.

What is pressing on my chest?

Where did this come from?

Make it go away, it's too much.

No, I can't look at it, it hurts too much.

I cried an ocean for your love.

Who ever said love was gentle?

I can see a little now and I want out.

Bring in the focus, take the pain away.

The storm passed and I can breathe easier.

Since when has the sky been blue?

Where did all this beauty come from?

What a beautiful light you are.

Thank you for saving me but I can do it on my own now.

2/23/92

Sadness for my parents. What kind of life have they been leading? What is going through their heads? Where is all this leading? What do I want? I can't wait for them to admit it. They may never.

I have a reoccurring dream about biting dad's penis off. It's so real. Then he can't hurt me. He's laughing at me, always laughing. Why doesn't he love me? I want him to love me. I want both my parents to love me. I want them to trust me.

I just spent a week with the nicest people. It was wonderful. I love being pampered and catered to. It really was a gift. In so many situations, I got what I wanted and needed. I loved being able to receive. People like me and listen to me. I liked having other people do things and handle things for me. It's not because they didn't think I wasn't capable but because they wanted to. I liked not having to take care of and worry about stuff. I really liked people doing things for me.

I don't want to have to fight my life away. I can't make them do anything. What does all this mean?

3/1/92

Why do I push men away and avoid intimacy? What don't I have to face by doing this? I get to avoid the fact that I am lovable. It's okay to be loved. No one will take advantage of me. I am worthy of love. I just have messed up parents who are incapable of love.

I can feel vulnerable in an intimate situation because I am here to take care of myself. I'm not going to let anyone hurt me. It's okay to be loved and feel loved. I am okay. I am a beautiful person who can be loved. I am a beautiful person who deserves to be loved. I deserve all the love I receive because I am a human being. It's okay to be vulnerable because I am here to take care of myself and I won't let anything happen to me. It's okay and safe to let love in. I am here for me. I don't have to be afraid of men anymore. They can't do anything to me that I don't let them.

I'm okay. It's all okay. Life's going to be alright, it'll have its ups and downs but it'll be okay. I can be loved and I deserve to be loved. No one's going to hurt me. I am here to protect me and I can let love in. I don't need to be afraid, I won't let others hurt me. I am a beautiful and lovable person.

3/19/92

It hurts. My parents are denying/lying about what they did. They aren't taking responsibility for their actions. It makes me mad. They claim they love me and want me to be happy. My mom wants all this to be straightened out. Fuck them. I've lived through hell and I'm tired of them not taking responsibility for what they did. I had to live with the terror night after night when I would hear my parent's door open. I knew what was coming. The torture, the humiliation, the incredible hate that my father felt toward me. No man that loves me would treat me in such a degrading way.

The insults of my being a whore and just a no good cunt. Being told that I was so rotten that I deserved such treatment. My dad would hit me and tell me I deserved it. I made him do such things. By the time he would reach my door after walking across the hall, I would already have left. I didn't want to feel what he was about to do to me. Making sure I enjoyed it so he could turn it on me and say I wanted it, he was just giving me what I wanted.

The searching my soul to try to figure out what I did that day to deserve this. It must have been something. Think, maybe I was too loud at dinner. Did I eat everything on my plate? I should clean up my room. This room is a mess, no wonder he's doing this to me. He treats me so good and I can't even keep my room clean. God, I am awful. My parents give me everything I ask for and what do I do? I don't do my homework and I don't make my bed. God I'm a rotten kid. They don't deserve such a rotten kid. I should leave this family so they can be happy. No wonder my parents can't get along, they have such a rotten kid with me. They don't know what else they can do with me. They try and try and I refuse to keep my room clean. No wonder dad does these things to me.

I feel vulnerable and re-victimized. My parents will never admit to what they've done. They are trying and trying to make it seem that I've gone crazy. Or that I have these strange delusions about my childhood from thyroid medication.

I can't buy into the fact that they love me when they don't respect me or trust me or my intelligence. Having private investigators follow me is not proof of their love. To me that is just desperation because they know they don't have control of me and I know the truth about them. I can't live a lie anymore. I will not allow anyone to treat me as a child. My parents are "feeling sorry" for me. They feel pity so that, as I perceive it, they can try to keep me in a victim role and have power over me.

But I will not take that on. I am not the one to pity. I am able to face the truth and I feel stronger and much happier for it. It's okay to be happy. God truly doesn't want us to be unhappy.

I can learn to live with happiness. Seconds will soon turn into minutes into hours into days. I deserve happiness. I don't need misery and despair anymore. It is truly okay to be happy! And I want to be happy.

LOVE AND FORGIVENESS

2013

I remember about this time I was learning to let the real me out. I could feel this other version of me that had been hidden away. I was standing by the tables in a Laundromat and there was only one other woman there. When we made eye contact, I let the inner me come to the surface for a couple of seconds before I covered her up again. It was a part of me that felt more exciting and brilliant. I did this little by little until I felt safe enough to allow the real me to be out in the world all the time.

During the spring of 1992 my dad was taken into the hospital after experiencing months of not feeling well. Exploratory surgery determined he had pancreatic cancer. It was uncertain whether he would live. Walking into his hospital room after he was out of surgery continues to be one of the most satisfying days of my life. The breathing tube shoved down his throat and the feeling of panic in the room. I remember thinking, as I felt some redemption, not so fun is it? How to let my vindictive side out without actually hurting anyone has been a question I've asked many times through the years. It was my power and strength wanting an outward expression.

This began a whole new direction in healing and forgiveness. I knew I needed to behave in a way that didn't form a regret later in life. My search for what it means to love another person continued. The kind of love that heals rather than destroys.

4/21/92

Dear Dad,

Parents are the first major influence on a child's life. There is no possible way for me to look at myself without seeing reminders of you. You have taught me a great many things about life. It was through you that I learned many of life's toughest lessons but learn them I did. Though I don't like the way I had to learn them, the universe can only provide us with what we need and not what we want. So it was that I had to learn and you had the responsibility of being my teacher of these tough lessons. One great thing I learned from you was acceptance and forgiveness. In order to have others in one's life, it is necessary to take the good along with the bad. It is only your expectations of others that cause your disappointments.

People are people and you must take them as they come because there is no changing them. Once you let go of your expectations and truly look at another it is possible to find forgiveness. For whom am I to judge when another's shoes do not fit my feet?

You taught me the true meaning of love and how to fully give to others. You taught me about respect and the importance of treating others how I want to be treated. Finally, you taught me about me and the importance of having faith and trust in myself. As long as I believe in myself, no one can take away my will to live.

And now the only gift I can give back to you is to free you of your burden of being my teacher. You've done all you could and now it is up to me to take what I've learned from you and integrate it into my life. I need to thank you for all you've given me over the years. I can honestly say I am a better person because you were in my life. After all is said and done, I can say from the bottom of my heart I'm glad I had you as my dad.

Love always,

Dusana

5/31/92

Sadness and grief. Sadness, not quite right. Am I okay? Love all around, reach out and touch someone. Where will I find you? I don't want to be alone all my life. Easy to find fault with me. Do I not let it in? It's all around me and I want it. Please help me let it in. Time, it all takes time. It will come. Soon come. It'll come. I can be patient.

I want someone to love me, love in the wrong direction. It needs to flow out from me. I want to love someone, so many someones [sic] around me to love. Love is healing. Let it run its course. I have been looking outside myself for someone to unleash my love when it can only come from me. Risk and let the love flow. There's so much to give. Love is acceptance. Love, love, love. I am love itself. I was created out of love and am sustained out of love. Life is perfect.*

6/13/92

I feel I should be different for someone to like me. I've had so many years of unrequited love. It makes me sad. I sure have lived that scenario enough to last me a lifetime. I kept picking men who couldn't give me what I wanted. I kept picking men who couldn't accept all of themselves or me. I am so used to doing things alone that I can't even fathom a man actually wanting to spend time with me. I've been second best for so long.

I've met someone with whom it seems that he's special and open enough for him to be a possibility with me. But there have been so many possibilities before, is this just another?

I was feeling sadness earlier today and it seemed to be my grieving for the notion that I am in fact not meant to be alone. It's so strange for me to think about having someone who wants to spend time with me because I've been alone for so long. I'm so used to doing things alone, am I ready to give it up? There's a chance that I may find myself in a healthy relationship with a good man in the near future. Whatever will I do? Enjoy it, sounds good.

---

* An example of free-flow writing: Letting the thoughts pour out without concern for editing or correct form.

7/6/92

Maybe there could have been something between Aidan and I, maybe not. Does it matter? He did teach me about love. Through him I was able to realize that I am worthy and deserve love.

Aidan really wouldn't have been able to give me what I want. He's too fearful to reach out to give me what I want. So I was wrong. It doesn't mean I'll be wrong every time or even the next time. I needed someone to love me in a safe way so I could move on.

But now it's time to move on. I'm one step closer to it never happening again. He never loved me. It's time to stop playing this scene out. It's time to stop putting up with less. Aidan never loved me and I was wrong.

Sex is okay and safe for me and I can protect myself. Within myself lies all the strength I need. When I draw into myself, I am able to protect myself and others. But I am also able to open myself up to embrace and welcome others into my life. It's okay for people to know me. It is all okay. I am able to protect myself while still being open to others. I can do it. And without hurting others.

7/7/92

Gentleness embrace me
Let me feel you all around,
In every movement you exhibit love.
It is mine to own.
The softness of your touch,

It engulfs me like a womb.

It is totally you, totally me.

Together we are love—

Separate we are alone.

Two beacons moving towards each other

Wanting each other totally.

Let me embrace you and take me into your world.

There is love all around—

We've been searching for so long but it is over.

We have each other and we are love.

Your physical-ness doesn't hurt me.

You cannot hurt me; it's been done already.

In me you see the truth and it wounds you.

I am all you could be if you were not afraid.

I threaten you yet I mean you no harm.

I can help you, teach you, let me in.

It's safe out here.

I'm here to guide you, let me help you to search you.

You're not out of reach.

I find love in helping others. Let it flow out of me safely. Keep me safe Lord. I want to do your work but I don't want to be hurt. With pain comes growth. Must I go through with it again?

What do these experiences mean? Is it a test or a means to an end? The sun beats down upon my weary brow. Let the wind pass through me and clean me out. Beauty in the world around me. I can do good work.

What do I hold onto and what do I let go? When do I let go? Has the moment passed? I want to help, I can help but I need to protect myself. Find the inner strength and move out of love.

I need protection in love. Let it flow from me. The love exchanged from me to you. It doesn't need to hurt. I can love without pain. You don't have to hurt me to get my love. I give it to you freely. It is my quest, my destiny. Love without pain, life without hurt. It is feasible and within reach.

Please help me to reach my potential, learn new things about me. Let the knowledge come to me, flow through me. The beauty that comes across from being one of God's children. A strength that while quiet is powerfully felt by all.

God, I love life, let it flow through me to cleanse away the past.

7/29/92

Life

I need to strengthen my joy, my love. Develop the skills of unconditional love and respect. I am doing things that I am not proud of. I need to stop. What am I doing? I need to love and respect unconditionally.

I want the repertoire that Jesus had with children and everyone. I want that love and understanding. I know it's in me. Please help me to develop it and bring it out. Please let it flow from me. I don't want to be hurt nor do I want to hurt others. Give me the strength to love. Please help me to let go my fears of loving. It'll be worth it. I am screwing up right now and I know it. I am not doing right at all.

I have so much undeveloped potential that I want to work on. Please help me bring it about. I know I can do it. It's in here. It's time to let go of the past and move with love.

Let me love, please let me love. The world deserves it. Let me look past injustices and love. Let me look past the war and love. Let me look past the chaos and love. And please let me look past the dishonesty and love. It is my destiny to love and I need to accept it.

I wash away my fears and go forth with love and respect. I thank you for gracing me.

Family:

My family does not satisfy me. I want and deserve more. They are people in my life who care about me but do not possess the skills to genuinely love me. And I want that love. I need to move away from my family and leave them behind. They are not what I want and I know that I can get what I want. It does exist in this world. I love my family but they will not bring me closer to what I want in this world.

Will I go back? Do I need to go back? No, there is nothing there for me. They will never be what I want them to be and it is time for me to make my own family. I can and will create the family that I want.

My mother will provide for me and my father will make all potentials limitless. I thank you for the race of this world!*

Love of my life:

---

* Inner or archetypal Mother and Father

He is in my life but our paths are still going in separate ways. With some work it can come about that we are equals. I need to know that if I want something to be real, I need to risk working on it. I need to learn to love to get out of my personal past. I need to take the opportunities that arise and do something with them instead of letting them pass.

I am afraid of ending up with a jerk or a child molester. I definitely have a fear of making a mistake. With hard work and trust, I will be able to make a union that I can be proud of. I need to look at reality and know that no one is perfect. Realistic not grandeur. Love that is whole and complete, not fearful. Do not settle, reach for the stars.

9/6/92*

Let the energy flow all around. Let my light shine on for all to see. Let not one drop of love ever be wasted. It's okay to love, you won't be hurt. It's okay to let go and let the dam break down. You don't need to worry anymore, this time is real. Just trust yourself. It'll all work out. It always does, maybe not in the way planned but always better. It'll be okay; you've let it go. Just trust yourself. You're not out to hurt yourself anymore. You're finally ready to give yourself what you've always wanted.

Take your gift and open it. The time has come, the time is now. It's okay to love, to learn. I have faith in you. You won't hurt me. It's okay to love, it's okay to laugh, and it's okay to dance your way into life. You're not meant to be alone.

---

* As I practiced new ways of being in the world, I frequently had to talk myself through the process of learning.

Take the cup and drink from it. Your glass is over-flowing. I'm not out to hurt you and you have nothing more to learn in this chapter except to love. It's truly over and the time has come to let go and love.

Say good-bye!

9/19/92

The constant thinking about love. I have such a longing for it. I'd like to learn to be able to count on another human being. I'd like someone to be there for me. I want someone else to believe in me. And it doesn't mean that these areas are lacking in me. It just means that I don't want to spend my life alone. I love me and I believe in me and I know that I am capable, possibly too capable.

I'd like to know that I can depend on another human being. I want to be able to love fully and deeply. I want my capacity of love to be at the upper limit. I know I am very passionate and I need many areas to express it. I don't want to be alone anymore. I want to share my life with someone. The good times, the bad times. Day and night.

For once in my life I want to know I am loved by another human being. I don't want to be afraid to love. I want my love to flow freely. I want it to blossom, to grow. I want all areas of my love life to be fulfilled, all encompassing. I need that intimacy in my life.

The frustration I feel is coming out in not so pleasant of ways. I don't want my frustration transferring to people and situations that don't deserve that vent. I need to trust that it'll come. I know that it is worth the wait and I am not willing to settle for less than I deserve. Some things are worth a little more effort and patience.

I'd like to be able to appreciate more all the wonderful things that I am already receiving. I hope that I am not being selfish here. Can I please receive, I'd like to be able to receive. Help me spread it out so that I am not asking too much of one person since I do need a lot. Could I please have it? Could I please have love?

10/20/92

The never ending circle, just where am I?

I never know if I'm at the end or the beginning.

-is this new or old?

-lesson or final exam?

-truth or lie?

What do I know?

What is my truth?

Will it match up?

Why am I afraid to let you know who I am?

I don't want the jewel to be found out

—do I have the courage to be a diamond?

The beauty lies in the sun

—fresh, alive, gold dripping down.

The jewel in the rough,

I shall make them shine.

Understand that rocky terrain brings about the jewel

—too similar for comfort.

Something that can't be denied, but is.

It's there in illusion, but I want reality.

A million cannot see the brilliance.
I'm glad I'm just one.
And you over there,
How and why did you get in this drama?
Are you what I need?
Is your tongue round or forked?
What is this web around me?
Gooey, sticky mess
But I am the spider that spun it.
The design is nice.

Let me jump on this roller coaster.
How could I ever have been afraid?
Merry-go-rounds never take you anywhere.
Though you do get off in a different place
The scenery never changes.
Sparks of light flashing all around,
It's too noisy to hear.
The highest highs plummeting to the lowest lows
With spirals and corkscrews.
Shaking you to another world
—at least I knew I was there.
The sun danced by me yesterday
But the mud kept it out.
I don't want to miss another sunrise.

11/17/92*

I don't want to be hurt again. What do you want? I don't know your intent. Where is the meaning? What are you talking about? What do you want from me? I don't know the answers. I'm not the only one to do this. Get me out of here. Stay away from me. I don't want to be in love, it hurts too much. What do you want from me? I don't know who or what to be. Just leave me alone, I'm good alone. Life makes sense to me alone. I know what to do, I know how to be. What do you want to take from me? What do you want from me? What are you trying to get? What do you want to use me for? What the hell do you want from me? What are you trying to get from me? What do you want? What are the double meanings? What are you saying that you don't mean? What do you mean that you are not saying? What are you hiding? What do you want from me? I don't know what you're trying to get from me. If you love me you want something from me, now what is it? I can't figure out what you want from me. What are you after? What is it that you want from me? What are you trying to get? I don't know, I can't figure it out.

11/24/92

Thank you for all the goodness and love in my life.

I am thankful for my life and all the adventures that I've had the opportunity to grow from. Help me to learn from more of my experiences so that I am able to give and receive love more

---

* I'd have my ideals and then life would amplify where I needed to smooth off my rough edges. In this case, a nice, sincere man was in my life and I had no clue what to do.

freely. I am thankful for all the things I've been able to let go of so that the past doesn't continually haunt me.

I am thankful for the intimate, loving relationships I've developed. I am thankful for being able to do things that I truly enjoy. I am thankful for the new body that I am developing. I am thankful for all the life sustaining forces that allow my life to continue. I am thankful for all the love around me. I am thankful for the natural forces that help to challenge me. I am thankful for the ability to change that which I am not quite satisfied with.

I am thankful for the destructive forces that aren't allowed to affect my life. I am thankful for the protection that surrounds me and I want to be able to feel it in times of need. I'd like to be able to recognize and rely more on the powers that surround me. I am thankful for my intuitive powers and I'd like to develop it to help the universe.

I am thankful for my power and confidence. I am thankful for the person that I currently am and all the possibilities of what I may become. I don't want to limit myself. I am thankful for my ability of self-expression. I am thankful for all that I am able to give to others. I am thankful that my course of life always turns out better than I could ever plan in my wildest dreams.

I am thankful for where I live and all that surrounds me. I am thankful that I am always given exactly what I need and that it is always at hand. I am thankful for my willingness to look inward. I am thankful for my willingness to change. I am thankful for the unlimited potential within me. I am thankful for my ability to interact and understand others. I am thankful for my energy and karma. I am thankful for the chance to change my karma. I am thankful for the ability to feel. I am thankful for the ability and experience of love.

12/16/92

What should I keep, what should I let go of? Direct me, take what isn't needed anymore. I survived being raped. I am happy. I can choose not to live in misery. It is a joy to let the love shine through. Thank you for letting me be one of the chosen ones. It is my pleasure.

I know what it's like to be raped. This keeps going through my head. The sadness is clearing up. The mud is gone, so much to go through. So much sorting to do. Keep it in its proper perspective. Amazing grace, how sweet the sound that saved a wretch like me.

I don't know why I was so lucky. Years of experience. Life is fun. I can be happy. I feel okay being happy. How did I get here? Months of traveling on the train of wishes to arrive at the station of bliss. Bliss does bring me joy.

EMERGING

2013

I had the goal to get my Master of Arts degree in Dance/ Movement Therapy. I took my two passions, dance and psychology, and found there was a field of study. In order to complete the requirements to get into the graduate program, I went back to school in the fall of 1991. I had always wanted to be a dancer but, with the arthritis as a child, it was physically difficult. I also had to confront the mental and emotional blocks towards expressing myself in that way. As I healed, I wanted to reclaim all the aspects of myself that had been taken as a child: mentally, emotionally, physically, sexually, and spiritually. Dance, amongst other practices, became a way for me to reclaim my body as my own.

The body can be seen as a betrayer to a child who is being abused because we are human and it responds to the good sensations associated with sexual stimulation. It messes with your head that something so scary can also feel so good. On top of this, the physical touching can meet a child's emotional needs for: attention, feeling special, nurturance, understanding, connection, etc. It's why the manipulations of the perpetrator work. Over the years I had to separate the twisted intentions of others from my own right to pleasurable emotional and physical experiences. Having them did not cause another's behavior.

As I read through my journals I've wondered, why aren't there writings telling what it was like to be around my dad and family through the cancer? My focus for my healing has always been to do it in such a complete way that it helps to rid the world of this convoluted pattern in relationships. My writings focused more on relationships with men, coworkers and friends during this time as that was where the effects of the abuse played out. I have tried not to use the abuse as an excuse to cause harm to another person, consciously or unconsciously. Though in my pain and frustration I know I have lashed out at others. It feels like I had a million questions as I learned new ways to interact with others. And, always, I learned more about love.

Though the cancer incapacitated my father, I still felt hesitant to be around him. I was there with my family as much as I could. There were so many questions about how the abuse and healing would play out over the years to come. The minimal support and apologizes I got from my brothers and sister evaporated when our dad got sick. I didn't know if this would change back when he got better. Or will he die? I just didn't know what was going to happen and tried to be part of the family while I continued on with my journey.

Based on comments I've heard through the years, when looking at incest from the outside, it's much easier for it to be a black and white issue than when you are in it. There is no right way. Each person needs to decide what is best for him or her to heal as completely as they can and in whatever way offers the most peace.

I had hoped we could talk about it at some point as a family to help understand how and why it occurs. I wanted it to stop and my personal goal had always been to do what I could to make this happen.

1/1/93

My dark side:

Ever present, evasive self, keeping others at a distance. Uptight with no room for fun. Everything in its place and only at a specific time. Elusive with no real caring for others. 'Go to hell, I don't care about you' attitude. Judgments and laziness in thought. Dependency and lack of self-respect. Accepting instead of changing things. Unkind, hurtful thoughts and actions towards others. Not having another's best interest in mind. Disrespect and disregard for life. Spectrums all part of spectrums.

I want to see justice done. I want every bastard that's hurtful to others to suffer. I want to see others suffering in their self-made misery. I don't want other's evilness to cause harm in my life. I don't want other's ignorance to cause me harm. I want to be safe and I will keep you as far away as I need to in order to stay that way. Stay away or I'll hurt you with my cunning remarks, my deadly glances, just you try to come close enough to hurt me. I'm going to slay you before you have the chance to slay me. You treat me right or get out of here.

Uptight or protective? If I hold on tight enough you will never be able to really penetrate my being. You can try but you'll never be hurting me, just the pretend me. I'll hide far away where you'll never find me to hurt me.

So go ahead and rape me, hit me, spit on me, fuck with me. It's not me you are hurting anyway. You can't penetrate my skin, my bones. My armor is much too thick. I'll never even know how good and beautiful I truly am so thick is my armor. You want me, well go ahead because you won't be hurting me, not the real me. My shields are up, causing harm, keeping you at a distance.

Let go and let God take care of that justice. It is not my job or responsibility to judge others. I took on a job when there wasn't an opening. I've been doing someone else's job and work instead of focusing on my own.

Love is the best defense against evil. It is the only lasting thing. The only thing that stays. It can rise and conquer above it all.

I don't like the way I think about others. It's spiteful and hurtful. I am not superior to others. Everyone is equal, is the same. We are all here to find happiness and learn. I had to learn those lessons and I made the same mistakes. Not everyone can be as willing or ready to change. My wanting it differently will not make it so.

Life is not a fight, it is a flow. Go with the flow. Let it willingly pass through me. Let it freely flow. I don't like bound flow because that is what I am. It's hard to live life like this. There are too many restrictions.

I don't like down-to-earth because it is loving and nurturing and this part of me was taken advantage of and abused by others. If I stay uptight and rigid, no one will hurt me. But I am more apt to crumble and fall when flow would get the job done more completely and with a lot more fun.

Teach me to break out please. Guide me, oh wise ones, to let it go and become me again. I never lost it. I just forgot how to be. I am afraid of sex because it was always forceful and hurt. It was never kind, gentle and fun.

I do not need to be bound anymore. It was needed in the past for survival but it is now causing harm and pain in my life. Holding on is not getting me where I want to go. It is a hindrance in my life.

Guide me in letting go please. This rigidity does not allow the flow of God's work. Transformation is on the way. Radical changes are in the forecast for 1993.

Let the light shine through. Changes have now begun. New imprinting* is on the way. The door to eternity has just been opened. Love shall heal thy all. New phase is on the way. Back to the basic eternal self. All loving, all encompassing.

1/4/93

What do I feel? What is going on? So much confusion. What the hell is love anyway? Why am I in a field of work** where I am once again the target of other people's rage and attention seeking behaviors? I only have so much to give. Ask, damn it, I'll give it to you but quit manipulating me. I don't want to be losing these

---

* Imprinting is the pattern we incorporate as children that is used as a template of how relationships, people or situations occur. It's one's way of making sense of the world. It can be changed.

** I worked in residential care for children with behavior problems.

physical confrontations anymore. It hurts damn it. I didn't do anything to you, why must you attack me? I am trying to live my life out as happily and peacefully as I can.

Why do you hurt me so? So much needless aggression towards me. I don't want to become some macho bitch either to defend myself.

See my qualities and respect them. Respect me damn it. Quit walking all over me. I don't want to be hurt anymore. I've had enough of this pain. I want some happiness. I want to know love and appreciation for whom I am right now. I don't know what it's like to be in a good, loving relationship. Does anyone?

I want a deep, loving friendship. I won't settle for less. I have so much. I should be happy with what I have. I'm always wanting more. I have everything I could ever want provided for me on this planet and all I am is a whiny little bitch always asking for more. I want, I want, I want, but how much of myself do I actually give to others? Not much, I'm so selfish. I'm always just giving to myself. I keep to myself and I don't let others in. I want deeper relationships yet I won't budge an inch.

I swear I don't deserve anything that I have. Do I have any sense of grace whatsoever in my life? No. I can never be thankful enough. All I do is complain and want more. I must truly be happy with what I have. Something is definitely shaking my foundation right now. I haven't felt this insecure in awhile. Just when I think I have the answers, something comes along to rock my very core, my root, my very being. What is it, happiness?

I want to go away so I know that I must stay and face whatever it is. Now what is life throwing at me? What is going on? Will I ever be real or just a mask to wear for the appropriate occasion? Deeper and deeper I go but do I ever find the truth, the answer? Where is it and how can I find it?

1/12/93

Wants, needs, desires. What is love? How does it last? The seconds roll past me but what will I do with them? What does my heart hold? Can I love all of life unconditionally?

Over the centuries many groups thought they could alter consciousness just by their thoughts and actions. Did it help? Will it help now? The 100th monkey syndrome.* It didn't hurt or harm another so there's no problem here. It's better than the alternative. Love and the power of change.

How do I go about it? What more can I do? What needs to be done? What do you bring here this time? Answers, more questions. I feel such peace. Who can understand the changes I am going through? It feels good. How long does it take? I don't even want to know the possibilities. No limitations.

Dreams about fire, Nancy and mom. Burning up of unneeded things, cleansing and slight readjustments. Mom, making peace, coming into womanhood. What does it mean to be female? Have I been too male for too long? I needed the control as a child. I don't need it anymore. I want to let go. I want freedom to move with this body.

---

* 100th monkey syndrome is a theory that when an X amount of people learn a new behavior, all people will incorporate it. Also known as critical mass. Originally it was a study of monkeys on an island.

Am I doing enough? Do I want it hard enough to work at it? I have the tools, am I utilizing all of them?

It's all illusionary. What we think we need to do. Life doesn't require a lot of work. Just the spirit to live and the willingness to fully experience it. Destiny or free will? I think I am freely choosing paths yet when I just roll with the punches, it all turns out better than I could have ever planned. Give up the expectations of how I think something should be and just let life happen. Follow the moment and adapt to it. Who knows what could happen. Just enjoy the here and now. It is all I have.

Does it matter what I do or don't do? I am just an insignificant small human life form yet I am the world, I am the universe. I am nothing and everything.

Love unconditionally or face the unconscious. Am I denying any part of me? Of course. I am alive. I am greatness and a void. I need the tools to properly get at the hidden and dark areas. It is definitely a part I want to develop. Misery and pain or goodness and love? I want bliss, eternal bliss.

A raging fire within me that needs its place to burn. Two potential fires in two days. I need to honor my fire, it'll bring me freedom. It'll come out in painting. Passion, raw female energy. The healing side of the world.

I can only take care of myself. They've put themselves in their positions. It is quite humorous. How *did* I get here? It's where I always wanted to be and here I am. I shouldn't be afraid of my beauty. I never notice it anyway. It's just there. It can't be given or taken away, just shared. To share is to live.

How can I give of myself freely to you? Does it matter if you deserve it? I can give and offer but it is up to you to decide if you want to take it. The beauty of the world lies within you. Difficulties to overcome but the beauty is there. Never ending or beginning, just beingness. [sic] Overall it doesn't matter.

I put myself here and you put yourself there. It is only from here that I will be able to help you. From there I'd be wishing to be here and getting both of us nowhere. From here I can offer and love you wherever you are. It is my pleasure to do so, to give you my offering. Why feel guilt when I love being here? It's wasted energy that could be helping you to get here too.

Relish and indulge it. It's definitely been well earned. With beauty comes ugliness. Let it out in non-harmful ways.

Why do I still hold on? It's not needed but to fully let go all at once would be too much for the ego to handle. It must go in stages. It's too raw and the potential to blow or fry the mind is too high. A little at a time but more rapidly than in the past. It can and will be done. It is time to let go of unnecessary baggage that holds me down and keeps me from loving you. It's in me and it is safe to let it out. It doesn't have to bring harm. It can bring love and joy to others. It's the other side of the coin that needs to be used.

It's female, it's raw and it is what I am made of. It is my true power and what I need to move from, to give from, and to take from. For only then can I truly give you the grace that you deserve.

2/2/93

Do I have pure intentions? What games am I playing? Am I even playing any? I hope not.

Why do I get allergic reactions to things? Allergies→irritations, frustrations, energy being blocked, flow cut off, disappointments, anger, grating, uneasiness, complacency, injustice, damage, cruelty, impoverish, lack of fluidity, bustle, no breathing room, tension, inconvenience, holding on, stopping the flow, not letting go through, blockages, denial, limitations, frustrations, inconvenience, lack of substance, lack of reality, pushing down, not letting what comes naturally, holding on tension, judgment, frustration, injustice, lies, cruelty, insanity, closing off, tension-inability to relax, constriction, scratchiness, inability to find the bliss, enjoy the bliss, holding on to what's not needed, not seeing it for what it is, irritation.

Irritation to lies or actually the truth that I see, I don't always like what I see but see it I do. Gut reactions, cutting through, inability to talk-not communicating, not expressing myself, keep myself down, let too much happen without taking a stand, be the warrior, be true to myself without hurting others, limit myself. God, this is great, doing too much, not taking care of myself, need time to play, have fun, be silly, be with people I enjoy. The truth doesn't hurt, it's easier to accept, reality is a wonderful concept. Don't let others influence you.

What has been irritating me that I haven't expressed? It is okay to complain. I really want my body back the way it was before the arthritis. I don't like that movement doesn't come easy and it is in fact painful. I don't like the limitations I place on my life because of the arthritis. I don't like the way my body looks, I feel clumsy in the way I move.

When I don't let my true feelings out it irritates me. Less masks, less limitations. I hate the fact that I am afraid of sex because it is painful and uncomfortable for me. Physically, emotionally, I don't want any hang-ups. I want to enjoy it and have fun during sex. It isn't meant to be a chore. It isn't work, it's easy, fun and carefree. I want to play with it.

Emotions still frozen, melting of butter, allowing the playfulness to come out. Free and easy. I want to enjoy it, I want to want it. I want to have no fear surrounding my sexual situations. I want my tensions, my blocks to melt. I can express my sexual nature. It doesn't have to get caught. Freedom to move. I want to reclaim my sexual side. I do have a sexual nature that was imprinted in the wrong way. It wasn't right but it happened and now it's up to me to incorporate what I've learned into my life. Change can happen.

I can find myself in a situation that will give me the freedom to let my incredible sexual nature evolve. I can put myself in a situation that will give me the freedom and security to take some risks. I can put myself in a situation that will allow me to love, to let my volcanic passion out. It can come out in a safe container melting away all unneeded reactions. I can put myself in a situation in which I am safe. I can put myself in a situation in which I am free. I am free to let my sexual energy flow. My passion runs deeply through me, filling and healing every crevice.

I have put myself in a situation in which my passion is free to let me grow, to heal, to love.

Thank You!

3/15/93

Mom,

I wanted your love and approval. I wanted your respect, your protection. You were my world and I was your nothing. You couldn't see your beauty or mine. We were too much alike. I was all that you could've been. Pure love, pure beauty, pure truth. All that was and is. We are alike in so many ways. I could never be good enough. I wasn't perfect to your eyes. I had outer flaws but internal love. Which is more important for the world? Love surrounds us in an ever-basking glow. Is my world falling apart or going too well? I don't want to screw it up. I am trying and succeeding. I am doing a lot. I don't want to hurt anyone. Just let me love.

3/16/93

What have I gotten myself into? The life of integrity and truth. What should be known and left alone? It'll be worth it when it comes but the wait is killer. Needless unhappiness. It's so stupid. Why does it hurt so? When does it get easy? All wrapped up in nothingness. It doesn't matter.

Where is my sign? Have I had one? The doubt, the worry, all so stupid. All so needless. What can be done? What does this mean? What am I supposed to think? Keep the walls down, please. It would be so easy to put it up now. I want more than I've ever seen and this is the price. But what an honor should I get it.

Communication. Did I do wrong? What is so great about love anyway? Why does everyone strive for it, put so much into it? What is the value of it? All it brings is pain. What is it now, it's pain. It's pain; it's all that there ever is.

I feel so alone. Where are the answers? We all want answers, even when there might not be any. I must go within. The truth is not always the easy path to take but it is the right one for me.

3/26/93

What a week. Thank you for the sign. I feel an ungrateful wretch for doubting. Where is my faith and why do I fail you? I always get what I most deeply desire yet my faith and patience are ever failing. I feel so unworthy of your love. I am ever doubting, making myself suffer over that which I know I will get when ready.

Guide me in this struggle. Thank you for the gentleness that surrounds me. I am ever blessed. What did I do to deserve all of this? I have so much when others have so little. Why? I am so lucky, so fortunate, how can I ask for more when I already have so much? What can I give? What do I need to do? I have the nicest life. What have I done to deserve this?

Help me to be more compassionate and empathetic to my brothers and sisters. I can be such a little wretch. I love people. I love life.

Do I deserve to dance? Why do I struggle with it so? I do not like having a deformed body. Where do these notions come from? If I give my passion over, I can dance just as well as anyone else. Does being different mean I shouldn't do it? Can't I express myself just as well as anyone else with my body? Does my body being different mean I shouldn't use it to express myself? It has so much to say, so much that needs to be expressed. So much to let go of. The pain is hell but worth it. Do I have the strength, the integrity to do this? It needs to be done. I want it so much, God grant me the courage to face my body. It can be so heart wrenching, so soul shaking, earth shattering but isn't that how I like it?

What journey am I embarking on now? It'll be worth it, help me remember it'll be worth it. Your pain has given me so much. I should embrace more. How fortunate that I have this pain. How loved I am to receive this pain. How can I curse that which is needed to help me grow? Treasure every step of this journey because the outcome shall be heaven.

Can I do this? Have I already faced the worst or is it just beginning? Can I jump into the unknown? I can't imagine being any more blessed but I know I will be. So, hesitant as I am, please bring it on dear Lord. Oh no, it is done. There is no taking it back. Grant me humor through what will come. Once again, what have I gotten myself into? Keep me strong and safe and please, please do not let me harm those around me because of my struggle. I don't want to hurt anyone else and I surely don't want anyone to suffer for my benefit.

How selfish can I be asking for more? My life just keeps on getting richer while others suffer. I don't want that to happen. Why does someone have to suffer? Please let this be for the good of everyone and not a selfish act.

What do I have to face? What has come before? God help me! Help me right whatever wrong I've done. Help me feel more deeply, love more fully, give more often and, of course, be ever more grateful. Help me understand the sins of others, their struggles and lost hopes. Grant me the sight so I may help others to be happier.

Yes, I know this must be at my expense but it is for the good of all. Renew and heal me, help me to be stronger than before. Release the knowledge from the past. The time has come to re-introduce it to the world. Help me to live it out. Help me to use it for others, not against others this time.

I am sorry for what has come before. I offer this life as my penance; do with it what you must.*

Thank you, I am safe, I am strong, I shall heal. Thank you for the love and trust. I shall do my best to honor your wishes. We are many, yet one. Thank you for the blessing.

4/3/93

I need to be so careful for my future children. I don't want to make a mistake. Trust, it's all about trust. Is he that great? I want a truly superb man. I don't want to worry. I don't want any harm to come to my children. I don't want them to live through what I did. It's too damaging.

I do love my convictions, lonely as they can be. But I am not willing to compromise on how I want to be treated. I will not! I expect to be treated respectfully and it's that simple. You don't

---

* This reads like it was a time during which I was studying about past lives. Understanding we have all been both the sinner and the saint at some point.

play me like you play other women. I am not that easy. I don't feel I am being unreasonable either.

I do have high expectations of other people therefore I also get deeply hurt. How true do I act in relation to my words? Am I consistent? Do I indeed do as I say I am going to? Help me to be truer in my own actions. Let my words and my actions parallel each other. I want to do as I say and say as I do. If I expect it of others, I'd better be prepared to live it myself. I am sure I must screw up sometimes and everyone can be allowed to be human but I want to be consistent on this basis.

Do I allow him to be human? Do I want a superhuman, damn right I do. Can I have a demi-god? I can't and won't compromise on this one. You can treat me respectfully or you can choose to be out of my life.

Reality is a beautiful thing. I must be true to myself. And I want to be treated in a certain manner. Case closed and come what may. Life with the nicest guy on earth or gladly alone.

Undated and year uncertain

I want to dance. I want to be a dancer. Fears and insecurity. I have beautiful movements. I am worthwhile as a dancer. My body can be very beautiful to watch.

I am not good enough keeps running through my head. Thoughts that others don't want to watch me. Thoughts that I shouldn't even bother. I do want the recognition as a dancer. I want my dancing to be taken seriously. I want my art form to be taken seriously. It is raw, it is real, it is you, it is me.

Through the head and to the body, my soul reaches to you. I show myself to you, will you accept me? Will you love me? Will you join me? I pause to listen but you're not there.

Spiraling, twisting, seething, motion-to-motion, gesture-to-gesture. Love that binds, wounds that heal. Growing, ever changing. Tumbling down, rolling to you by way to justice. Jump, jump, jump. Careening down a slope never to end. My feet hurt, my hip hurts, do you hurt? Do you bleed? Do you long? Do you yearn? See me, hear me, feel me. Inch by inch, mile by mile.

5/6/93

Where are we going? What does it all mean? Why are we here? Why am I here?

I hope I am doing, being enough. I want to be learning fast enough. Does one fail if one has loved just once? We are all connected. Why don't they see that? The wars, the fights, it's useless and gets us nowhere. The suffering, the pain, the hunger.

Why do we hunger for the wrong things? Am I wise, am I not? What am I? Who am I? What can I do? I want to help so badly.

Am I willing to suffer? How can it be considered suffering when others benefit? Help me not to hurt others. Help me not to push others away. Help me not to turn another away or myself away. Help me feel the connection, strengthen the connection. For only then do I know I live. Let me love more fully, give more fully, forgive more fully. Help me to see more fully, to know more fully, experience life more fully. With life comes pain but sometimes that is all there is to know.

Help me to use sarcasm less to push others away. Help me to become even more real. Give me understanding. It's a suggestion not a demand. Help me understand another's fear so I can alleviate it.

Help me to move out of love, out of respect, out of caring. Please take away my pettiness to see another, experience another, love another. Let me move with the peace of a dove. As the earth gives, so let I. As the stars know, so let I. As the moon understands, so let I. With the love as old as time, so allow me to move. Transform me, purify me, let your goodness shine throughout me. Allow me to walk intelligently with love and awareness.

Please forgive me the harm I've done others. Please forgive what I've had to do to survive. Thank you for allowing me this wonderful experience and opportunity to grow. It has brought so much goodness, it is well worth it. Help me to obtain the purity I had as a child. Help me revive the love I felt, the clarity of life, the lack of restraints. I am free to come out, free to breakout of my self-contained prison.

What I've done to keep people away. Well, no harm can come to me from another human as long as there is love. It is the right way, the only way. It is the way it must be. The things we do for love. Is it enough that they are around me? Can they see me or have they been hurt too much?

There is more, so much more. A strength seldom heard, seldom seen, seldom touched. Thou who hath loved is not a failure. Thank you for the peace, for the transcendence, for the calm. Thank you for it all, I guess you do know best.

5/7/93

I feel alone, apart. I feel I don't have a family system operating in my life. I don't like that I have gone five days without a single message on my machine. I feel no one ever thinks about me. I feel no one cares and no one did.

What is the matter with this planet? Why are we all so fucked up on priorities? Where has our value system gone?

Vent, let it out. It wasn't supposed to have happened. I shouldn't have needed to worry or think about it. I shouldn't have needed to waste energy on it. It should never need to be spoken. I should have felt safe. I want someone to care about me. I want to feel the love I should have felt as a child. I want to be able to care, to love as fully as I wanted to as a child. A child's love is so precious, why does it have to be taken away? It is so pure, so complete. Why did it have to be taken away from me? How can I get it back? I want your freedom back. I want your joy back. I don't want to be afraid. I want to let the love flow.

5/13/93

Taken from me, stolen in the night.
What is my true nature?
Where do I stand?
My burning desires—
Joy, fun, carefree
—escape my reality.
The pain, fear, the terror of your touch.
I was not meant for this, I was meant for love.
How do I relearn, where do I find myself?

Quivering, chills, get away from me.
You're too near, I don't want to be here.
Why don't you leave?
I am not the one you should want,
I didn't mean to attract you.
Why must you touch me daddy?
Where's my mommy?
Who can help me?

There's no one there, does anyone care?
Will I ever be treated better?
Do I deserve more?
Evil as a cover, you can't touch me.
If you knew how good I was, you would hurt me.
At least the evil me doesn't get hurt.
At least the evil me doesn't feel.
At least the evil me can't be touched.
My good side gets hurt.
My love destroys me.
My good side gets the demons.
My loving side brings understanding.
My loving side brings respect.
My loving side brings me you.

The rain pours down,
I am alone.
You creep in silently to pull the bedcovers down.
The pain is intense,

I want to vomit, I stifle my screams.

What is the use, no one cares.

There's no one to help.

I scream out, you hit me.

I try to bite you, you push harder.

I am silent.

5/18/93

Love and pain. Those I love repeatedly let me down and hurt me. So much pain around love. All I can ever see or feel is the pain. Where was the joy, the fun? Where has it been? Love is supposed to be positive and pleasant? Really?

How can I reach out when all there has ever been is pain? How do I learn to trust again? One day at a time. Can I take care of myself enough today to have fun? Just for today, can I take care of myself so that I don't get hurt? I have never known love to be fun. Relaxation, peace, easy, love. How do you trust someone?

It feels so good to feel as though I've been seen. I feel like someone has seen my potential without questioning my means to getting there. I do like being validated. You have the ability to touch the deepest part of my soul. You allow me to see the inner beauty of my soul. Am I truly all that you see? You have helped to ease my pain just by your being there.

I don't like what I've been taught about love. It's an ugly, dirty thing. I don't see the beauty in it at all. It's full of spiteful, painful situations. God I was hurt deeply and badly.

6/18/93

I wonder if I'm getting another memory. I've been so sad and irritable lately. I've always been so sad around others. Do I just look at the negative side? It's easier to look at the bad side. It's familiar, it's known. It keeps me from looking at all that's missing in my life.

I have known the most misery in my life from others. That in itself can keep me wanting to be alone. The price paid for having others in your life. I think I've been hanging around the wrong people. Have I found my own yet? People with little expectations of life can keep you down.

I want life to be better than what it has been. I want more. I want to go the distance, I want to try. I don't want to get stuck. Attitude will get you everywhere. I am a hard worker and I do have a good attitude most days. And when I don't, I try anyway.

Surround yourself with people who are where you want to be, not where you were. I need someone in my life on a more consistent basis that is where I want to be. Do I need someone else or do I just need me?

I am not where I could be nor will I ever be. There will always be more to attain. Miracles are only ideas with a lot of hard work behind them.

6/27/93

Changes in relationships. I've been a bitch lately. It hasn't been my main concern to make bridges with others and it's starting to bother me. Where do I lie on the scale? I like to have fun and be free but I'm afraid that it might be at another's expense more than it needs to be. I don't feel I've been as open and accepting as I could be. My compassion and empathy seem to be lacking. Somewhere, somehow.

Where do I fit in relation to others? Am I okay with where I am in life? What do I need to work on next?* Where does the beauty lie?

Others seem to have wisdom, is mine so much more? I am so young, am I searching too much? Many things it's just not my time to understand.

What type of people am I currently bringing into my life? Doesn't everyone see what I see? Am I that perceptive? Actually I feel I need more development in that area.

I've felt lately that I am missing the obvious. I need to do something and not quite sure what. Something has to change. Problems that aren't there and solutions that are.

What is my responsibility and what are other people's? Help me not to take on other people's crap. But let me fully take my own. I think I need some fine-tuning of the adult in me. My behavior does come down to the fact that I don't want to hurt anyone else. I don't ever want to be the cause of someone else's misery.

Do I know what I want? Will I know it when I see it? How do you know?

---

* Figuring out which healthy interpersonal skill I wanted to learn as part of my healing and recovery.

7/9/93

What a strange phase I've come out of. Weeks of dissatisfaction and imbalance—more of a feeling of disharmony.

Now I feel good, I feel confident, much more grounded/ settled. Very content. What will come, will come. Where is everyone else on the journey? The process is important.

Emotions, connections, integrations. The evil lurking in the shadows is gone. So much more, life of wonder and joy. Sometimes it just is with no major reasoning. Or no minor earthly reasoning.

No matter what, I need to go. What will happen? Where will this friendship lead? Time will tell. Space and time.

I am much more comfortable. I think I geek [sic] out less. It'll be fine. It'll be a learning experience. I'd prefer a positive one; it will be a positive one if only to strengthen my convictions.*

9/8/93

It was so nice to be treated with such respect. To be valued. Finally, a man who knew how to treat me. It was so flattering. God it felt good.

Can I get that feeling for myself? If it's out there, it's in here. I am a valued employee; I can or could live up to what others see in me. More responsibility, more intelligence. I will become what I want in a role model. I love that person. I can be admired. I do more because it needs to be done, not to pump myself up. I fell between the cracks on too many occasions.

---

* Realizing you can learn from positive situations too.

I can be more truthful, people want to know and it is their responsibility to be prepared for the answer. The development of a great woman.

Where do all the influences come from? That was a great and needed experience for me. Add it onto past knowledge. There are men like that out there.

I feel good. I am a confident, mature, intelligent woman. It's okay to go forward. I have choices and can create life to be the way I want it to be. Live life the way you think it should be. It is my life to be done with as I choose. To be spent the way I want. It's better to get off the well-beaten road and forge a new trail for myself.

Didn't I go through similar things with my family? Didn't it work out best when I left them and let them go? Only then could I rejoin them. Only then could I start to care.

9/9/93

It is not forever. A year of dramatic change. It is the emotional that is keeping me back and it is time for more change. It is time for the outward to manifest from the inward. It is time to let it go.

It was helpful at one time but not anymore. It's keeping me back from truer, less petty relationships. I still am very petty and not as loving and accepting and gracious as I could be.

Your surroundings do matter. It is good that I left. Next time I need to take more time for me and forget the outside stuff. Relax and let go.

Thanksgiving 1993

Dad's cancer is back, it doesn't look good.

More struggles with men and relationships and what they mean. It's something I've always wanted and it's hard for me to wait. I keep trying to figure it out instead of letting it happen. Men I've been attracted to, men I haven't. I must be true to myself. I will not settle.

I know the feelings I want; I know the unity and closeness I want. I really don't need to worry. I am feeling connected, a part of things. I fumble, I stumble, I fall, I get back up. I don't need to worry as much. It feels good. I am coming home to myself more and more. It is making more and more sense. Dad or family or both? Good-bye dad, hello family?

It's been hell, it's been lonesome, it's been lonely but it's been worth it. I won't settle, it's out there. It will find me. I won't find it, it'll find me.

2/4/94

Boulder, CO

Destination of destiny?

Fear, will they see me? Have I been taking it too easy? It'll be a challenge. Shedding of my defenses. Will I fit in? Will I find friends? Will my life be any different? Will it be better? Can I find the life I desire out here?

I know I will work hard. I know I am capable. I have a lot of loving support around me. Do I have what it takes, what they want? I want to learn, I want to grow, I want to be more.

I am prepared; I do know what I am doing. I have accumulated wonderful experiences in the past two years. It'll all fall into place. Everything always works out far better than I could have ever planned. I do know what I want and won't settle for less.

2/7/94

Interview over with. I don't feel great about it. For some reason Sandra felt it was necessary for me to know that dad was in the hospital one and a half hours before the day started. I feel it could have waited.

Two years I have worked towards that interview and I went into it not feeling emotionally great. That really hurt.

Discern between inside and out. This is definitely out. Inside comes when I think others are thinking particular, though untrue, things about me. A day that should have been happy and great for me wasn't.

That hasn't happened in a long time. How would that information from Sandra benefit me at all for my interview? Did she think it would aid me in doing my best? Does she hate me that much? Why did she think I needed to know at that particular point? I know it will all work out for the best but it still hurts. What would possess her to do that?

2/12/94

Okay, what is it? Sandra majorly [sic] touched some issue since I am still upset with her.

I wish she were more than what she is. I wish she were more like me. She's so goody two-shoes and tries to be so perfect. Is it her, is it me, is it dad and his illness? I can't let this go.

I am upset that a day that should have been happy for me wasn't. I feel undervalued for all the hard work I've done for the past two years. I feel upset that she wasn't there for me. I feel I am not allowed to be me. I am not allowed to see the world my way. I am not allowed to live my life my way.

Why are they clinging to the old ways of life? There is so much more out there. Reach for it. God they frustrate me. How can they live with so much denial? Dad is dying, don't they know these things? Can't they tell? What planet do they live on? Of course I'd be upset. I have a right to be upset.

How can they live their lives that way? Reality is knocking, let it in. I get so confused with them. How could I grow up in that environment? They contradict what I see so much. They pretend that it's not there. How do I relate with them? Don't they hear what they are saying? Don't they see what they are doing? What reality do they live in?

My family, ugh! Do they even know who I am? I wouldn't have done that and that's what bothers me. I was disregarded. Not everyone can be me though. To live with others!!!

That's her extent. That is how she reaches out. Going through the motions but not necessarily sincere. I feel so many people who know me less like me more than my sister does. Why don't I accept her gifts as readily as I accept others? My family's gifts usually prove how much they don't know me or I feel our distance because of the gifts.

They don't reaffirm me or my traits as a human being. Is it the gift or just because they are from a family member? The latter. Because they have been a part of my life for such a long time I feel they should know me better, but they don't. To see each other is to see our pain. To see our loneliness and isolation. My family totally lacks trust, a trust I have taken so long to find. A trust I need to survive. A trust that is worth living for, dying for. It makes life more joyful for I can let others be close to me. I can reach out to others and know I will be received and welcomed. Too much fear in the world. It is a friendly, fun place.

I can trust, I do trust, I choose to trust.

2/13/94

Blood spills out of my pores.
Your love is there waiting,
Time ticked on yet I didn't see.
Steadfast and free.
I run to you now,
What took me so long?

Over and under,
Wild and free.
The wheat in your field,
Golden and true,
The warmth of your sun.
Welcoming me, encompassing me
Filling my soul.
I bask, I bathe

Your golden rays shimmer on my back.
Endless light welcomes me home.
Draws me near.
Keeps me safe.
As endless as the sea,
As pure as gold.
A treasure to behold,
Gracious and true.

2/19/94

It was a different relationship to say the least. No one based
so much on love but on sex. The constant pain of uncertainty
lingered in my mind. Night after night. Day after day. How could
I maintain the front?

It was not okay, it was not fine, it was not supposed to happen.
My life is not meant to be lived this way. Your torture at night
torments during the day. Don't you know what you're doing to
me? You're killing me but I don't want to die. I'm too young, I'm
too vulnerable. I must grow old, I must wise up. Only I can stop
the agony. Alone I must fight for the world. I alone shall free the
slaves. I alone shall free my soul.

Death's shadow looms ever so near,
I look over your shoulder and it is there.
Silence in the night,
Cool intake of air,
Quickening my pulse.
I feel you near, I pull away.

I close up as not to let you in.
It never works, it never will.
You can get to me when others can't.
You wretch my soul from my body
And spit upon the remains.

I want to die.
Your slow murder rips my guts.
Do you care so little for me?
I am your flesh and blood.
Do you not care?
Do you know how?
Will you ever leave my side?
Will you ever leave me alone?
With death does it end?

Will your death bring me peace? Such a difficult and deep relationship. So intertwined, too intertwined. The damage was done long ago. Can it be repaired? Too deep for a child. The interplay of my life with yours. Back and forth we go without comfort or speed. One day it'll make sense. It already does, but so much happened. Pain and misery everywhere. When can I go away? I don't want to take you with. I want to leave you behind. I will always remember. For it did happen, it did matter but I count too.

I want my chance, I want to be free, I want my life back now. I can have my life back now. One sacrifice for another. I sacrificed my life for you, now you must sacrifice yours for mine. I need to be let go. I need me.

3/4/94

I didn't get into the master's program. Time will let me know why. Another year of undergraduate work.

I am feeling resistance towards the idea of letting it all go. To be revealed and known. It's a goodness I can't get used to. I am moving towards the unknown, a new and different life. How will this move change me? What opportunities will open to me?

A lot of oldness there too. Knowing people and everything I have. I don't want to get rid of the person I am, I just want to become more of who I am. So many unknowns. Learn to live all over again.

What do I want my life to be like? I want closer, more open, more accessible friendships. I want truth and kindness. I want people around to support me. I want my house, my home. I want something that is mine. I want someone to share my life with. I want kindness, gentleness, a loving and giving life.

Later on that same day....

I don't like looking at the section of my life right before I started getting my life back. It scares me how out of control I had gotten. How much I had let others rule my life. How little regard I had for life. I was ready to throw it all away. I didn't have my own. I was lost. I was going nowhere.

I am coming to a point where I shall again rediscover my beauty. I have been running, pushing away those who see my beauty within. It was a part of me that was hurt and that vulnerability scares me.

Will I be safe? Can I come out again without being hurt? Will it be okay this time? Will life be the way I see it to be? Will I be valued this time? Will I finally be treated the way I deserve?

Graduate school will reintroduce to me a person who has been gone a very long time and I have missed her. It's been so long since I have been free. Someone who wants to shine again. Someone who has rejected love for years. It will finally be okay to be me!

I can't live the life they want me to. I need to live my own life. I can't pretend things are okay when they're not. I need to live with reality. The good, the bad, and the ugly. Major change, minor change, round and round it goes. Life continues on. Things die, people die. Life is brought forth to be reborn.

I can't be the person they created anymore. I need to be me. I want to experience all of life. I have lost my family in the last few years. One by one they drop out of my life. Gone forever are the days of childhood. But I need to let go of my childhood as an institution to say hello to the child.

What don't I like about being strong? It's lonely. I have to give up all that I have been taught about life. I have to find out a new way of relating. I can't stay in the safe world of those around me. I have to admit that I am worth more than what I am allowing the circumstances around me to give me. I have to say good-bye to things and people that just aren't doing it for me anymore. I have to say good-bye to things I have loved but aren't what I need anymore. I have to give up parts of me that I love.

I love them but they are not people I want to be like. I hate it when they show their true colors. I have to give up the things

I love most. Yet I don't feel that it is a loss but a gain yet to be experienced.

2013

During my twenties, I was able to find my intelligence again. As the memories came forth from my body, the energy that had been used to keep them repressed was available to be directed into other pursuits. As a child I had been an average student and never felt particularly smart. When I went back to school as an adult I not only had more skills to utilize, I could actually feel my brain working in a different way as the fog cleared. It literally felt like my brain had more energy to process information. I relished feeling accomplished in this area after years of feeling stupid.

I was also able to be more present in my body. Though I was never officially diagnosed with PTSD, I could recognize the symptoms within myself. They still pop up in my life when a situation repeats the dynamics of my childhood and continues on for an extended period of time. My anxiety level increases and my thoughts travel down the familiar self-defeating path. I know I am dissociating when I feel spacey and numb. It's like my brain is a couple of feet above my body and I can't feel it or my extremities as clearly. I am not taking in information from my environment as completely as usual. I am walking around with a feeling of, 'huh, what?'

I learned to counter this by taking deep breaths. I learned to feel my feet on the ground by wiggling my toes and shifting my weight from one foot to the other. Putting my attention toward my hands by making a fist or pushing against something.

Feeling my bottom on whatever I was sitting upon. Noticing my environment and doing self-talk to let myself know I was safe. Using my senses to become present in the moment. What can I see, hear, smell, taste, and/or feel and naming at least three of these things in my head.

3/19/94

What will the next four years bring? I sure am going for a change in my life. It's time to go. I'll land on my feet again. I do like what I've done with my life. I really have had many interesting experiences. I have taken what I needed and integrated it into my life. I really do have a lot of experience.

3/31/94

The circles of life. I need to go with my gut. It works for me. I enjoy walking my talk. I enjoy being a person of integrity. I am very excited to move. I am curious to see the changes that will come about. More insights into my soul.

People don't leave me as often as I perceive them to. They are there and will come back sometime. We will meet again. The important ones always come back. Life is falling into place for me once more.

I need to find my answers. I do know how to interact with people. I have great social skills. It feels good, it feels right. How I've been living my life lately has been satisfying. I cry more for things that I don't get than for things that are taken away from me. I cry for my unfulfilled desires. Things go away and then come back. I've been given so much in the last few weeks. So many gifts from people around me. It helped to talk about my dance solo. It's that asking for what you need thing.

4/23/94

Look for the bad and ye shall find it. New mood or different mood?

I feel really good about my solo. It's falling into place somehow. Funny how life does that. Pieces I didn't know were there suddenly fit together. I do know what I'm doing. I pick a black dress and weeks later I pick a song about a silhouette. It will all happen. It will get finished. I have what it takes to perform a compelling dance. I have the presentation and the energy. It's the onion with many layers.

Universality, follow your dreams, go to the bliss. Don't settle. Find it within. Go against the grain. Find your own groove. It'll come through. It will have something to say. It does have a very deep and important meaning to me and for others. It's about a beautiful dancer dancing.

Undated

Pathways we take, each blending a different tune. What are the forks and why do we choose our roads? Destiny or freewill— is it ever clear? What life brings you and the places it provides. Ever changing choices, what will this one bring and does it matter?

Views of life, who does have the correct one? No such thing, it just is, never any right or wrong. It just is.

What was down the other road and how did I get here? Why are you here too? Did I put you here—are you even real? Which view are you? Should I go along for the ride? Let's just go and hope for the best. That's all I can ever ask for.

Movement is life and I have chosen life. Move west young lad. What will this bring? Can I do anything about it? I'm only here for the ride. It has been fun. I can't believe all the excitement, the adventure life brings without being asked.

Who would have ever thought life could be so perfect. I couldn't have asked for a better life. It's been so perfect for me. I've been given so much, so much. It's always just what I need. Why worry, it's perfect. Everything is oh so perfect. It's all about justice; I'll get what I need.

How have I accomplished this? I was making so many unconscious choices but they always brought me what I needed. Hiding here I am not alone. Do I want to give it away? I like what I have yet I am hoarding myself instead of letting others enjoy me. My greatest wealth in life is me and I am so good at keeping me to myself. Do I let the world see me yet? Do I ever let myself out? I love myself so much that I just cherish myself. Am I a prisoner to myself? I don't like to share myself with others.

Answers don't always matter. Let's just go and hope for the best. If I let you in, will you let me in too? Can that last wall come down so I can be totally exposed and vulnerable to the world? I know I can protect myself and I will so why not just let it happen. Embrace life, don't fight it. Let go and let the universe take care of me. It knows more than I can ever hope to. Be an instrument to let life flow. Creation of my life—the only thing I will truly ever make. The only thing worth making. I might not know better but the universe does, so let the master take over. Who know what is coming down this path anyway. Why plan out? What will be, what will happen? I think it's destiny with a little freewill thrown in for flavor.

2013: I moved to Boulder, CO at the end of May 1994.

NEW BEGINNINGS

6/13/94

And the way of the world was etched upon her brow. "You look angry," they say. Taken for granted, pushed aside. Am I wrong to search for my life? To want more? The strength in me scares me. What is expected of me? I am here to find out. There is much more in me than I know. I am sad. I have to relinquish the life I've known. See what must be seen. In me and in others.

The world is becoming smaller. I am small, I am weak.

Falseness in their world. But it is what they know. Strange how it all comes out to play. Generations past mix with generations present. I will never understand them nor they me. I left their world behind and now I am the enemy. They don't speak to me, barely acknowledge me. All I did was grow up. But it is a love I miss. The two that adored me now abhor me.

What can I do for the children?* I want them to understand that I haven't left them. It was nothing they did. Do they know that? Will they know it when their parents tell them otherwise? I wish I could relieve the agony they will suffer when the world they see doesn't match up to what their parents see.

---

* The next generation

6/23/94

And the trumpets blared. I think I am starting to thrive again. I'm laughing again. God I needed that change. I'm feeling happy again. Why did the move make a difference? What will come with my family?

Life is so interesting. Where will I fit into my family as time goes on? I finally feel separate from them all. The emotional separation happened long ago. It's good that the emotional and physical match up. I don't want them in this life of mine yet. I feel free and I am enjoying it. I feel people care about me. I feel wanted and accepted. It feels good living here.

6/27/94

I like it out here. I love the mountains. Being so close to grandeur helps my mood. Driving through them always puts things in perspective for me. Looking over past journals I've noticed that I know what I want. I don't trust these things will happen. I project onto others what I want and when they fall short I get upset with them. It is not being fair to the people in my life. I was lonely too. I don't think I knew how lonely I was.

It's starting to matter less what never came before. It's just how my life and personality are. I know what I want and am not willing to compromise. Given the choice, I'd rather live the life as it's been laid out for me than to settle for less than I want. It's not really what I feel I deserve but the quality that I want. The self-assurance that I want. The interaction that I want. The way I am living my life is right for me.

I love being a woman and finding my feminine aspects. I've had some great experiences that have taught me how things should be done. I'm just doing my job. It's what I'm being asked to do and that's what needs to be done. What that makes me is inconsequential.

I have a fear that my dad will be sick and my family won't contact me until he is already dead. This feels pretty legitimate because of the lack of information that comes my way. I find I don't know about things until after the fact. Dad knows that I would say good-bye and that I love him so if it comes out that way, no real harm done. I can't expect much more from my family. It's not like it would be a pleasant experience for me to spend time with them as he's dying. They have been excluding me or am I finally getting my wish? I really don't want to be close to them. I could totally see them not calling me. It feels more like a fact than a fantasy.[*] It's not anything I wish or hope will come about, it just is.

They certainly don't need me to cope with the situation and I'd probably hinder them from reacting how they'd like to. Communication within the extended family will be bad. Not everyone will understand why I wasn't there which would lead to further isolation because it'll be viewed that I don't care. There really isn't anything I can do to make them act courteously.

I feel a letting go of trying to get others to act certain ways and a peace with my actions and other's actions. People are going to act according to their nature no matter what I do. Just as I do,

---

[*] Another thing I learned from *The Courage to Heal* was to discern my fantasy thoughts from facts.

it's in my nature. It doesn't mean it's good or bad, it's just how I am. It's how others are and there is nothing that can be done. We are human beings. It's how life is. And God knows it's all subject to change without any notice.

7/9/94

I am afraid of the power greater than I. Will I measure up to what is being asked of me? The love and strength is over-powering. But it lifts me up.

What if I fail? Do you see me as I am? I want to remain unobtrusive. Is that the word I mean? It won't be me doing it. It'll be something through me. Will I be able to find me again? But I am an instrument for your love.

I'm confused about this. I just need to trust. It'll be a greatness moving through me. I know it won't hurt me. It's a greatness that can strike me down at any moment yet I live. It is something I want though. It's a power that can do anything. I thank you for it.

7/21/94

Thoughts, feelings, actions. Watch them go by like clouds across the sky. Nothing needs to be done about them. Nothing needs to be said. I worry about that which I can do nothing about. It doesn't matter. It all works out.

Anxiety equals lack of trust. Lack of faith. Sit back and watch it go. My intentions are true. If it works, it's great. If not, oh well.

Control and release. I seem to be trying to help in all the wrong ways. It'll come. Relax and let it flow. Make the effort, it feels good.

8/6/94

He's dead, he's finally dead. The man who raped me, the man who hurt me more than any living soul could is gone. I don't have to be nice, I don't have to pretend nothing happened, I don't have to pretend anymore that he was a perfect father. He'll never hurt me again.

The very thing I had always wished for finally came true. That relationship is done, it's over. I can't believe it's over. Can I now love the way I've always wanted? Can I now get on with my life? Can I now let a man love me? Am I free to find my own way now?

My emotions are all over the place. It feels really good to be back home now. I missed the mountains. To have such majesty, such beauty constantly around you does not do any harm.

It's so hard for me to be around my family. Five days and I was more than ready to leave. They have no backbone. They really allow me to look at myself and my principles. Is the money that great? I know they will always let me back in. They are not the disowning type-or are they?

They didn't call when dad was dying. They kept stating everyone was there, is that as in everyone who mattered? I feel I am being excluded in many ways. But I want to be in my nephews' lives. I do feel an exclusion.

They didn't let me know when Charlie was coming to town before I moved. They didn't let me know Sandra was also coming to town in May. They did offer a plane ticket home this past week but I was a busy with work and volunteering. Diane did write a letter to let me know what was going on. I'm dying to know what's happening with the baby. Has it been born yet or not? Make your own family. I still have Monica and the boys.

It'll come together somehow, someday. I don't need to make any decisions today. I am happy with the life I have though I would like someone to hang with, to talk with, to love with, to laugh with, and to cry with.

8/10/94

My dad and men, so intertwined. I don't know where one starts and the other leaves off. I want the hero, the man of principle. I want the truly gentle man. I want the kind man. How do you make that decision for life? I don't think I've ever been given a choice.

What is it about me? I just want someone I can talk to. Most people don't understand. It's the way life is. I am not to be pitied for the way I feel. It just is.

My heart hurts, my heart hurts a lot. The back and forth. What am I looking for? Am I going to want it when I find it? So many conditions that I want. But am I being fair?

Do I judge too harshly without knowing? Or am I right on target? So many opinions in the world, which is right? They all are, it's a matter of perspective.

I don't want to be hurt again. I want to be treated in a decent, kind manner. Protection, I want to be protected. He has never let me know I can count on him. Words yes, actions no.

Can't I mellow out on all this? I am so tired of this merry-go-round that I have my mind on. It's round and round and it doesn't go anywhere. It's all non-sensical babble. Who gives a crap what anyone does to me? It doesn't change me. It's not good or bad, it just is. But around and around I go thinking he cares, she doesn't care. I am so insulting to my friends. What do I expect them to be, superhuman? I am so rude. Judge, judge, judge, judge, judge that's all I do. None of these thoughts get me anywhere. What do I need to do? Doing is not being.

8/19/94

Briana was welcomed into the family two days ago. I hope it'll be okay for her. God I hope nothing happens to her. I will protect her as much as I can.

I feel better about a girl being born into the family with dad gone. I hope she has a better chance than I did. It's so much fun to watch the kids grow. It really is a miracle, the joining of two gene pools to create a life. What will they look like? What personality traits will they develop? In what way will they create their own life?

What have I mourned already? There is so much I have gone through in the past few years. I am really happy to be in Colorado. To have the mountains within reach is incredible. The purple mountain majesty, I know what that means. How can you not feel good with that beauty surrounding you? I really am fortunate to be here. I feel better being away from my family too. I love them dearly but I do better away from them. They are who they are, I am who I am. It's easier for me to accept them when I don't have to put up with their meanness. It's easier for them to accept me too. Well, maybe they aren't mean; they just have a strange way of showing they care.

They are so afraid of living. Life isn't safe; you need to take risks and chances to be there for others.

8/26/94

Dear Dad,

In your death I've been looking for answers. Answers about love, answers about hate. How can one love so blindly? Does love always bring sorrow? If I love will I get hurt? Mom loved you very much. Enough to look past the pain and harm you caused in my life. I have always wanted a deep, satisfying love relationship but with it will I too become blind to the evils that lurk in a man? She loved your good and your bad and put you above all others. Will I too become so blind as not to stop someone from hurting someone I love? Could I love someone so much that I would allow them to torture a child of mine?

I wanted to know how this happened. What was going on in your life? Do any others see your nasty side? Everyone talks about you like you were a saint, but you weren't. Didn't they see your dark side? Does anyone else on this planet know about it?

Patient, kind, gentle, who was this man they described? My eyes still look angry. Maybe I understand too well. Maybe I know too much. The things you taught me about love and respect are not what I wanted to learn nor is it how I want to live my life. What was handed down to future generations?

You looked so sad in your coffin. What was life like for you? I really did want to be there when you died but I didn't know about it until after the fact. I would have liked to help with your transition to the other world. I think I could have helped. It's nothing to fear. It's all that we want on earth and more. I wish you could have found some peace and beauty in the world. It is here all around us. The next world is just another step. You are loved here, you'll be loved there. It is a thin, thin line.

I loved you and I did learn a lot from you. Hearing what others saw in you, I know I got your best traits. I hope I am able to take these further. I have learned to go after my dreams. Through it all I did learn to be a better person because you were my dad. I learned to find the life I want to live and not settle for what is given to me. I am glad that your suffering is over. I really wish we could have talked about the abuse and your life. I don't understand it but I do forgive you for it. I hope you find peace in the afterlife. People come and people go but the spirit remains the same. So many ways to die. So many ways to live.

1/18/95

And the rain came down
Endless in a sea of sorrow
I touched the heart
The raven pecked at
Dutifully in the winter's night.
I sat upon a gardens wall
When the begonias started to fall.
The tide went away
Yet I stayed.
Turning, stretching toward the noise,
I prayed to silence it all.
Yet the drips continued,
Down, down, down.

Let the snow melt away
To shine a new dawn.
Morning doves coo the welcoming peace.
Last nights storm leaves its debris.
Trees knocked down
Never to stand tall again.
Who lives with this destruction?
It is you and I.

Life doesn't always deal you the hand you want. But sometimes
it is the winning hand anyway.

2/1/95

I have been leading my own life through others. I've been fearing what has happened to another will happen to me. The difference is I don't allow it to happen. I am leery around people. I hesitate but I acknowledge I do it. I can trust myself.

I do try to make good out of bad situations, which isn't necessarily a bad trait, I just take things too far. I give people too many chances. I do get out when things don't seem to be going the way I want. I can take care of myself. I do watch out for others. I do act when it is appropriate.

I can find my own way, my own path. My life can be different. It is not inevitable that I end up with a child molester. It's just confusing seeing the two generations before me end up with child molesters. But I am a different person.

That life doesn't have to be my own. It can be better for me. I can take care of myself. I can forgive others. I can forgive myself. It doesn't have to be that way, I can go forward.

2013

With abuse there are questions from others regarding: why didn't you say something, why didn't you leave, why did you stay? Unless you go through it you don't understand the mental prison that gets built around you. Its function is to keep you safe in that you are surviving through the day. You are still alive. For me this prison was a familiar way of life and my family was a safety net of sorts. In the following entry this is the net I am referring to as I imagined what would happen if I let it go.

4/7/95

> If I cut the net then they will abandon me.
>
> If I cut the net then they will turn on me.
>
> If I cut the net then they will lie about me.
>
> If I cut the net then they can live without me.
>
> If I cut the net then they will abandon me.
>
> If I cut the net then I lose my ties to them.
>
> If I cut the net then I won't be part of the family.
>
> If I cut the net then I have to face the consequences.
>
> If I cut the net then everyone will know.
>
> If I cut the net then I will be alone.
>
> If I cut the net then I'll have nothing to fall back on.
>
> If I cut the net then I'll have to rely on me.
>
> If I cut the net then all I have is me.

I'm sure one day this will all make sense but until it does, this sure is hell. More information.* What do I do with it? I have had so many fortunate things happen to me. So why do I feel like hell?

I feel weighed down, beaten down by the world. I feel I've been given a bum deal. I don't want to live with the negativity. I don't want to live alone. I have given up all hope of relationships. They never seem to go anywhere. I don't know how else to be either. I can't wait until I reach a certain point but I will never be there. There will always be more to work on. God I feel like hell.

---

* A new memory surfaced about this time.

I want to feel a part of a family. I want to feel loved and supported. Why can't I feel it with my own? I wish I knew what was going to happen. Will it always be me against them? Why can't I get clear answers from them? I need answers, I need something more concrete. Couldn't I have one of them on my side? Couldn't just one of them remember for me? I feel so all alone through this. Couldn't one of them say, yes Dusana, I do remember the rape. Couldn't one of them be there for me? They were all there, couldn't one of them help me? Couldn't one of them stick their neck out for me? Couldn't one of them be kind or considerate towards me? Couldn't they help me now? They couldn't in the past but they have no excuse now. They could come forward now but they don't.

Where does this leave me in relation to them? Where do we go from here? What do I put up with from them? What do I confront them on?

They aren't a part of my life because I won't be a part of theirs. I can't live my life like that anymore. Where do I fit into their lives and where do they fit into mine?

4/9/95

Where do I go from here? I am feeling so vastly different from others that it is painful. I spent last night with some people that I grew up with. I felt I didn't have a lot to say to them. How can I talk to people about what is really going on in my life? I feel so boring, like I don't have a lot to share with others. There's just too much of my life that I feel is way too personal to share with casual friends.

Do I let people in my life? There's just so much that I don't feel others will understand. I hope as I get older that I am able to find a group I fit into.

I'm so impatient to know how my life is going to turn out. I want to be twenty years older to know that everything turned out okay, that I made all the right choices. But I guess I need to decide how to act now to hopefully get the outcome I want in twenty years. What do I have to do now? And where am I going?

5/17/95

Argh!

God I'm so pissed off and frustrated with how my family is. I've been crying the past two days each time I see something remotely similar to what I want from a family. Why can't they see? Why can't they admit it? I feel like I am hitting a brick wall. Why can't they be nice considerate people? Assholes-that word keeps popping up for me a lot. What is with their bullshit?

They are so weird. Where do they think they are going to get with all of this? Why can't they put the two boys first? They really are uncaring. Do I honor others too much? Do I lose myself in trying to be everything to everyone? Can my family ever be honest? I will do whatever I need to do to protect the children. Why didn't that happen for me? Wasn't there/isn't there one member of my family that would stick their neck out for me? My family is as insane as ever. It's days like these that I don't want to be by them.

6/16/95

Father's day is on Sunday and I've been grieving all week. I haven't been able to sleep and I've been edgy at work. I've treated myself to a weekend away.

I keep trying to find answers to what, why, how did it happen? I have finally allowed myself to scream. Will I ever be able to be with a man without ghosts haunting me? Is there a man out there to satisfy me?

I feel so small and alone. Infinite wisdom lurking around the corner. I don't feel attractive anymore. Or it's more a feeling of 'what's the use of it?' And the question that keeps going through my mind, 'am I busy because I'm alone or am I alone because I am busy?' It fills up my time but is it a life? It's the life I have but is it the life I want?

I would love to build a foundation on which to let things grow. I keep wanting *to get on* with my life. What does that mean?

The father archetype. The ever-loving, all-knowing protector. You failed, dad. And I'm so sorry that I am the one to know it. I saw your humanness. You never could be all things to me. You could never be what I wanted you to be. You were up against a high icon in my eyes. I feel like a bitch for having standards that I don't know if anyone can live up to. People do when I look around. There are a lot of people that do satisfy a need in me. At least they can see their own humanness and laugh about it. That's what drives me insane about my family, their need to be perfect.

Is it just my own need? The need to be everything to everyone? I have mentioned that or at least thought about it in the past. I can laugh at myself and the human side of life. Things happen over which we have no control.

I'm staying at a 120 year old hotel in Fairplay, CO. It's comforting to sit here and think about all the people who have slept in this room. It's a good representation of the coming and going of life. That veil that keeps us serious. Pan* would laugh at my pain to show the web that I've gotten myself stuck in. I have defined myself but is this whom I want to be? What would it feel like to be unstuck? To be in the moment, to be ever in a state of flux.

7/7/95

Dear Mom,

There's so much I want you to know about me but I don't know if it's possible. There are so many areas and things I leave unsaid to avoid parental concern.

I am alright mom; I want you to know that, to believe that. I want you to see me, to know what I feel. I feel I have to keep up a brave front for you. There is more depth to me than you will ever know. I wish I could show you my best side but it is the side that you always criticized. I know it doesn't fit into the boundaries of society but it

---

* Another archetype character. I was so invested in the story I told about my life that I couldn't find another way of looking at it.

is who I am. I am not a perfect little lady. I am a full-bodied woman with a passion for life. Who cares what others think, I am having fun and I am not hurting anyone.

Why won't you let this side of me come to life around you? I always felt you wanted to silence this part of me but it is the biggest part of me. You got the daughter you always wanted in Diane, now why can't you let me be me? I am rude, I am crude, I am imperfect but I like me that way. At least I am a thread woven through the fabric of life and not a pattern to be copied.

Maybe I don't appreciate you enough.

Mom, can you look at me? See me? Could you show yourself to me just once? I have always felt guarded around you, never wanting to disturb your life with my life. Do I hold any importance in your life except as a piece to show off? Do you know the importance of my life to me? Do you know how the things I do affect me? The meaning they have for me? Do you know what I am working towards? Do you know me at all? Not just my goals but the motivation behind them? What do you say to others about me? How do you describe me? Is it at all similar to how others describe me to you? Would you recognize the person my friends see in me? If they described me to you, would you know it was me? Do you know me mother?

I hope your trip here can be the start of answering these questions. I hope we can work at seeing each other in a non-judgmental way. I love you and would like the two of us to start to get to know one another. ~Dusana

8/2/95

The cars whizzed by,
plummeting into the depths of insanity.
Do they know where they are going?
Or are they led blindly by societies demands.
The soul knows the way it must go to reach the promised land.
But is it a vast wasteland ever demanding more?
Yet here I go again plummeting into the darkness of my soul.
Alone to the outside world but held
within the strictest confidences.
I know you are there yet you do not speak.
Is there a word I could give you to let me in?
Or shall I walk in your shadow forever.
It is not mine to ask but for you to give freely.
Spinning my own deception onto the souls of others.
The gap is too large to bridge but too close to feel.
The pain, the suffering, let it in to
experience the joys, the mystery.
Hide out in your shell, the vast wasteland of the soul.
Look into my eyes, my love, and see what I see.

The harm you caused shall never go away,
But color my vision forevermore.

Your reality is not my own, yet it pains me.
Stricken with your sorrows you strode along to no end.
The pain you wore like a badge of courage,
Keeping me at a distance yet drawing me near.

8/6/95

Sporadically we touch each other's lives.
I leave a little bit of me with you each time we depart.
Are we really away from one another?
I can bring you readily here.
Your touch, your voice comforts me in my darkest hour.
I miss you, yet you are here protecting me.
Keeping me safe.
I shall never be alone.

8/7/95

What am I going through? Confusion about life. Where am I
headed? There's an uncertainty in my future. It feels like a wide,
open void. Yet I do know what I am doing. It's the things that I
want and I feel that they may actually come true.

Could it be what I am feeling is hope? I am uncertain of this
hope. It feels strange to me. There is a wide open void ahead
and I don't know what is on the other side. Something is going
to happen and for once I don't know how it is going to happen.
For once, I don't know what is expected of me. I don't know

what to feel or do. How strange for me not to know. Something wonderful is going to happen and I am scared to let it happen. It is so different from what I have seen, what I am used to. I have a hard time believing in it. That it will finally happen. I feel like I want to shake off how I've been living. All I've learned, all I've seen. But I feel frustrated with how things have been.

While I enjoy the life I have made, I am ready for more. Ugh, how many times have I written that and it didn't go anywhere? A clearing, I feel a clearing away about to happen. The circles of life will happen no matter what I do. They keep spinning and I need to spin with them. I don't have much control over it but I can trust.

Dream: Dad was dead but still moving around for the preparation for it. He came downstairs and I still made sure he was comfortable. I spoke of it being a nice way to go so unfinished business could be dealt with.

Interpretation: I am still taking care of the dead. I feel so embarrassed for him that I saw him as a failed human being. Being the way he was. I saw it, I witnessed it. He failed as a human being, what a way to live. People I loved, and the way they lived. The life they lived, how awful.

1/16/96

Dear Dusana,

I am writing this letter to release my resentments and negative emotions and to discover and express the positive feelings that you deserve. I am also writing this letter to ask for your support without demanding it.

I don't like the way you push men away and won't let them see the real you. I hate the way you keep a distance and put on an uncaring front. I don't like the way that you demean men to keep the upper hand. I hate the way you always need to be right. I hate the way you can't allow others to help you. I don't like it when you keep yourself alone when there are men who want to spend time with you. I hate it when you pull away from a man. I hate your fear of intimacy and the nauseous feelings you have when you are too close to a man. I hate the way you need to be better than others. I hate the way you push others away emotionally and keep up the front that everything is okay. I hate your lack of clarity around men's intentions. I hate the way the past comes into the present. I hate the way you keep me alone. I hate your fear of something more. I hate your fear of happiness. I hate the way you hurt when you are happy. I hate your lack of awareness and the way you use humor to keep others away.

It hurts when you don't give yourself the chance to be known. It hurts the way you push others away. It hurts to think that you don't think you deserve happiness. It hurts to think that you don't think you deserve something great. It hurts to think that you think you deserve any of the treatment you have gotten. It hurts to think that you aren't good enough. It hurts to think that you don't deserve a nice man. It hurts to think that anyone ever treated you badly. It hurts to think that anyone ever hurt you. It hurts to think that someone didn't love you. It hurts to think that someone didn't care.

It is painful to watch you not give yourself what you deserve. It is painful to watch you fall short of your capabilities. I am afraid that you will always keep yourself alone. I am afraid that you will never trust again. I am afraid that you won't allow yourself the things that you deserve. I am afraid that you won't allow yourself the happiness that someone like Dean could give you. I am afraid that Dean won't want me. I am afraid that Dean isn't interested in me. I am afraid that you won't let someone help you with your sex issues. I am afraid that you won't let someone love you. I am afraid that you will drive someone away.

I am afraid of life. I am afraid to be close to a man. I am afraid to love someone. I am afraid to trust someone. I am afraid of being hurt. I am afraid of the future. I am afraid that no one will love me. I am afraid that no one will want me. I am afraid that no one will give me the patience and understanding that I deserve. I am afraid that I will be alone.

I am sorry that I don't allow you to get the things that you deserve. I am sorry that I don't allow men to get close to you. I am sorry that I don't trust you. I am sorry that I won't allow you the chance to prove yourself. I am sorry that I don't allow you to be happy. I am sorry that I keep you alone. I am sorry that I don't allow you to interact honestly with others. I am sorry that I don't allow others to see you clearly. I am sorry that I won't let Dean in. I am sorry that I keep men away. I am sorry that I don't treat you fairly. I am sorry that I don't let you prove yourself with a man. I am sorry that I make you nauseous with intimacy. I am sorry that I don't let men near. I am sorry that I don't let you be vulnerable around men. I am sorry that I make you keep the upper hand around men. I am sorry that I don't let you respond honestly. I am sorry I keep you away from men. I am sorry that I don't let men in. I am sorry that I don't let you be happy. I am sorry that I don't give you what you deserve. I am sorry that I give you the short end of the deal. I am sorry that I don't trust.

I love the way you understand. I love the way you are willing to work so hard for what you want. I love your humor and your positive attitude. I appreciate your tenderness and love. I appreciate your friendliness. I forgive you for keeping men away. I forgive what you have needed to do to keep yourself safe. I would like to thank you for keeping yourself alive. I thank you for your perseverance. I thank you for your understanding. I thank you for being committed to healing.

I realize that you have had a hard life and do things to feel safe. I would like to be able to trust and give yourself the happiness you deserve. I would like to help you fulfill your wildest dreams. I would like to help you fulfill your greatest potential. I would like to help you bring a nice man into your life. I forgive you for feeling nauseous from intimacy.

I love you,

Dusana

1/28/96

Why don't I date?

Fear of the unknown. Who would I be if I were loved? Where would that put me? This person I have always known has never been loved. I just don't know. I wouldn't know how to be. I wouldn't know who I was anymore. I would have to learn about the world in a whole new way. I would have to learn to relate to others in a whole new way.

I wouldn't know myself anymore. I wouldn't recognize myself anymore. Who would I be if I actually gave myself a chance with men? What could I blame my family for if I was loved? They wouldn't be at fault anymore. I would be loved in spite of what they did to me. I would be loved in spite of what they thought of me. They wouldn't win. They wouldn't have me anymore.

I wouldn't have me anymore. I would have to rediscover who I was in relation to the world. I think my world is crumbling into *a million pieces* again and I have to pick each one up and look at it. Who would be the Dusana that is loved and taken care of? Who is the Dusana that men find attractive? Who is the Dusana that men want to be around? Who is the Dusana that needs another human being in her life? Where did she go? Where is the Dusana that lets another human being know her and love her? Can she come out and play?

I push away that which I want the most. My words and actions don't match up. The integrity of a lifetime. Being true to oneself. Letting the world take care of you. You don't always have to do the work. You can let another come in and assist you.

You have already made the statement to yourself that he doesn't know. So let the man know you. Let the man understand you. Let the man love you. You already have the answers to the questions that keep running through your mind. You know what is going on, now what can you do to stop it? Why don't you ask for what you want? Fear that I won't get it. Fear that I won't be listened to. Fear that I'll be laughed at. Fear that I'll be ignored. Fear that I'll re-prove to myself that I don't matter.

2007

A Million Little Pieces. That was how I was going to start the book I was going to write. That was going to be my title. My healing from incest equated to walking into the hallway, picking up a crystal vase and smashing it on the floor. It breaks into a million little pieces and I have to pick each one up, look at it, and put the vase back together. I imagined the vase sitting on a round table, Duncan Phyfe style, with a crocheted doily under it. The floor is a sleek, white marble. Very elegant surroundings for the beginning of my personal hell. And now some guy who made up a story has taken my title. There is no originality left in this world. My thoughts are being thought by someone else at this very moment. If I don't grab them, someone else will.

1/31/96

Seasons change, so does my mind. The enemy invades from the east, sanity from the west and never the two shall meet. The men of my life suck, or so I want them to. They want me, I don't want them. I want them and they don't want me. What evilness changes my body and mind so?????

The past is a blur that I don't want to receive too clearly. The future is uncertain. Do I have a future to bet upon? To have someone see me so vulnerable scares the crap out of me.

How about the cancer, is it cancer, is it not? Explore life and all its wonders. Do I care? Do I really want to go forward with this? Do I have a choice? I don't want to die.

He came to her in the night
and took the soul that she was saving for another.
He took it and never looked back.
He took it when he had no need for it.

He took it and he ran.

The winter's song is sung silently through the night.

Are they there?

They listen through the night but no one ventures out.

Afraid of the big bad wolf.

He's only a mouse in sheep's clothing

but they do not know that.

He keeps his reign so stealthily that no one dares to breathe.

She alone fights through the night.

She alone is awake.

She alone leaves the house in one piece

to venture forth into the world.

The casualties left behind to suffer forever in their doom.

The bright light marches on to find the

wonder that has eluded the rest.

When it is found it cannot be touched.

It stays forever on the edge of her reach.

Will it crumble if she grasps it and brings it near?

Do I stay and venture forward into the unknown or stop in the comfortable zone and veg out? Complacency in the third domain. To know what another is thinking and love them anyway. The ultimate compassion for the living.

2013

Sometime during the winter or spring of 1996 I confronted my mom about the abuse again. I was hoping with my dad being gone and some distance, my family would come around and admit what had happened and finally support me. I had been holding out for it. I needed and craved it to the depths of my soul.

It didn't come. My mom stated she's sorry but she doesn't remember it. I've never mentioned it to her again. I held out hope for it to be different with my siblings and we could rebuild our relationships.

2/2/96

Dear Dusana,

I'm glad that you were born and I'm glad that you are in my life. You are so very special and dear to me. I love to be around you and I love spending time with you. Your smile brightens my day as only the sunshine can. You are a breath of fresh air every time you enter the room. The love that surrounds you is breathtaking and you are a wonder to watch as you bloom and grow.

Just the sight of you sends shivers of anticipation down my spine as I await what you can share with me today. I am blessed to have such a wonderful, loving person in my world. How you came to me I will never know. I am just thankful that you are here.

I look forward to each coming day because it brings to me a chance to know you more. You are the love of my life and my one and saving grace. Thank you for coming to me and sharing your wisdom with me. I will continue to love and care for you as the angel from heaven that you are.

Thank you for being you.

I Love You,

Dusana

3/18/96

Who am I? I don't know anymore. There was the person I had to be to survive. But who was I before that? Who am I really? Where did I go? Was I supposed to be someone other than who I am now? I am tired, I am confused, I am no more.

The world is changing day to day and I don't know where I fit in. What do I know? What are my interests? I feel boring, I feel stripped, I feel pathetic. If it weren't for my mother, I wouldn't have contact with anyone in my family.

Does life have any meaning anyway? What were the walls that I had built around me? And where am I without them? Where do I go? How do I reach out to another? How do I find my way to another?

I can relate to another. I can be vulnerable with another.

5/24/96

Confusion has reigned heavy on my heart over the years. I do know what I am going through, I do know where I am going. To the place that always was. My knowingness. I do know things about others and it amazes me. It's my feeling of 'Wow'. It's my ability to accept, it's my frustration that others don't see it.

Acceptance/frustration. Accept the knowing. Frustration from not being able to speak the knowing. Yet I want it more.

I don't feel I express my knowledge in a clear and precise manner. I am not thorough and complete enough. I am afraid of my joy, of my heart melting. Yet those two are happening.

By appropriately using my armor and allowing my joy, I can allow the knowing that is already there to reveal itself to me. What makes a great therapist? Do I want to be a great therapist? Where do I want my degree and education to take me?

I am starting to recognize faster my tendency to remove myself from my present moment. It is a more subtle difference that occurs between the present and when I am in the past or future. The power of the mind amazes me. It is all in the mind.

Where does healing come from and how does it work? Relax and quit doing. Allow it to be done for you. I am totally in a different place.

The proving is dissipating. Projection toward my mom? Always feeling the need to prove that what I perceived to be happening, did happen. I feel I am finally coming into my own.

Melt the heart and relax into the joy. Allow it to happen without trying to change it. I can find the words that will allow the hidden parts into the light. Acceptance or the need to challenge? I move from acceptance. I move from love. I move from warmth.

Do I need to accept or do I need to challenge? Which will be more beneficial to the other? When asked for advice, I feel that it is not 'I' that is responding but I am a vehicle for higher knowledge that needs to be known. When asked, it is my time to speak. Otherwise, keep the ever vigilant watch on what is unfolding before me. Pattern to throw in the wrench and watch the action.* Used wisely it can be healing and enlightening. I am ever taking in and learning. I just don't recite it the best.

Whatever limitations were there are vanishing. The need for them has left the building.

Can I recount what I've done? I have trusted and I have hoped and I have had faith. I have held true and kept on trying. I have lost faith and regained it. I have held a belief in myself that I could become a more powerful being. I have believed against the odds. I have noticed traits I admired and later replicated them. I have held an ideal of who I wanted to become and aspired towards it. I have moved beyond society to find the world and life I cared to live in. I have never given up forever. I am willing to find the positive. I get away from that which I find unpleasant. I keep making new goals and move towards them. I do not hold onto thoughts of how life should be but try to deal with how it is. I look life in the face and figure out what I need to do. I laugh and I cry. I seek to move toward others and not away. I let the goodness of life in. I am grateful and I try to be honest.

---

* I've been known to be a bit of a trickster or instigator.

WHY LIVE? WHAT IS LIFE ABOUT?

2013

I had some health issues during the spring of 1996 with pre-cancerous cells that freaked me out as I had had three family members die from cancer in the two previous years. This sent me on a search of what it would mean to die and ultimately, what it means to live. If death is inevitable, which I hear it is, then how do I want to be living my life?

5/30/96

Grief and sorrow with fire coming through: secrets, dreams, diversions, actions, and leadership.

Fear of death: Heading in the right direction. Taking my ground and standing firm. Knowing who I am and what I am to be. Not letting others stand in my way. The fight for the right to be who I am. Freedom from suffering. Realization of dreams. Desire to know the truth. Fear of persecution. Fear of being alone. Fear of not being on the right path. Desire to hang onto the past. Hanging onto the past diminishes the future. Realizations of dreams. Unabashedly me. Action to be me. Calling others on their shit. Thanking them for their opinion but knowing my truth. Fear of being called on my insecurities. Saying I want to know the truth but fear in facing it. Will grief and sorrow continue all my life? Can I heal from it? What is my responsibility in attracting another? Can I admit that I am worth it? It feels so selfish.

Don't be selfish. Don't take everything. Save some for others. You are so selfish Dusana. Taking the best for yourself. You're not special. You don't deserve this. You'd better prove why you think you deserve this. I want to know. I hate you. I hate you for all the things you take from me. You think you're so cute. Everything was fine until you were born. You're powerless to change anything. You can't do anything right. You're stupid and ugly. I hate you. I wish you were never born. You walk around like you know everything, but you don't. You don't know anything. You don't think right, you don't speak right, and you don't act right. Learn the games. You deserve everything you get. You've got to prove yourself around here. Learn to play the games or you are going to get it.

Above seemed to have come from Sandra.* The above came from Sandra. Don't add words that signify that you don't know when you do. You do know, there isn't a need to hide behind not knowing anymore. You can own your wisdom and intelligence. Timidness around your guides and helpers. They are there for a reason. They can provide what is needed. They are willing to speak when you can listen. You are in a position of authority. Take it and go out on a limb. Offer what you have. Don't take what is not yours. But accept and honor what is yours.

---

* My inner belief about what my sister thinks/feels about me.

5/31/96

What would I regret/miss most about not living:

I would regret that I never allowed love in my life. I would regret that I didn't let people know how I felt about them. I would regret never allowing myself a healthy, loving, healing, intimate relationship with a man. I would regret not having the chance to extend that relationship into marriage. I would regret never bearing a child. I would regret never raising a child. I would miss seeing my niece and nephews grow. I would miss the love I was able to allow into my life because of my niece and nephews. I would miss being able to love my niece and nephews. I would regret not being around to show them guidance. I would regret not being around to assist them in becoming responsible adults. I would regret not being around to be a role model for them. I would regret not finding the population I want to work with. I would regret not sharing what I have learned on my journey. I would regret not finding people who understand me. I would regret not living up to my full potential. I would regret not finding true happiness. I would regret thinking I could overcome a disease and then not doing it. I would regret what I haven't learned yet. I would regret not taking better care of myself. I would regret not standing up to what I believe in. I would regret not speaking my truth. I would regret not fighting for my truth. I would regret not finding a deep, passionate, true love. I would regret not becoming the person who could find a deep, passionate, true love. I would miss time with my friends. I would miss time by myself. I would regret not sharing my story with more people. I would miss chocolate. I would miss driving. I would regret not being truthful with myself about myself. I would regret not facing my biggest fears. I would regret not manifesting my deepest desires. I would regret not speaking my deepest wishes. I would regret not asking more of others. I would regret not being open to the universe and my purpose in it. I would regret not laughing more, loving more, living more. I would miss dancing. I would miss my interactions with others. I would regret not finding out what is really important in my life.

6/19/96

Our desperate searching for love
Brings us to the edge of desires.
Never reaching our depths
But showing us a glimpse of our deepest reserves.
Yearning drives us on endless journeys to squelch our needs.
Not quite it but we fool ourselves to believe it is what we want.

7/17/96

Childhood heroes crumble in the daylight.
Were they ever there at all?
Light beckons me toward the horizon
To the never ending past.
Footsteps tread lightly on my dreams at night
Yet crush in the daytime as reality keeps them at bay.
"Where did you go," I asked
But the knight did not show his face.
The battles of life keep us apart
As I live out my days alone.

Do I hope or do I live graciously?
Can I hold both?
To hope withers out graciousness,
Graciousness scalds hope.
Hope is the future, graciousness is now.

7/30/96

I am 30! I have earned each and every second of time that I have been alive. The hopes, dreams, wishes, ambitions, and consequent failures of what is to come. The realization of life as it is, not as one wants it to be. The acceptance and inspiration to continue, to go on, to be a part of the struggle.

The birth of the moment, the freshness, the crispness of existence. The accomplishment of surviving my twenties. Knowing I won't ever exist in that form again. Similar possibly but never the same.

New being, needing nurturance, care and attention, and the space to grow. Food, shelter, water, love and a sense of belonging. To be needed, accepted, and wanted. Any moment can be special, any moment can be boring.

8/04/96

Garish display of wealth. Power hierarchy, is it right? Does one person know more than another? Do they have the right to dictate to another? Isn't that how wars and invasions and dominance have endured over the millenniums? People thinking they know more than others. Thinking they are right. Feeling superior instead of equal.

It is amazing the preservation of the statues. They are everywhere and they are intact. People from all over descend upon Prague. Where were we when they needed us? If we go against the communists, would they then notice and come after us? Would our nation have been safe?

English everywhere. Do they mind having to incorporate another language? Would it be better to hold their ground and say, "no, you learn Czech?" Can they think and stand up for themselves or do they prefer to be told what to do? I like how they make you pay for your mistake. Don't have a ticket for the bus? 100k. Trying to steal that? If you wanted it bad enough to steal it, you can buy it. There's no just giving it back, you pay for it.

8/08/96*

I now know what it feels like to be loved. Twenty-four hours that I will hold with me and cherish for the rest of my life. An acceptance and appreciation for who I am. A kinship that went beyond words, went beyond time. A mutual understanding between two women. Yet I felt more a part of her family than I have ever felt in my own. Sweet, happy, gracious Eva. My presence was a gift to her. And I am happy I was able to give it to her.

8/18/96

I don't want to go home. Entering the world of the known/ unknown. Rising dissatisfaction of left relationships. Wanting to be alone, yet knowing others like me to be engaged. The

---

* I visited my second cousin while in the Czech Republic

unknown is how I will be, how others will be towards me. The struggle at school, I am whom I am. Misunderstandings, misattunements. [sic]

The desire not to give up my independence. What to do with my family? Friends I am not impressed with, other situations I am not impressed with. Things I have found here, can I keep them? So many more things to explore.

This holiday has wrapped itself around me as a lover's arms. All encompassing, endearingly holding me as it sees me, keeping me safe and cherished. Exciting and new. A boldness that is unabashedly honest. A completeness and wholeness not experienced in quite this fashion. It is more to me than a lover because I don't want a lover to see me as I am, as I have been. I don't want to be known. I want to keep my distance from others. I don't want others to know who I am, to understand me. I am tired of the effort.

It is never clear, it is never known. The years roll on and I remain alone, such as it is, such as it will be. Such is not bad. I can never convey what this trip has meant for me, and I will not try. Except by a gesture here, a word there and the looks that render what I have learned. It does not matter. There is a freedom with this expression.

2013

During the summer of 1996 I had the chance to do a house swap through my place of employment. A visiting professor was coming for the summer and his family needed a place to live. In exchange, I would have their house in Manchester, England.

I used this base to explore England, Scotland and Wales. I also headed over to the continent for two weeks. It was a dream of mine to go to Europe and it seemed like the natural thing to do for one of the summers of graduate school.

This became a turning point with my healing. It was a clear symbol of saying good-bye to the old and discovering the new. It was the summer I turned thirty and entered a new decade. I was more than done with my twenties and hoped people would start to take me more seriously during my thirties. I hoped I'd have better experiences than the gut-wrenching healing I had just been through.

I personally do like the word closure though I know it doesn't work for everyone. It doesn't mean I don't think the issues will return again but that a particular aspect of an issue is done. I have found my peace or acceptance surrounding an ideal, a belief or an experience that is no longer functional in my life. I cannot view the world in the same way I had before, a new reality needs to take place. I know there are more layers of the onion to come but I am done chopping the one and need to find a way to use it. By using the word closure, I open myself up to new possibilities instead of continually experiencing my life through the same old filter. A new way of being needs to emerge from my experience. It's why I love New Years and turning a new decade. It's the symbol of the Phoenix.

It was the summer my hips really started to hurt as the effects of the childhood arthritis had worn them down. I had to stretch every morning and was taking the maximum dose of pain relievers and they weren't even touching it. I remember being in a train station and the counter where I needed to buy a ticket was 15 feet away. I looked at it but I couldn't get there because the pain was that bad. I learned to sit and enjoy my surroundings until I had rested long enough to get up and walk again.

I felt like a sitting duck. I remember to this day how empowered I felt when I got through the seven weeks without anything traumatic happening to me. I felt I had conquered something. I have noticed my writing is different after this also. Not only had I matured chronologically but I had healed many of the places where my development had become stuck. The age I *felt* when writing becomes more contrasted after this. Some entries sound much younger than I actually am as I reclaimed another part of myself that had gotten stuck at a particular age. Certain aspects of the abuse were more traumatic than others. At these points my emotional or mental development was truncated and my thoughts reflected this.

During the fall of 1996 I wrote a deposition for my brother Charlie's ex-wife to warn about what he had done to me as an adult and the incest within the family. I didn't trust my family had the ability to keep children safe. Though my two brothers had apologized to me for what they had done, I was concerned with the level of denial within the family. This was the beginning of an estrangement between me and the rest of my family that was to last for a year and a half. I didn't talk to anyone until I invited my mother to my graduation in May of 1998.

I had been in therapy since the spring of 1995 and would continue for about another six months. The counselor also viewed life from a spiritual as well as an emotional/mental perspective.

Through various techniques, I learned to deal with the intense emotions and my defeating thoughts. During some sessions we used Eye Movement Desensitization and Reprocessing (EMDR) to help me feel the emotions without getting stuck in them. I was able to move from the negative thoughts associated with an emotion to more positive ones. As I found out over time, this needs to be repeated. I wasn't sure this well would ever dry up. Even after therapy concluded there would be more layers of the onion to chop.

Through all of my healing, my life became my classroom. I had to discern what was happening in my life that was an outward reflection of an inside belief. When I didn't do this fully, it would come around again for another chance to heal. It has allowed the healing to come a little at a time. Looking back, I couldn't have done it all at once. It would have been too over-whelming and debilitating. Life is kinder that way. Months and years of more positive experiences are intertwined through the negative.

9/20/96

Blood drips down on my soul at night.
Stifled screams silenced in the gulf of madness.
You come to me unasked, undeserved, and unprotected.
Knife's shooting pain envelopes my being
as you thrust away.
What am I to you?
I am your child.

Put the pain away for a rainy day.

I can look at it then.

Far away from the sorrow you bring

I find my wings of flight.

Touch down in the cool, soft meadow

To be engulfed by love.

You will never touch me again,

But for that matter,

Neither will anyone else.

Sunlight, daylight.

Will you ever come?

Bring to me the day

So different from the night.

I can see what I want to see at noon.

The sun's rays stream down

and caress my wounded soul.

The sun brings me warmth.

The sun shines upon my light.

The sun is my strength.

9/23/96

Transition back to the American way of life. I hate being back. Where's my freedom? Where's my independence? Where's my aloneness? Daily life with its routines and schedules and demands. Solitude of my house. Lock myself inside and throw away the key.

The convenience, the availability, the 'I want it now'. What do I notice about the States? Fall colors changing, blue skies, sun, snow on the mountains. I know where I am. There are no surprises. I know how to do it. I know what I need and where to get it.

There are people to call, people to see, and people with needs. People who want to see me, very few people I want to see. Relationships to tend to, to nurture, to develop. Numbing in my feet. Pressure to be in couplehood, [sic] pressure to be healthy. Inside or outside?

What does having a therapist mean to me? Something's wrong, something needs to be worked on, something about me isn't right. I'm not dealing with something, I can't cope, but this isn't true. So where does this leave me in association to therapy?

10/8/96

Sensitive, male oriented domination know it all. I am right and you are wrong, I know it. You don't. I am doing this right. You aren't. But I'll pretend that I don't know—but really I do. I am a sneak.

I am not going to let you know what it is that I really want. I'm not going to tell you what I want from you. But I'll make an example of your actions, just you wait and see. You're not okay. I want you to be different. But you'll still never be good enough. Just try and please me but it can't be done. I won't let you make me happy. I will find all your faults if it is the last thing I do. You'll never do it; you'll never make me happy. I know what you're up to, I can see through you. I know you better than you know yourself. I'll show you. You can never do it. You can never be enough. You'll always be wrong. I'll always be right but I won't let you know that I am right. I'll play dumb. I'll pretend that I don't know what's going on.

"You are just wrong. No, I don't want to talk about it. You're just wrong, sigh, if you did it my way you would be right. But you won't so just forget it."

I'm giving up on you. You're worthless, you're clueless, you don't know what you are doing and you'll never be enough for me. No, you'll never be enough so don't even try.

There's something you're not telling me and I need to know. I think it's something about me so I need to know. Tell me. You are not right for not telling me. I need to know, tell me, tell me what I want to know. Tell me what I want to hear. Tell me. I need to know more about you. You are wrong for not telling me. I am right in my need to know. I am right. Don't even try to tell me otherwise, I am right. I know better. I know more than you but I'll never let you know that I know more. I'm perfect. I have nothing wrong with me.

I will shut you out so I don't have to see me in your eyes. I don't want to see me in your eyes. Don't show me to me. I don't want to know. I don't want to see. I don't want to hear you. I don't want to see you. I don't want to see you looking at me. I don't want to see me. Go away, quit looking at me. You're seeing me again, please stop. Stop looking at me. Please don't see me. Please don't touch me. Please don't hear me. Please don't know me.

You are only willing to show me so much; I want to know the rest. What else is in there; is it about me? What do you know?

I know it is something. You're not revealing all you know and it hurts me. Don't you trust me? Why don't you trust me? Is it something that I did? What did I do to you? Please tell me. I want to know, I need to know. I need to know this isn't about me. I need to know more about you. I need to know that you are okay. I don't know that. I am curious about you, who are you, where did you come from?

What is all in there that you are afraid to show? What has all happened to you? Are you okay? What has life been like for you? How can I make it safe for you? What do I need to do to let you know who I am? When will I be enough for you? When will I be good enough for you? When will you come out and play? Can I join in your reindeer games? I want to understand you, I want to know you. I want to be with you, I want to share my life with you. Cough, gasp, choke, spit. I want to be with you. I want to comfort you. I want to hold you. I want you to share you with me.

10/23/96

Wee hours of the morning. My sanity echoes through the chambers of my heart. I see my brilliance reflected in my life. Leave me alone, I will get it. The flowing through without grasping. Not needing to grasp. Allowance and acceptance. The richness of my soul abounds in my smile.

To give and to receive. Following my path away from the life I have led. To where I cannot say. But with grace and love I move. I go where I need to. I do not stay where I can't.

How do I bring this back out into the world? There has been a brilliance and an intelligence in the life I have led. I appreciate where I have been and what I have learned. It has been amazing and I am okay.

I am okay. Of all the things in the world that I thought I would never understand, that was the biggest. I have lived my life and I am okay.

There is so much sanity and brilliance in the way that I am. I have skills I have learned. I have taken what was given and made the best of it. Little acts, big discoveries. It can be the very thing that we feel we shouldn't do that can bring the biggest changes.

Amazing changes happening rapidly. Exploration of the parts of me that don't want what I have always thought I wanted. What do I get from not getting what I desire? Exploration without desperation. I am brilliant, I am sane and I am loved.

11/17/96

Beautiful child of the sun. Light up our darkness. Wonder child of light. Taken too soon from the web. Let the strands of golden sunlight guide your journey. Keep us safe from harm. Light onto us your laughter and smile. Beautiful child of the world. You bring to us refreshing breath for the stale air that permeates our planet. Star child twinkle in the night. No more darkness to fill your soul. It should never have been done to you. You didn't do anything. We are the ones to blame. Let your light and wonder fill our souls. Teach us to laugh and sing. Let your light shine upon us and take us to the promised land. You are free to be all that you can be. Share it with the world. It is your gift. Hear us through the words of others. They speak our truth for us. See the world in its ever-changing colors and trust. You shall be shown the way.

I don't want to leave. Let me stay with you. Let me leave a part of myself with you. Let my light and energy be ever present in your soul. Take a part of me and remember me forever. Know that you too can be like me. From the darkness to the light. Find the wonder with each passing day. There is more to come. Welcome me to your place and know that you will be loved.

3/17/97

The sun beats down upon you, my love, in your shining glory. Rest into the being that you are. Share your gifts of love and laughter with the world. Teach, console, give, receive that which is around you.

Your answers are within and ready to be shared. Love, flowing joy. Exuberant joy. Exciting joy. Boundless joy. Expansiveness beyond compare. Be who you are and the path will open to you. Walk the path with honesty and confidence. Drop into the knowing; bless us with your presence, love, compassion and understanding. Presents to be given to yourself and others. Your beauty abounds. Breathe it into your fingertips.

Your loving eyes engulf me with knowing understanding. Is there anyone I can't be? What can I do to lose your love? Is there nothing I can do to make you leave? Your look of love surrounds and penetrates me. Can I be that beautiful? Can I contain beauty? Is the universe big enough for the beauty that waits within?

Waiting for the right moment to let it out. My beloved is myself. There is nothing I wouldn't do for my beloved. Nothing I wouldn't do.

6/18/97

Stealing my soul away from me. Creatures in the night crawl into bed with me and take my essence away. I hold on but it's no use. They are stronger than me. They are bigger than me. They control me. They can do whatever they want. They take my life from me. They, they, they, they, they, they, they.

Outsiders in my life. Controlling me, taking me away from me. Eating away at me bit by bit. Chomp, chomp, chomp, clamp, clamp, clamp. Down onto my soul. Fitting it into a box, stuffing it down. Forming me into a shape that is not me. Other than me. Where am I within this configuration? Where does this fit into my life? How does this fit into the wholeness that is me? Where am I within this culture? Demands upon me that do not fit whom I think I am. Am I this person or whom you think I am? Which perception of reality is true? Who am I? Where am I?

2013

The following eight entries are undated and the exact year unknown. They were written while I attended graduate school from 1995 to 98; my journals have less in them especially from 1997-98. On the other hand, I was also finishing up with school so I was busy with classes, internships and writing my thesis. There may not have been time to write about my process of recovery. I numbered them but they are not necessarily in order.

Some of the entries pertain to discovering within my body where I had held the stress of the abuse and what that part of my body needed to say. What isn't expressed gets repressed but the energy of the emotion needs to go somewhere. There are two directions for this, outward or inward. My tendency is to be self-destructive with my thoughts and physical ailments. I have also been a pro at self-sabotage.

During graduate school I worked on reclaiming my sexuality. It was something that should not have been taken away from me at such a young age. To have any negative connotations associated with it was heart-breaking to me. It was something to enjoy not fear. I read books about healthy sexual interactions, studied Tantra yoga, wrote my graduate thesis on Sacred Sexuality (creating the intimate relationship necessary for vulnerable, passionate sex) and learned to tolerate ever more increasing states of arousal. These were challenging in that they could trigger me to have flashbacks or were an impetus for hidden emotions to be released. I used techniques to stay present in the moment and learned to trust the process. When needed, I've asked my partner to stop.

I struggled through graduate school with never feeling seen or understood by most of the female teachers. They knew about the incest and I felt pigeon holed by them. It seemed I was supposed to be acting in a certain way, almost as though they expected me to have Dissociative Identity Disorder.[*] They thought I'd break under the pressure of school. They had me go through it

---

[*] Formerly Multiple Personality Disorder

differently from the other students and take classes out of the usual order. I never felt they believed in me and I thought about quitting school many times to get away from the negativity or thinking I needed to change myself to be accepted.

Looking back through the years I can see that all my lofty beliefs and intentions would get muddied by my self-loathing. No matter how much I wanted, craved and yearned for life to be better, there was a part of me actively working to ensure that I never got it. I believed that such a despicable creature as I certainly didn't deserve it. I could tell myself all the positive affirmations I wanted but until I felt the depths of my self-loathing and hatred, they would never stick. My healing has often been the case of one step forward and two steps back. Each time I came face-to-face with it I had another opportunity to heal and learn that maybe I am not the worst person on the face of the planet.

I

Tension in the face. Chisel it away. Don't let me see. What don't you want to see? The pain. The humanness. How sick my dad really is. The lies, the pretending to be the truth. If I put on this mask he won't touch me anymore. He won't be able to hurt me. He can do what he wants but it won't penetrate me.

With this layer I guard against the pain. With this layer I guard against the truth. With this layer I guard against the lies.

They can't hurt me. I won't expect anything from them then they can't hurt me. I am hidden deep down in my face. No one can see me. If they saw me they would see the truth of our family and they would take him away. Then everyone would hate me because they like him more. Why else would they side with him if they didn't like him better?

They don't care about me as much as they care about him. If he went away they would all blame me. They would probably throw me out and take him back anyway. It's me against the world and they don't really want me around. He wouldn't be the one to leave, I would.

Where would I go? What would I do for food? Where would I live? I would have no one to talk to and no one would care for me. I might as well be invisible. That way I won't bother anyone with my problems. I'll just be very quiet and not disturb anyone. No one else cares what he does so it must be okay.

Why did I have to be born into this family? They all like him better than me. I'll just go along with this and maybe they'll like me too. The more I go along with this, the more they will like me and maybe someday they'll like me more than him and they'll stop him from touching me. I'll be just like them and pretend I don't see his mistakes. I'll pretend I don't notice his lies. I'll pretend that I don't see him for whom he truly is. I'll pretend that I don't notice anything wrong around here. I'll pretend that this is normal.

No one else will see me and my beautiful self. No one will even know that I am here. I'll just be very, very quiet. The further inside that I hide, the harder it will be to find me and no one will be able to hurt me. I'll just go deep inside where no one can find me.

Where are you? You can come out now. No one is around that can hurt us anymore. We are safe now. I got us far away from them and what they think doesn't matter anymore. They don't bother us now. You can come out now and see the world the way you always wanted it. It is calm here. There is no one lying to us here. It's like Christmas everyday. There is love and goodness all around. There are people to help when we need it and they listen to you. It is peaceful and warm. Like fresh bread every morning.

There are people to love us and care for us and accept us. I don't need to hide you anymore. What they don't see can't hurt you anymore. You know the truth and it is okay. You don't have to hold on so tightly. You can relax and start to live again. You can open up and let life in again. You don't have to be afraid. I love you and I am here to take care of you again. I can listen to you and we don't have to worry about being hurt.

You can feel the emotions and not be afraid of them anymore. You can see the world through your eyes and know that it is correct. You can feel the world around you and know that it is correct. Relax into the joy around you. Trust in the world around you. Feel free in the world around you. Laugh with the world around you. Be present in the world around you. Let go to the world around you. Let go of the fear that surrounds you. Be a part of the world around you. Interact with the world around you.

Be free my love, be free.

II

Badness takes over. Wins the day. Badness, evil, live, life. Control, intelligence, love, lust, life. Control over destiny. Not a half hazard event. Control over how I want to live my life. Control over what happens to me. Control over what happens to others. Control over the uncontrollable. Control and love. Control and life. Control and power. Power to choose how I live. Power over my life. Power over others and their life. I know how you should live your life. I know what is right. I know what is wrong. You need to listen to me. I know a lot of stuff that is of importance to your life. I know a lot of stuff about how you should live your life.

I know. I know. I know. Listen to me and what I have to say. Listen to my words, listen to my voice, listen to what I have to say. Listen to me. Can you hear me? Are we speaking the same language? Do you understand what I have to say? Do you know what I am talking about? How can I explain to you what I have to say? Do you understand me? Am I all alone out here? Is there anyone to understand what it is that I have to say? Am I all alone here? Am I all alone? Am I all alone? Alonealonealonealonealonealone

The world just keeps on spinning. The world and my money. My money and the world. Ever spinning, ever intertwined.

Confidence to know what you are doing. Confidence in what you are doing. The confidence to go against the grain, to live out your dreams. Confidence and integrity. Confidence and love. Confidence and speed. Confidence to go against the law. Laws of nature. Laws of the world. Laws of the universe. To know the laws and ignore them. To do what I want. To get what I want. To go after what I want.

Belief in myself. Belief in my actions. Belief in what I know. Belief in my presence. Belief in myself.

To know authority doesn't rule me but I rule me. I act in my integrity. I live in my integrity. Can I risk flunking out of school to be who I am? Can I be who I am? Can I be all of me? Can I let all of me out? Can I speak my truth? Can I speak my intelligence? Can I speak my integrity? Can I say that you don't know jack shit? Can I let you know what you don't know? Can I see through you? Can I know what I am doing? Can I not do what you want me to do? Can I do what I want to do?

III

If I trust you....

    I will have to trust myself
    I will have to let you in
    I will have to learn to depend on someone else
    I will have to let you know me
    I will have to allow you into my space
    I will have to wait for you
    I will have to differ from you
    I will have to be different from you
    I will have to have different needs from you
    I will have to need you
    I will have to accept you
    I will have to trust you
    I will have to open my heart to you
    I will have to believe that you won't leave
    I will have to believe that you will see me accurately
    I will have to believe that you want to be around me

IV

Crying, crying into my heart. Where did all the pain go? Into my joints, into my body. I bring it on to keep you away. Go away dad, go away. I do not wish you here anymore. Then what happened? Distractions, distractions, blackness, darkness surrounds my joints. I can't see through them. I can't see you. I can't see your ugliness. I can't see my joy.

I used to play a lot. Is that why you came to me? Did I turn you on? Was I too pretty? Was I too fun?

I can't see me anymore either. No one can, I am invisible. You can't get to me now. I am impenetrable. You can't touch me, you can't hurt me. You can't get to me now. No one can. I have a little game I play with myself. It is called keep away. Its goal is to keep me away from you. You can't find me no matter how hard you try. I can laugh at you but you'll never know. I can tease you but you'll never know that I am doing it. You won't know what I am thinking or doing anymore.

I want you far away from me. I want to be rid of you. Nothing you do or say will ever hurt me again. It is a force field around me that you can't get through. No one can. No one will be able to hurt me again. No one will be able to hurt me again. No one will be able to hurt me again.

You walk around high and mighty but I know you and you are shit. I know what you do to me even if no one else does. I can do that too you know. I know something about you that no one else knows and you can't take that away from me. No matter what you do you can't take our little secret away from me. I will always have that. No matter what you do I will always have something on you.

I know that you are not perfect. I know the truth about you. No one can ever take that from me. I will always remember what you did to me. You can't take that away from me.

It is all I have to remember him by. It was all there ever was. The lies, the hurt, the shame. You can't take that away from me. I'll die if you do. It is all I have on him. It is all I have. What will I be without it? Where would I go? Who would love me?

Please don't take that from me. Please don't. I need that to survive. Without it I would die. I need to know that I have this on him. He's such a pompous ass. He's not perfect and neither am I. We are human. Why can't he see me? Would he stop if he could? I don't think so. He just can't. He doesn't know any better. Quit hurting me, you're stifling me. It's not fair. Don't do this to me. I didn't do anything to you. Why are you doing this? I didn't do anything to you. You can't do this to me. I am your daughter.

Hold onto what you can Dusana, just hold on. He can't do this forever. If I can hold on a little longer he'll stop. If I hold on then he can't hurt me. Hold on and then he will love you. Hold on and then he will care. Just hold on and your nice dad will return. Just hold on no matter what. Just keep holding on.

V

Hello right hip. You sure have been talking to me for a long time. Have I been listening? I must not be because you sure do like my attention.

What is there about you that constantly demands my attention? I do have other body parts that need me too. In all fairness, I think that it is time that we have it out once and for all. What is it that you have been trying to tell me?

I am hurting. She hurt me bad. She left me in the middle of the night all alone with him. I couldn't fight back. She could have. She could have rescued me once and for all. We could have gone far away where no one knew whom we were. We could have been happy. We could have been a family. We could have loved and talked like normal people. We could have expressed ourselves. I really wanted to leave. I wanted her to take me away. I didn't care what happened to him or the rest of the family. They didn't have to know where we were. We could have started over in a new place and I would have been happy. I could have made new friends. People would have accepted me and my pain would have gone away. I wouldn't have to hide all the time. I wouldn't have to pretend all the time. I could be open and real with other people. I would go to school and mom would work. I would help out at home and we would be happy. Just us two.

We wouldn't need anyone else. We would have each other. I would work real hard and make mom really proud of me and all that I could do. She wouldn't have to worry about anyone treating her badly because she would have me there to take care of her. She would be happy again like in the old days.

We had fun when I was young. We used to laugh a lot more before he had to ruin it for all of us. The laughter died out when he started to come around me. He ruined it for all of us. We used to be really happy. We used to have fun. We used to be a family. Why did he have to ruin everything? I wish he would go away. I wish we would go away. I wish that no one knew who we were.

Then I wouldn't have to pretend anymore. I could be truly happy. No one would know me and I could be whomever I wanted. I could act like I wanted not how they wanted me to act. I would be free.

I am mad at you for leaving me. You left me the same way that she did. You left me to deal with all the dirt, all the junk. I've been holding onto it for you all these years and I'm sick of it. You whine about me. You complain about me. You abuse me and now you want answers from me. Well, I don't feel like giving them to you right now. You can just figure it out for yourself. I don't care anymore what you are going through. Quite dropping it off on me. I don't want your problems anymore. Take care of yourself instead of everyone else. Go deal with your own stuff for a change. You are so perfect. You have your problems too. You always have this high and mighty routine. Well you are just like everyone else.

You disgust me and I don't want to hear it anymore. You've made all of your parts deal with your shit for years and we're sick of it. You hold on and hold on hoping for change. Well it's not coming. It's just you and the cruel world so you better learn to live in it and quit depending on us so much. You are a body and an animal just like everyone else. We are here and we are willing to help if you quit blaming us for our humanness, our animalness, [sic] and our bodily functions. We aren't just here to be dealt with. We are here to be enjoyed, laughed with, giggled with, adored. Forgive yourself as you forgive others. You have a body and you are human. Now deal with that. Let's have a little compassion towards ourselves and a little honesty and a lot of love.

Thank you for the time,

Your right hip.

VI

Dear hip,

I hear you. I hear your pain. The pain of days
gone by. What you have had to endure for my
sanity. I am sorry. You have done an excellent job
keeping me safe. But now it is my turn to keep me
safe. You have done all you can for me. Now it is
up to me. Your pain is incredible. I have a hard
time believing that you are the manifestation of
the chaos in which I was raised. But believe it I
must if I am to alleviate your pain. I know that
you are trying to work the pain out and I am
trying to be patient. There's so much I want to
do and the pain does not motivate me.

I know I need to rest in order for you to heal.
There is something to be said for the slower life.
Time to enjoy that which surrounds me. I feel my
toes, I feel my feet. Everything trying to come
back to life. I have built a beautiful life for myself.
It is time to enjoy it. As I slowly let the confusion,
the insanity in which I was raised permeate my
body and work its way through. The pain I feel is
the delayed pain that I could not feel as a child.
It is pain that deserves its time to be felt, to be

acknowledged, to be accepted. It is pain that can be let go of. The body's manifestation of reality.

What is felt, what is thought, what is believed. I may not know exactly how to heal my body but I can find out. Do what you need to and I'll try to listen and abide by this. You can take as long as you like but please don't drag it out. Please allow me to have some fun on my vacation.

Love,

Dusana

VII

It's okay. Nothing here can hurt you. You are a prisoner of your own mind. You've walled yourself in and won't let anyone get to you. You are safe now. No one will hurt you.

What's it like to have a nice dad? What's it like to have a nice family? One that is open, honest, and supportive? I beat myself up for things that I didn't do. Look around at the world that surrounds you Dusana. There is no one here to hurt you. The world is as you perceive it. Your world is calm, honest and open. People aren't hiding things from you. People aren't lying to you. People aren't coming within your boundaries.

You can melt your defenses. Can you name the last time someone took advantage of you? No. It doesn't happen anymore. You can relate to the world in a whole new light. You have done it. You have made your world safe for you. People enjoy you. They like you around. They want to be near you. You need to see what other people see.

Your defense has been not to see yourself. Not to appreciate yourself. You have cut yourself off from you and are always second-guessing yourself. This is not needed. The world is as you see it. You can let others in.

I don't see myself as others see me. I keep a distance from myself. It's okay to have special skills. It's okay to be more than other people. It's okay to have the gifts that you have. It's okay to want more than other people want. It's okay to get more than other people get. Everyone else sees that you deserve it. Can you start to see it?

You have worked hard to get where you are. You challenge yourself more than other people do. You want to see what there is in this life. Don't be afraid to be who you are. Give yourself a break. It is okay that you aren't perfect. You can't do it all. Take time for yourself more often. This world won't fall apart if you take a break once in a while.

VIII

Do not disturb, leave me alone, stay out of my space, I don't need anything right now, let me rest, let me sleep, let me be quiet, I am alright, peace, glow, honesty, love, light, pain, hamstring, can't, won't, shouldn't, but maybe.

Can't see, no, don't, it's wrong, he is wrong for you, no man will ever be right, stay away from him, you don't know what you're getting into, you don't want to do it, I won't give you permission, you shouldn't want a man, they're just trouble, don't see him, I forbid you, play happy, don't make waves, play along with what I tell you, listen to me, hear what I say, listen to me, hear what I say, listen to me.*

March, 1999

Focusing on the body is not of service to me. It has been of service to learn to honor myself, trust myself, forgive, increase my sense of inner peace, become secure in myself, enjoy life, keep my focus away from my gifts, keep myself ordinary, relate to normal people, not have to challenge myself, integrate more, decrease stress.

The physical has kept me from going over the top on addictions. It shifted my attention away from the material side of life. I learned compassion and appreciation toward growth in struggles. I learned to trust and strive for my dreams. I learned life could be more. I learned beauty, trust and wisdom. I learned to not make excuses. I learned inner growth. I learned honesty and integrity. I learned to do fearless searches and inventories. I learned that I am alone and that is okay.

To know whom you are not in order to find whom you are.

5/29/99

Things I can love about myself and my progress in life:
- My sense of humor
- My power
- My ability to perceive
- My knowing

*   More free-flow or stream of consciousness writing to bring to light the unconscious tapes running in my head.

- My intelligence
- My strength
- My gifts
- My special-ness
- The hard work I put into myself
- That I am a totally different person than I was raised to be
- My lack of fear at a core level
- My tenacity
- My being-ness
- My big-ness
- My ability to have more fun than anyone else
- The support that I am able to offer others
- That I follow through with relationships
- I try to make my life better
- I follow my natural rhythms
- My ability to remember songs
- That I can dance without being drunk
- That I can do a lot of things without being drunk
- My ability to love
- My ability to forgive
- My life experiences
- My zaniness
- My ability to be loud
- My ability to confront
- My ability to care for myself
- My ability to surrender
- My ability to receive

- My ability to treat others fairly
- My sense of responsibility
- My calmness
- My inner peace
- My sense of protection coming from the universe
- My refusal to be pushed or bullied
- My attitude
- My quick-fire wit
- My love of adolescents
- My ability to love and be loved
- My hair
- My work ethics
- The person I am
- The person I can still become

7/30/99

Dearest Daughter,

On this most spectacular day of my life you were born. You entered my life with an ease and grace for which I will ever be grateful to you. The joy you brought me and your father was all encompassing. We felt like the luckiest parents on the face of the planet. Our love for you knows no bounds and we will always be here to protect you. And while we can't keep harm out of your way, we trust your innate strength and intelligence to help you through to prosper and grow. Whatever comes your way, we believe in your truth, compassion and grace to make you a winner in our eyes.

Daughter, you have brought a sense of completion to my life that I have never known. It is the highest honor to be chosen to be the person who will challenge and nurture and support your greatness. Your presence and potential humble me and I only hope I can meet the challenge that being your mother will bring. But however I shall fail, please know that I love you deeply and want what is best for you because that is what you deserve. You are worth all the love in the universe because that is what you bring to the world.

The dreams I have for you are second to the dreams you must have for yourself. I honor your choices in life and support the decisions you make which will further your growth as a human and spiritual being. I may not always understand what you are doing but I have the utmost faith in your ability to know what is best for you.

Your intelligence and capacity to love confound me and I hope one day I can be as great as you. You are an inspiration to all you meet and touch. Your mere presence allows people to see that there is a better, kinder way to be in life. The strength you portray allows others to find this strength within themselves. It is your ordinary greatness that helps others to see that anything is possible. Life can be so much more than mundane existence.

Go on wonder child of the universe; spread your magic upon all you touch. The transformation in others will be miraculous. You truly have a gift for changing the lives of others for the better with your presence. I am extremely proud to be your mother and giving birth to you has been my greatest accomplishment in life. I love you deeply and trust you innately to go forth and spread your joy and magic to all you meet.

You are a very special child of the universe and I want you to always remember this. There will never be another you and we are all better off having the chance to know you. You will never know all that you bring to the people you meet and are truly loved by them. I hope at some point you will be able to let this in to transform your own life as you have transformed others. You are a dream come true in my life and in the lives you touch. We have all been waiting for the miracle that is you and are forever changed for the better because you are here. All I want is the best for you since this is the quality you bring to others. All that truly know you are extremely blessed and those that don't are forever at a loss for that missing piece of love that you bring.

We are all better people at having known you and are forever at your debt for the joy that you bring. I don't feel I can ever do enough to match the joy you bring me. I shall forever be grateful for the chance of being your mother and the honor it bestows upon me. Not only do you deserve, but you are worth, all the love in the world. You are worth all the goodness that comes to you. Forever honor this day in which you were born and the world was blessed in whatever way you see fit for what you need. You are worthy of all the greatness that you are.

Enjoy it and thrive sister, thrive.

Love,

Mom

2013

Reading through the following I am just sobbing. I think this was written fourteen years ago for me to read, understand and appreciate today. My pectoral muscles burn as these emotions are released. The armor for my heart lessens as my ability to let love in increases yet again. It was the fifth anniversary of my father's passing.

7/31/99

Dearest Daughter,

I look upon you with wonder and awe at what a beautiful girl I've shared in creating. A humble soul am I against your greatness and love. I want all there is in the world for you. True happiness and a loving man to share it with.

You are a bright shining light in my life and I will do all I can to ensure that no harm crosses your path. I love you deeply with a love only a father can know, yet I give you up to love another freely and completely. May you know a love in your adulthood that is all encompassing and complete. A love that is honest, respectful and true. With a man who will adore and cherish you in way that I cannot. A father's love is deep yet yielding. It can only go so far towards fulfillment. For true fulfillment, you will need an honest, giving and respectful man to offer to you what I cannot. A man who honors your soul and spirit and shares his own with you. You are free my daughter to find the love of your life. I have loved you as completely as I can, now it is your time to be free. I have done my job, now it is your time to be free of me.

Go forth and let a man love you and I will know my job is complete. I am extremely proud of the beautiful woman you have become but you need to be free of me. Because of this I will leave you now. Our time together is complete and it is your time to find love and happiness. I have taught you all I can about love, now it is your time to learn about a mature love that will complete you and the desires you have for life.

Go now in peace and know I will always love you but it needs to be from afar from now on. With this you will complete my life. I did not live in vain because I created you and it has been an honor to watch you bloom and grow. But please, do not let me hold you back anymore. You do us both a great discredit when you do so. You were born to do so much more than I was and it is your time my child.

Go forth and let your talents and gifts flow freely. The world needs what you have to give. It's been selfish of me to take for myself what you were born to give everyone. For this reason, I give you back to the world for I now see that it was not mine to take. It was your gift and it was unfair of me to use it for my own benefit. For this I am truly sorry. I had no right to take from you but am extremely proud of what you've done in spite of my ignorance. I am sorry for all I put you through and can only know in death what I could not know in life. You truly are a great soul and I was honored to be your father but I took it too far and am so sorry for the grief and suffering I caused you.

You are an amazing person and I'm sorry that I stopped you from seeing this. But it is time for you to see yourself in your complete brilliance that is you. Shine forth your love on everyone you meet. I will keep you safe in death in a way that I was unable to in life. I am so sorry for all that I have done and am grateful to you that I don't need to ask for your forgiveness. It is your greatness that is your ability to forgive.

Be born again my child and live your life the way you always thought it should be. Go forth and be proud of who you are because you are a shining example of all that can be. Never be ashamed of what you have been through because of who you have become because of it. You are an incredible, beautiful woman who would make any man proud to call you his wife. You don't need to apologize for anything about your life because of the person you are. My only wish for you is that someday you can see yourself as others see you. Only then will you know what a truly amazingly beautiful and unique person you are.

Hold your head high and never, ever apologize for anything you have ever said or done. It was always your greatness acting and if others can't or haven't been able to handle this, it is their own smallness not yours. Expand and grow as only the great can. We will all be following you as we can. But don't ever make yourself small because others can't handle you. That is not your job.

You were put on this earth to bloom and grow to show all of us what is possible in life. You do us all a disservice when you don't do this for us. Your brilliance is in being all that you can be. And trust me, this is a lot. You may not be able to see your potential at this time but I can and you are breathtaking! Please understand this about yourself. Right now your mind can't comprehend where you are going but it is to the top.

I will be beside you to support and love you in a way I couldn't when I was alive. But you are awesome Dusana, always remember that. And you can be that again and I won't touch you. I'm sorry you felt you had to hide it away but I can't hurt you anymore. You are safe to be your greatness now. You are safe.

Go forth my wonder child and create, create, create. You have so much to give and it is time you start. The world needs your brilliance and intelligence.

I love you so much.

Respectfully,
Your father

10/11/99

The changing seasons of my life allow a
sparkling clear version of you.
You can't be all that I need and must be true to myself.

Do I want to see you again?
I don't know.
Disappointment wipes away the desires of my heart
To show me a new version in which to view the world.
Less expectation of you and more acceptance.
Life showing itself to me again as it is
and not how I want it to be.

So what's the use of having convictions and intending life to be a certain way? Can't intend life to be a certain way, just how I will be amidst it all. I can't intend the perfect lover into my life but I can intend to be a conscious, supportive lover. I can intend to be open to friendships offered me. I can intend to work hard and diligently to change my body. I intend to use my mental and spiritual strength for the benefit of mankind.

2013

In August of 1999 I had my right hip replaced followed by the left one in January of 2000. My parts had worn out and it was time for a new life to begin for me. I couldn't go on with the physical pain any longer or imagine living another 60 years with it either. I had tried other types of healing but as I passed on the words of my doctor to other people contemplating the surgery, you'll know when it's time.

My mom came to help with my recovery and this offered another opportunity for emotional healing. It had been over ten years since I moved out of my parent's house and we hadn't spent that much time together in between. I was able to hear things she said and recognized I had heard them while growing up. The dynamics of our relationship were also clearer with the healing I had done over the past seven years. The entrenched grooves I found my way out of for healthier interactions to develop allowed me to stay true to myself.

2/7/00

> Dear Mom,
>
> I do not appreciate nor agree with your view of men. They are not selfish pigs. I know many wonderful, giving men. I find it mean of you to say to a single daughter, "you don't want a man" because I do. I can't help if this will disappoint you or make you love me less but I need to move forward with my life and this includes marrying a wonderful, supportive man who helps me out.
>
> I do want a man in my life. I deserve the right to try and see what it is like to live with a man. You had your chance and you made your choice for a partnership but my view of marriage is different from yours. I wrote a whole thesis on what it is I want. I do want a man mom, I do.
>
> I want a partner and friend in life. I want someone there to see me through the good and the bad times. I don't want to be alone anymore. It's not fair for you to project your attitudes onto my life and expect me to accept them because I don't anymore. Your view of men and mine

are different. I think they are quite wonderful creatures. I love good men with honorable characters.

We are different people, mom, and we view the world differently. We want and receive different things. I can't live in your world but will honor that you want to live in it. And I honor the world I want to live in.

I cannot deny it any longer to satisfy your beliefs. We are different people, mom, and I choose to live my own life including my own beliefs. I want a man in my life.

Thank you for showing me where I was stuck but I need to listen to your beliefs without taking them on as my own. I do want a man in my life. I am ready, willing and able to attract my life partner.

I love you mom but I can't be you.

Dusana

2/17/00

What have we come to? The world is speeding up and becoming more and more cut throat. Where is the love? Where is the caring?

Argh, I need a de-briefing from my mom being here! I want to love. I want to give. I want to share. Sensual softness of puppy piles. Where is this world spinning to? Morals and values screwed up. I need to love. I need to care. I need to make a difference. It can be a better world.

Focus on love, focus on happiness, focus on caring, focus on connections.

My world shrinks down, my world expands into love and caring.

2/18/00

Life with a major disease is really hard. Not feeling good enough, feeling unworthy, feeling I am less than because I am different. All the worrying about what men would think, not feeling like I could give what was wanted in a partnership. Feeling like a failure because I am not the same as others. The pressure to prove myself and my ability. Not sharing myself with others because of fear. Not wanting to be seen in my disability.

As though there is something wrong with it taking years to get to the place of success. I have not been living to my fullest potential and it hurts. I have been cheating myself out of the bounty of life. The cycles of life come and go. Deep, all-encompassing love that takes my breath away. I would be so grateful for it and take care of it. I know how special and divine it is. I would cherish it and appreciate it. This has been years in the making.

I have so much to share and give. It is time to move forward in life. To love another and share our created life together. It is time for a change and allow my hearts desires to manifest. It is time to be curious and explore. Find out what is behind the curtain. To go for it and ask different questions and answer them. To let myself be fully known and know another fully.

2013

During the 1990s I learned to accept the harsh realities of my childhood and live my life in a new way. Through trial and error, I learned to trust my instincts regarding which friends I told about the secrets of my childhood. There are others that still have no clue. I realized people don't know what to say. I internalized the damage, or secondary wounding, that comes from people saying absolutely idiotic remarks. Not only was the abuse itself wounding but the reactions of others caused another wound to grow over the first one.

I experienced confusion while getting the memories and accepting what I was discovering. Was it true or not? I felt guilty for accusing my family of such horrific crimes. It perpetuated what a bad person I thought I was. As I told people about the abuse, many would assume I was being overly critical of my family. "Everyone's family was messed up. Could I really blame them for not admitting it? Why couldn't I realize how hard it would be for them? No mother could ignore this happening right under her nose. It was too much to hear about. I had no right to subject others to the horrors of my life. Wasn't I over it yet? It was just the latest trend to get yourself on Oprah."

The pain of the rejection became too much of a risk for me to take anymore. The shame of it all—what I had lived through, the way my family treated me and the length of time it was taking me to heal—led me to be silent once more.

Until recently I would occasionally wonder if maybe I am someone with an undiagnosed mental illness. If it was a mental illness, what an awful scenario to be accusing another person of doing. My family would prefer it to be this reason. While watching *Silver Linings Playbook* it dawned on me that if this was a mental illness, shouldn't my family have been there for me? Shouldn't they have been more concerned and intervened? Shouldn't they have cared instead of leaving me to work through it alone?

The next twelve years were spent living out my intention to hide the shame of the abuse and the secondary wounding. The questions remain: is it safe for me to share and can I just be normal? In the case of learning about another person's life, a simple "I'm sorry you had to live through that" or "thank you for sharing with me" are sufficient replies. It is not the time for a trauma competition. It would take a few more years to learn to repeat to myself, as often as needed, I'm sorry I can't do my healing in a way that makes you happy.

I was offered a job in a small town in western Colorado and I moved in July of 2000.

11/4/00

What am I trying to forget?

- How alone I am
- How much I have lived through
- All the struggles I've been through
- How much I have to give
- My responsibility
- My duty to serve

Why do I want to forget how much I have to give? Because it's being wasted right now. How I am using it is being wasted. I'm not doing all I can. I have so much to give and offer. I continuously waste it.

You are safe to bring it in. It is true you couldn't where you were before, but you can now. You need to now. It is what you are here to do. It is time to help, it is time to offer your services, it is time to show others the way. Challenge others, challenge yourself, there is always more to be. Be more loving, be more dedicated, be more compassionate, be more accepting, be more trusting, be more faithful. You have the market cornered on respect.

Bring the love into your heart and shine it outward. Stand up and meet the challenge. Share what you see. You will be protected. It will benefit others without harming you.

Quit squandering your gifts. You are here to show others the way. Your being silent does not benefit anyone. Speak up and be heard, others have been waiting to hear what you have to say. Build an awesome team. Build a strong community. Offer to the adolescents all that you collectively have to share. Be a source of wisdom and inspiration for the staff and residents. You will never know how much others appreciate and accept you. Show your love and wisdom. You got it right with six months. Dedicate yourself for six months and you will see wondrous results. You are all very close. Everyone just needs a little more encouragement and support.*

---

* The place I was working at was going through a difficult transition.

Find out ways to make it better, it is what you are here to do. You are exactly where you need to be. You have been planning for this moment for a long time. Shine my wonder child and allow others to bask in your glory. They will grow and learn to benefit others with their own essence and being. It is what you are here to do. You cannot serve or demonstrate any greater deed. It is what you are here to do. Lead now.

1. Have the desire to do something
2. Make the firm decision to begin that action
3. Do it

12/31/00

Death, letting go of the old, big, strong, sensual, sexually liberated woman. Born my new child of the world. Welcome to the new millennium. Be free to be yourself. Let yourself come fully forward. To love, to live, to laugh. Let yourself be fully free. It is all over with. All the struggle, all the doubt, all the self-hate. You know what you know. Bring it forth to share with the world. To love freely and completely. To be happy beyond belief or reason. To be fully and completely loved.

Laugh my child of the sun. Travel, love, be free to explore the world and your soul. Let the abundance of the universe in. And bring it forth into the world unconditionally. Explore my child and learn all the intricacies of your soul. Learn what you are here to share and give. It is time to bring it forth. Relax, you are in a place to explore it and learn how to utilize it. Give back all you have been given. My magical, mystical child of the world. Be creatively open and offer yourself to the betterment of the world. Live, laugh, love 'til the ends of the earth.

The end for now! Good-bye 2000

READY TO FIND LOVE

2013

I attempted to enter the world of dating. I searched one of the online sites and came up with a match. I smile now at my experience and the question posed below of whether you can love someone you've never met. Fast forward through the years and how this has played out to the current sensation of catfishing in the online dating world of social media. I'm glad I learned on my first try to decipher fact from fantasy.

3/01/01

The plane carries me further from you
But brings you closer to my heart.
Is this real or another one of my pipedreams?
The grieving and sorrow lay heavy on my heart.
Do unbreakable walls break?
Am I really lovable?
How will my life look different if I am?
Raw, vulnerable new.
How do I relate to you as a lovable person?
What do I do?

Take me and show me all that I am.

All I've been denying myself.

What I can't yet see.

Show me the way.

Let the dust of my heart settle.

Twenty-five wasted years gone forever.

What have I been missing?

Help me learn to love again.

Drained beyond repair,

Worn beyond recognition.

My soul waits in anticipation of your attention.

Renewal stirs below the calm surface of the turbulent undertow.

Take me down and let me be reborn.

Let me see me.

Let me hear me.

Let me feel me.

Leaves turn gray upon my skin.

Endless searching for my family

So dear to my heart it hurts.

Will it really satisfy my soul?

Or is it the illusion I cling to?

Won't I be a great mom?

Will a child ever call me that?

What is love anyway?

3/2/01

My love,

How can I explain to you all I have been through? How and when will it happen? Will you accept me? Will you stay by me? Will I stay by you? Am I ready for this? Are you ready for me? Do you know me or only who you want me to be? What life will we build together? Is it possible to love someone you've never met? Can I entrust my life to you? Can I allow you to take care of me? Do things for me? Pamper and tend to me? Do I know how to give to you?

3/4/01

More middle of the night stirrings....

The layers built upon my soul keeping me at a distance from myself. I cannot endure another disappointment. My greatest fear is that you won't be there for me. Am I setting myself up for another failed relationship based on dishonesty and broken promises? It weighs so heavily upon my shoulders and body. The endless sorrows I have endured at the hands of others.

Friends never really giving of themselves to me. Hearing how wonderful it will be and it continuously falling short. Will you be any different? Will you leave me?

There are a thousand ways to leave someone, which one do you practice? What will I have to endure with you? The giving to others as I get none. Where is the effort towards me damn it? Am I so demanding? Am I so hard to please? Do I ask too much?

Am I that difficult to get along with? Tell it to me straight just once, someone, somewhere. .

Be the answer to all my prayers. I am tired of being alone through this. I want my saving grace here on earth. Please, let me have it. Am I not listened to? Can you not hear me? I don't understand your plan for me. I want to share my life with you, can you do that? Can I trust you? Do you want to hear me? Do you care?

Quit settling for less. Get the friendships you want. Stay away from all else. The other people are soul killers. They add layer upon layer of debris on your soul. You don't need them.

Do you really love me? Can I be loved? Is this what we've both been waiting and searching for? I will not waste it. It is the greatest gift of all. Fill me up with your love, care, and understanding. Bring to me all you desire and watch your dreams come true.

I love friendly, warm service. I love being given to with intelligence. Reminders of who I am in a busy life. How to lead a soulful life in a dead society.

3/8/01

Well my love,

I fall deeper in love with you every day. The depths seem eternal and I welcome the chance to explore them. I feel you holding me, caressing me, loving me. Can I possess such gentleness with such intensity? Will I ever share this with you? It has been forever since love has been given and received by me. It is so refreshing to have it expressed. I am an expert at being a friend with a man but was not given the opportunity to love. I thank you for this.

It is an honor to love and be loved by you. My dear sweet man, thank you for expressing to me your inner thoughts and feelings. It is so healing to be given such a gift. I cherish them and you deeply. The journey we have both taken to arrive at such a gift. Four more days until I am in your arms. Will I ever want to leave? Will I finally find my home? Fear, anticipation, and excitement all rolled up into one. Fluctuations of emotions and concerns.

3/19/01

Bleeding heart, woe of the masses. So much pain and suffering in the world. When will it end?

Please, no one see me right now. I have nothing to give, nothing to offer. Alone in my solitude, when will I be free? Nothing, nothing to give. My heart hurts.

The pain and suffering that surrounds me. How can I make it through the day without breaking into a million pieces? I hold this for you my dear.

What is the point of this life? How do I live a sane life and be satisfied with what I am doing? What I am contributing? There has got to be a way. To contribute to the health, safety and well-being of the world. Is my living it enough? Or do I have to constantly have to be giving, pouring it out?

I can't get to this point again. It is not good for me or those around me. Hold me, caress me, care for me. Just don't leave me. I have had enough people leave me, I don't need another.

Wearing me down to build me back up. Find the jewel once again. A heart that collects other people's sorrows for them. Hopes smashed into tiny little pieces for all the world to see. God it gets so tiring. How can I do this for others in a way that is easier for me?

And a beautiful day dawned for all to see. The troubled world forever gone. All sorrow, injustice and pain gone from the earth. The spirit and the essence of all the people reborn into a new shape, a new form, a new beginning.*

3/29/01

Weary soul forever tormented by dreams, desires and expectations. You are not what I expected my dear. Yet you are here for me. Ever willing to give and I find I do not want you as a person. Is this a cruel and unusual joke of the universe or am I an ungrateful bitch?

Centered, balanced, growing tree. Eyes strong and wise. Tree filling up the center of the being. Duality struggling inside of me.

Crown of thorns forever biting into my soul. Bleeding out my hurts and anguish. I do not want you to see this. You cannot see this. You are incapable of it. You do not know me and I remain

---

* We met in person and reality didn't match the fantasy.

alone. You do not understand me and my heart bleeds. I am left alone again.

Sexual center exploding in white light. Creative forces coming through. But I do not want others to meet you, to see you, to see my despair. It hurts so much being loved by you. I am being taunted. I am being made to suffer for my sins of vanity. I am suffering for how great I've thought I am.

Love being kept from me. Satisfaction ever out of reach. I am an awful person. I've been given someone who loves, accepts but does not understand me. You didn't get it, Jim. You don't. I'm not being met. I don't want to be alone again. I don't. The reason I would stay with you is because I don't want to be alone anymore. And that is no reason to stay. I am not comfortable continuing with this when we have such varying degrees of feelings. It is not fair to you.

Flames covering my body. Hot, passion erupting around. Encompassing the mind, body and spirit. How deep is my love? Can I work through the revulsion? I want to talk with people who know and understand me. I don't want to explain. I want to be with someone who gets it without an epic novel about my life. I want to be understood.

4/18/01

Male body, downfallen, beaten down, unforgiven, woeful singing dances his way into my heart. Outer manifestation of my own inner turmoil. How can I hate myself so much? Man hated for what he has done. Lied, cheated, stolen.

Taken from the souls of those he loved the most. He has not forgiven himself because he doesn't believe that they can forgive him. The patterns of my life. Men I have loved. I have witnessed the forgiveness but I do not allow myself to experience it.

It is okay that you were driven. It is okay that you want the world to be a better place. It is okay that you work your ass off to accomplish it. It is okay that you are good at what you do. It is okay that you intimidate others. It is okay that you are loving. It is okay that you are compassionate. It is okay that you are forgiving. It is okay that you are human. It is okay to love. It is okay to be a fool. It is okay to lose. Much bigger than the confinements of whom I think I am. It is okay to be giving. It is okay to be accepting. It is okay to love. It is okay to be loved.

You have been forgiven. Only you still carry around your faults. Everyone else has forgotten them. It is okay to be loved again.

REACHING FOR MY DREAM

2013

Through the years I continued to have health concerns
with pre-cancerous cells. My doctors had been recommending a
hysterectomy but my desire to be a mom and carry my own child
prevented me from listening to their advice. In 2001 the cells
were positive again and the recommendation was presented once
more. I knew I would regret it if I didn't at least try to get pregnant
before having a hysterectomy so I decided to conceive through
donor insemination. At one point I had to switch doctors and
found one willing to allow me this dream, within a time frame.
In September of 2001 I started the journey of becoming a mom.
I was writing in two different journals, one for myself and one
for my unborn child that I planned to give him or her when they
were older. The entries for my child will begin with, To my child.

9/4/01

To my child,

It is the night before my first insemination
to conceive you. Will you come this time or
wait? It is the great unknown that I am jumping
into. I feel my capacity to love expanding as I

contemplate becoming a parent. It is what I have wanted for so long. I can't believe the dream can become a reality.

I am so grateful for donor insemination and the chance to be a mom. I can't wait to feel you grow inside me and then watch you grow after you're born. I have so much to teach you and so much to learn from you. What will our life be like together? I imagine a lot of love, laughter, fun, creativity, and respect.

How many times will I fail you? When will you first detect I am not perfect? Will we grow apart, will you hate me? Will I drive you insane the way my mom has at times?

Being a mom is such a huge, important role that I am ready, willing and able to meet. I welcome you into my life and will love you more than you will ever know. I am here for you always.

Love,
Mom

9/11/01

To my child,

Are you growing within me? I have a few signs but is it just wishful thinking? The other night all my dreams involved either my, or someone else, being pregnant. It would have been around the time of your possible implantation. Time will tell.

Today is a newsworthy day in U.S. and world history. Four airplanes were hi-jacked. Two smashed into the World Trade Centers in New York eventually resulting in two 110-story buildings collapsing. Another plane crashed into the Pentagon. The last one crashed in rural Pennsylvania allegedly headed for Camp David. This incident was a shock to the world. There's been TV coverage all day.

I spent most of the day watching the news coverage. It's been 13 hours and they're just starting to be able to move in to try to find any survivors. And there miraculously are some. People were calling on their cell phones that are trapped in the rubble.

A few passengers on the planes were also able to use their cell phones to call with bits of information before the crashes. Seat position and types of weapons and such. What a world I am bringing you into!

It is currently unknown who initiated the attack. It apparently came out of the blue. Was it foreign, are we going to war? Or almost worse, was it an internal job?

I hope with this and other disasters that people love each other more. I'm not sure where the country will go after this. There's talk of spending more for defense but that mentality will not lead to peace. I've observed that the acts of the underdog towards groups of power are getting more extreme. Thousands of innocent people died today. The division between the have and have-nots will lead to the demise of this society. No super-power stays that way forever. People's values are skewed. We spend more money on defense strategies than on our children. And defense is just a substitute for real power. True power comes from each person having what they need to thrive in life. Defensiveness gives people something to hide behind.

I wept when I first turned on the TV. It was such a shock to watch the tower collapse upon itself. I was so grateful that your Aunt Monica doesn't work there anymore. But the loss of life and destruction to the psyche of the world is unfathomable. I said a thanks for living in a small town far away from a major city. Not that that makes me safe but I don't feel like so much of a target.

Life does go on my child. Always believe in the power of the human spirit. People overcome major tragedies. The human spirit is very resilient and life will go on. I don't know what changes will need to be made but the phases of life go on. It's part of the circle. With that I will continue with my quest to be a mother. I have faith in me and you to survive.

People are coming forth to donate blood and do what they can to move forward. Who knows what the next few days will bring.

All air traffic was grounded today, the first time in my lifetime. Your grandmother would have been eight the last time this happened. It's quieter without airplanes flying overhead. It's become such a part of life that you almost don't notice them anymore, until they aren't there. I sat outside looking up and didn't see the familiar white streaks they leave in the sky.

Tokyo's stock market is open on Wednesday already. Stocks are down as a result of what happened in the U.S. On Tuesday, stock exchanges around the world closed down. They will still be closed here on Wednesday. What will the financial repercussions be in the future?

Leaders around the world offered condolences to the U.S. It warmed my heart that in Russia, our former enemy in my lifetime, people came forth and laid flowers at the U.S. embassy.

No one is ever exempt from hard times. You never know what people have lived through. Have I raised you to understand this? I hope so. May this bring world peace. I'd love to see it in my lifetime but if not, I wish it for yours.

There's so much beauty and capacity for love, let's hope we can all move that way. I hope I was a good role model of this for you. But alas, I am human and I'm sure you, more than anyone, knows this. Life is a continuing journey and one always has the chance to be a better person. Let's hope I was able to pass something good on to you.

I hope this event doesn't have a negative impact on you if you are indeed growing within me. If you are, I will do my best to concentrate on the good of people and the world. You deserve that chance.

Love,

Mom

9/20/01

To my child,

You did not come this time. I was distraught. It's amazing how a person can tweak reality to what they want to believe. I thought I had some morning sickness. I thought I was really tired. I thought I was pregnant.

I am not. Will I ever be? Will this dream come true for me? It has always seemed so far away from me. Will I ever be part of a loving, healthy family? It doesn't seem possible that I will get the one thing I have always wanted and longer for.

I want to be pregnant. I want to feel life growing inside me. I want to create life. Will you come in two weeks? How many times can I do this before I give up?

I have to trust that I will have this dream. Please come into my life.

Love,

Mom

11/3/01

Feelings of unimportance and insignificance. How long has it been here? How long will it go on? And what proof do I have that it is actually true—none!

It was so much about them and not me. Why did I take that one on? Oh, this has been going on a long time. What would happen if I were significant and important?

I would be loved and feel loved. I would be happy. I would be fulfilled. I would worry less about my friendships and just be available. I would be more available period. My heart would grow. I would love myself more. I would know I deserve good things in my life. A man who loves me, a child or two or three, fulfilling work. A full life. It is happening. Slowly it is all coming into my life. And I am grateful. I actually believe that it all could happen. Things I have been dreaming of for so long. They can actually happen.

I get to be a mom. It's what I've wanted for so long and it's actually happening. I get to be a mom.

I get to be a wife. Okay, that one I may have to work on but I am closer.

My heart has been breaking open over and over the past few months. I am ready to love. I feel more able to love now. I feel good and happy.

11/9/01

My child,

Will you hate me just because I am your mother? Do you know what a significant relationship I hold in your life? I have helped shape who you are today. Have you forgiven me for the times I have failed? Do you admire me at all? Was I able to provide for you in enough ways? Did I do a good job?

I don't know if you will ever know how much I wanted you in my life and how scary it is to think I could totally screw this up. I know so many people who hate their mother. I don't want that for our relationship. What a huge job parenthood is. You never can be it all for one person.

I am waiting once again to see if I am pregnant with you. I was inseminated on 11/5/01. It's the birth date of my good friend Jennifer. Have you ever met her? It's also the date I bought my first house. I hope it's lucky for me again.

I had another IUI done on 10/5 and you didn't choose to come then either. One of these times will work. I've got to have hope.

I switched doctors. The former one was trying to tell me what to do with my body and didn't want to go ahead with the IUI's without some more surgery. I didn't agree, so I went to another Dr and had it done. I won't bore you with my medical concerns though.

I'm not feeling well but I think that has more to do with the cold I have. Another week and I'll know if you are on your way or not.

I love you,
Mom

12/25/01

To my child,

Merry Christmas my love. My greatest wish for this Christmas is that I am pregnant with you in the coming year.

It's been a tough holiday season for me with not having a family of my own when it's the one thing I desire most in this world. I am so excited to be a mom and have you in my life. I have so much love to give you.

I still don't know how I will manage this on my own but we'll figure it out. I'm hoping my friend Annette moves up here and can take over my business if I need to be on bed rest with you. It'll work out, I have faith in that.

I keep thinking of next Christmas and what my life could be like. You'll either be here, be on the way or forever not an option. I pick the first two.

I have so many questions about our life together. Do I ever get you a sibling? Do I ever find a dad for you and a mate for me? Am I enough for you? Do you know how much you are loved and wanted? Are you glad you were born? The world is an amazing place, do you know this? Do I succeed in letting you be you and not my version of you? Are you happy, confident, giving and understanding? Was I a good parent?

This Christmas I noticed more homes decorated with lights. Especially with the colors of red, white and blue. I hope people can keep the spirit of the season going throughout the year.

I can't say that our way of life has changed much. People are more cautious with money but I can't say there's any hardship except for the emotional ones. All of our luxuries are still available. Little petty arguments still happen. So life during wartime isn't that different for us. I hope by the time you read this that the world is a more peaceful place all the time.

I am awaiting you.

Love,

Mom

12/25/01

My Christmas wish is to be pregnant in the next year and safely deliver my baby.

This past year has brought the death of my feeling unwanted, unlovable and insignificant. I feel at peace. My gift to myself this holiday season has been time and what I will give others is peace. My intention for the coming year is to walk in peace, talk in peace, respond with peace, and emulate peace.

I have so much more love in my life than I did a year ago and I am grateful. I am content and fulfilled in my work life—it is all coming together. I love where I live, I love I am going to be a mother and I love that I am at peace with being single.

The gifts of being single: I've had time to become a more spiritual person and interact with others from this space. I know the importance of relationships and how to truly give to another. I know how to listen and just be with another. I know appreciation and the importance of seeing another. I know what it is to be alone and how to make another feel their importance to me. I know genuineness and laughter. I know inner peace and understanding. I know how to love. I know happiness. I know how to be slow. I know how to enter the world of another. I know quietness.

I can be fully me. I can lead my life. I can change in the blink of an eye. I've been able to do the exploring I want to do. I've been able to be a free spirit. I've gotten to develop me. That's my greatest gift of being single. I've gotten me!

2/8/02

To my child,

I'm watching the opening of the winter Olympics held in Salt Lake City, UT. It's the first major event since the 9/11 terrorist attacks and I'm feeling emotional so I thought I'd write. People from 86 countries were killed when the World Trade Towers collapsed, so it's great to see the world coming together. The Olympic torch was run through the valley. I went to Glenwood Springs to see former gold and silver medalist George Dicarlo swim it across the Hot Springs Pool. He won his medals in 1984 for some sort of swimming. I also watched in be run just blocks from where I live. It started at what will be the location of the old hospital by the time you read this.

I was inseminated on Tuesday, 2/5/02. Shoot, I forgot to look at the clock, but probably somewhere around 10:20 a.m. I read an article about George Harrison dying. It was an old magazine. I took fertility drugs to help my aging eggs. I had to consider the chance that I could end up with multiple fetuses. But I only have a few months to get pregnant, so I want to give myself the best chance to have you enter my life.

Anyway, the opening ceremonies are just reminding me of triumphing over adversity. Others thinking they can defeat you but your spirit coming through to thrive. And it is just about people being their best. I love it when people strive to be better than they have been or currently are. And the U.S. representing true freedom. My child, always cherish your freedom, no matter what your life circumstances turn out to be. Find your individuality and freedom and express this always.

The Czech Republic carried the U.S. flag. Got to love those Czechs! Let's see, you will end up being 25% Czech. God, I never thought about not knowing the percentages of your nationalities from your paternity. I don't know the break up of my 50% mutt-ness but with my father being 100% Czech it's not hard to figure out. I wanted a donor with Czech or Eastern European decent. The one I picked is part Russian, close enough for me.

France also carried our flag on the other side of their flag. I love the support from other countries for what we have gone through. Ireland is also carrying our flag. Also part of your heritage. I love the lightness, or lilt, of the Irish.

The opening ceremony is so much about unity and coming together. I hope the world I bring you into is different from what has been. They are also honoring the 5 Native American tribes that inhabited Utah. And the spirit of the

West. Coming west for a better life. That is what I did.

Love,

Mom

3/8/02

My Dearest Child:

Happy Conception Date, should you choose to come this time.

It's a long shot. There's not any indication that I'm even ovulating but it was either go for it or skip this cycle. I decided to take the chance.

I haven't had a decent night's sleep in a couple of days. I thought it was more important to toss and turn, feeling sorry for myself and thinking all sorts of awful thoughts of how this will never happen for me. Essentially driving myself insane trying to figure out the right combination for your existence to start. I'm glad I waited to write to you when I was in a better frame of mind. I wouldn't want you thinking your mother was some sort of neurotic nutcase.

Do I ever allow myself to fully live my dreams? I swear I will never figure out the destiny/free will thing.

I finally looked at the clock at 3:30 a.m. after being awake for quite some time. I was awake the rest of the night. I just couldn't decide what to do.

211

Have the IUI or demand an ultrasound to see if anything is indeed happening with the ovaries.

I got up and it was snowing. I knew I was headed to Junction as soon as possible in the morning. I was taking along one of the daycare kids. She told me yesterday that the reason I was fat was because I was going to have a baby. She had to be a good luck charm!

After she arrived and I packed a ton of things to keep her entertained, we headed out. We traveled through snow, rain, clear weather, hail, and more snow all in an hour's time.

Bethany had to be in the room with me much to my dismay. I set her up next to me with books, puzzles, and her own binder. I figured this would be interesting. While the Dr. fuddled away trying to get the other half of the equation into me, I was reading, *Oh, the Places You'll Go* by Dr. Seuss. Not a bad book to be conceived by if you ask me. The Dr. was impressed by my ability to read and smile through a rather painful and uncomfortable procedure. He said I was a good mom. "Great, now let's get me a child." It was around 10:45 a.m.

Now it's time for bed. Let's hope I can sleep tonight.

Love,

Mom

4/6/02

To my child,

I'm not sure you will be able to come into my life as I dreamed you would. I would love the honor of conceiving and carrying you but I'm not sure it is going to happen. It's getting to the point that I have to wonder how far I'm willing to go to make this happen. I was so happy when I found out I would physically be able to have you. I wasn't sure I could with the arthritis. I never believed I would be able to do it. I met friends for dinner the night the orthopedic Dr. said I could go ahead. They commented that I was glowing. And now a year later I see that dream slipping away from me.

I had a doctor's appointment today and didn't get the most encouraging news. I am so sad to give it up. How do you come into my life? I know you're out there somewhere.

Why won't you come to me? Okay, you can't this cycle because only my half of the equation is here. I ovulated early and except for heading out for a one-night stand, you don't get the chance to grow this month. What am I doing, what am I doing?

Can I hope this will be the last heartbreak of my life? One can always hope.

Wow me Lord, show me the splendor of the
life you've been holding for me. I can't see the
happy ending but you can. Show it to me now.

Love,

Mom

2002

I was recently playing the game of Life with my niece and
nephew. In the game, as in life, I ended up childless. Unexplainably
though, I ended up with grandchildren. I thought this was pretty
cool since, as the saying goes, most grandparents would have
skipped having children and gone straight to grandchildren if
they knew it was going to be so much fun.

As in the game, I feel I am on to something with skipping
parenthood. I get to be a powerful influence in a child's life but
still get to send them home at the end of the day. I've also spent
enough time challenging my own definition of what it means to
be a mother and having never given birth, I am certain that I
am one. I found that part of me and live her everyday. I create
and I love.

That intense love I hear about for one's child is in everyone
one of us and some people take the road of parenthood to let
it out. Others of us are challenged to seek it in other ways. It's
allowing that love to come forth for people and things that
aren't guaranteed to love us back that is the challenge. To stop
for a moment and really see the person in front of you with total
honesty and acceptance for the God created person that they are,
now that is love.

5/9/02

My child,

Here I am days before Mother's Day waiting to see if you are coming this time. I'm having a hard time being hopeful. I want some sure sign you are on your way. But I don't know what it'll be.

Will you ever know me? Will you come? Will I live through trying to have you?

I feel so alone. My friends are wonderful and supportive but I am the only one living in my body, feeling every twinge and cramp. Wondering if it is you only to get another negative. It's hard, it is so hard waiting. Do your mother a favor, don't wait until you are 35 to go for your dream. It's heartbreaking to think it might never come true.

It's been a year since I decided to have you. This is the month you would have come had I gotten pregnant the first time I did DI. With each insemination I count ahead and think of what stage of the pregnancy I will be in and when. I think of how I'm going to tell people. I think of what I can and can't do because of the pregnancy. And each time you haven't come. I'm trying not to think this time.

When do I give up this dream? When it comes true.

Oh to be a mom.

I love you,
Mom

5/11/02

My life is going really good right now. I am happy. The happiest I've been in a long time. I love being alive and letting me flow outward. I am settling into what an amazing person I am. I love getting older. Everything I wanted when I was young just happened with time. "Just", ha, and a lot of work.

In my life, not out. Being around people who love and know me. Know what's going on. Relax into the moment. God I am amazing. I love how I feel. Strong, powerful, safe, gentle, loving, giving, sexy, right as rain. I'm tired of being messed with. I'm tired of being ignored. I'm tired of not being cherished. I'm tired of others not giving their time.

Relax into the wonderment that is you. Express joy with each passing moment. Love thy neighbor.

5/17/02

Can my heart break open yet again? Am I happy? How did I get here and where am I going? How do I deal with the insanity? Is this elusive dream really what is best for me in life? Desire, what good is it? What good is a beautiful vision when that is all it remains? And what do I know anyway? God, how do I see you in this moment? Is my life working or isn't it?

6/9/02

Moments of contentment pierce my soul
Bleeding happiness into my very essence.
Shhh, listen.
The silence speaks to me about love.

It will all work out in the end.

Know and be known, love never ending

But ever growing.

My rich existence surrounds my every move,

My every word, my every deed.

Love is the endless bounty from which we eat.

Come to my table and get your fill.

You deserve it, you are worth it, you have earned it.

I love, therefore I am.

Caress my soul with your tenderness,

Bathe me in gentleness,

Soothe my aching needs with quietness.

The shadows float by at the edge of my vision. Wisps of smoke, who is there? Are you coming to speak to me? Will you materialize at some point? What gifts do you have to bring me? I wait in stillness and silence.

Who is there watching me? The wind caresses my face and gently lets me know it is there. Sweet love, ever wanting to be near me. Expressive and appreciative in its very nature. Speak to me everyday.

6/21/02

Lies told to me by my mother:

- I'm not beautiful
- I'm not worth caring for
- I am unlovable
- No man could love me

- No man could desire me
- No man could want me
- I was ugly
- I was unimportant
- I was not worth her time
- I was not worth her energy
- My breath was a waste of air on the planet
- I was stupid
- I was useless
- I was worthless
- I was boring
- I was a useless human being that wouldn't amount to anything
- I wasn't worth her time
- I wasn't worth her energy
- I wasn't worth her effort
- It was useless to place any hope on me, I wouldn't amount to anything
- My life was a waste of her time
- My life was a waste of her energy
- My life was a waste

I was ugly, I was fat, I was stupid. No man would ever want me, no man would ever care for me, no man would ever desire me. I was ugly, I was ugly, I was ugly. No man would ever love a piece of shit like me. I would forever be laughed at, I would forever be scorned, I would forever be an outcast. No one would want me as a friend. I would always be alone. And even that was too good for the likes of me. No one would ever take me seriously. How could anyone with how stupid I sound? I would never amount to anything.

Why haven't you ever truly been able to tell me you loved me? Why is it always in a book or a card? Why can't you have the guts to say it to my face? Afraid I'm going to reject you the way you've always rejected me? Love me damn it, love me. Show me, hug me, adore me.

It is too late, now get away from me.

What you taught me about love:

- I can't rely on it
- I can't depend on it
- I can't count on it
- It will end up failing me at some point
- It lies
- It thinks of itself first
- It is more important than me
- It is not worth trying for
- It's not anything that I will ever have
- Just give up
- Don't bother, don't try

6/27/02

Coming to terms with my life and accepting who I am. How did I get here and where am I going? Fate stepping in again. This doesn't feel good. This feels like shit. I hate being alone. I hate not having someone to do stuff with. I hate feeling like I should be doing something more.

8/18/02

My dear child,

I've taken a break from trying to conceive you as the inseminations have yet to work. My latest test for the pre-cancerous cells came back more normal than what they've been and I get a little more time to conceive. I just wanted to have fun this summer and not think of this part of my life.

Here I am toward the end of summer and unsure of how to proceed. I keep wishing I could see ahead five years so I could know how you came to be. Do I ask a friend to be a known donor, do I meet some wonderful man and fall in love, do I have a one-night stand or do I adopt you? Those are my options as I see them. This could change in a couple of months, but right now I don't want to continue with the IUIs. It's been a major stress on me to figure out my cycles, order the sperm, get time off from work and then not have the procedure work. Not to mention it is painful. Sex is a more appealing way to conceive you. I don't want you to hate me for what I feel I had to do to have you.

Plus the grief I am experiencing as I realize I may have to give up my dream of how this happens. I always thought I'd meet someone and fall in love but this hasn't been the experience for me. I wish there was a reason but there isn't. It's how my life has been. And even though I've never met this wonderful man, does that mean I have to give up my dream of being a mom?

How do you come to be when the route I was trying isn't working? I don't feel I am done trying to make this dream happen but I am having a hard time living with the ambiguity of my situation. Life is such a miracle and it is not up to me whether it happens.

God grant me the serenity to accept the things I cannot change.

I am waiting and I can't wait to meet you.

Love,

Mom

8/31/02*

All that is and all that ever will be, here now, present in this moment. Unfolding at the right speed, at the right time, and in the right sequence.

Murdered child, you haunt me with the truth. The naked, ugly truth. I can't bear to see. Don't make me look at it, yet it is coming. It will not harm me.

---

* I started to date again and came face-to-face with my thoughts, beliefs, and emotions regarding men and relationships.

I feel ugly and unseen and ignored. I am dirty and rotten and don't deserve happiness. Your mama didn't love you enough to save you and now no one else is allowed to love you. Loving you would mean you are worth something and you had crappy parents. But you needed your parents to survive. You keep yourself alone.

Don't let me walk out that door. Walk with me.

I keep myself alone so I don't have to face myself. I keep myself alone so I don't have to love. I keep myself alone so I don't have to be known. I keep myself alone so I don't have to be challenged. I keep myself alone so I don't have to believe in men because believing in them would make me sad that the ones who should have loved me didn't. Am I just a scared little kid afraid to be loved?

My heart opens up in a million little ways everyday. Expanding at the speed of light. Drumming, beating on.

10/31/02

Doubts and fears haunt my mind. Questioning this, questioning that. Will I ever be able to enjoy the gentle unfolding? Racehorse off on the track. Impatience, tick-tock, tick-tock.

Special soul reaches out to another, bringing lightness and joy to the lives of others. It is so important. Eye contact and presence. It is my gift to you.

Ever ready to give up. Can I be in there for the long haul? Don't over analyze. Don't make up things that aren't true. Just don't.

Love, love, love, love, love.

11/26/02

Endless love waiting to fill and renew your soul. Will you ever come? Is it my destiny to walk this earth alone?

Sadness prevails but I will survive. I gave it my best shot. I know I have what it takes to be in a relationship and be a good partner. I am kind and giving and loving and patient and forgiving and steady and just a good person. And I love me. Thanks for that gift Stewart. You helped me to see me better. But it is time to let you go. I tried and I was there and I was understanding and I was patient but enough is enough. Real love awaits me.

I am fun and worth hanging with and have so much to offer the right person. And I am loved and my heart can open and I can love. But it isn't worth it to me anymore.

And I love me. I am a good person. I like my company and it's okay to be alone. I am at peace in the world.

12/16/02

Take my broken dreams and mend the seams. Let's go toward life from a different perspective. It is time for a change.

My intentions for my life. I accept love into my life. I live from a position of fulfillment. I accept love, joy and fulfillment into my life. I am included in a family of love and health.

What I don't want to go back to? The questions, the focus of not knowing, the endless giving to others, the demands I place upon myself, the striving for more, the loneliness, the aloneness, the trying so hard to make things happens, the small town-ness, the being good, the demands of me, the lack, I don't want to go back to the lack. So don't. Go back to fulfillment!

There is enough to satisfy me, there is enough. There is enough, there is enough, there is enough. There is enough love, men, time, energy, space, love, love, love, people, nurturing, support, love, love, love. There is enough love in my life. There is enough friendship in my life. There is enough caring in my life. There is enough support in my life. There is enough love in my life.

12/17/02

Cold soldier coming home to love.
Tired, weary soul battles her way through love.
What is it and how do I let it into my life?
Slowly, carefully, with each in breath and out breath
Feel it, catch it, hold it.
Let your heart be soothed by the kindness of others.
Melt into the relaxation of their touch.
Let the years of endless sorrows go.
It is time to be free.

Promises you made in the cold darkness of time don't hold up anymore, dear child. They are yours to let go of at will. You don't need to carry it anymore. It was a temporary gift you gave to those you loved. But the gift doesn't need to exist anymore. You served your time, now be free.

Crimes committed against you long forgiven now set them free. Set yourself free. Set the world free. You have been forgiven, the world has been forgiven, happiness and dreams have been forgiven. You are free to live the life you have always dreamed of. Welcome to the other side of the rainbow.

Your sins have been forgiven, your sins have been forgiven, your sins have been forgiven.

Wounded heart on the mend. Carrying me back home to myself. Know me in ways I've never been before. See me in ways I've never been before. Hear me in ways I've never been before. Trust me in ways I've never been before. Have faith dear child, have faith. The world can be a vastly different place than you have ever experienced before.

Heart of hearts, fill me with a love I have never known before. Warm these tired, old aching bones with love and joy. Fill me to the brim with wonder and delight. Show me life can be different.

Shhh, be quiet young child. Listen and be still. Look, listen and walk tentatively towards your new life.

12/19/02

What is working?

- The beauty I create
- The love that surrounds me
- My truth
- My persistence
- My dedication
- My integrity
- My devotion to making the world a better place
- All that I have learned
- My standards

- My expectations
- My understanding
- My respect
- My acceptance
- My giving
- My availability
- My responsibility
- My warmth
- My open heart
- My witness

What isn't working?
- What I teach others as acceptable behavior to treat me
- My silence
- My neatness
- My not saying—enough or no
- My not asking for what I need
- Time to sleep

12/31/02

2003 Intentions:

It is time to be utterly and completely fulfilled in love. To learn from love, the spiritual aspects of life. To offer this knowledge to the world. To grow into myself at a deeper level. To live daily with spirit in my heart. To be heavenly blessed on a daily basis.

I am not doing anyone a favor by being small. Allow myself to come fully into myself as an invitation for them to do the same. Show the world how to love and the steps I took to get here. It's okay to be blissfully happy in love. It's okay to be me and lovable. Thank you for the spiritual protection and guidance this next year. It's okay to love and be loved.

1/3/03

Silence settles on the soul and eases the worries of the mind.
It all comes and goes but love is eternal.
The path I cross, the direction I take,
The choices I make lead me to salvation.
My soul being able to speak, to cry, to love, to be.
Hold me in your arms and comfort the prisoner long held
Without bail, without pardon, without parole.
Unthink the prison walls little one
And be free.
No one should have locked you up.

I deserve to know, you deserve to know, we all deserve to know. How else can we be free? How else can we love? How else is there to live?

Pictures of my life flash through my mind as cherished friends. We've been through so much together. How the hell did I do it? How did I keep it together? How did I move on? Am I the person I dreamed of being? Look at what you have to offer to find out. What is wrong with being loved? What is wrong with being checked out? What is wrong with being attractive? I've worked hard to get here. It is time to reap the rewards. Love and its seven languages.

1/11/03

There is no good reason for me to be alone and unloved. I think I have let myself suffer quite long enough for something I didn't do. It is time for me to be loved for all that I am and all that I have done with my life. I stop and see myself clearly and I see an amazing human being. I am proud of who I am and what I give to others. I am surrounded by love. It is right for me to be treated well by others. I deserve to be treated well by others. I am treated well by others. I deserve to be treated well by others. I am thoroughly loved by others. I am utterly and completely satisfied in love.

DESCENDING

2013: The following entries are from doing a self-inventory after a failed relationship. It was time to find the underlying beliefs driving my relationships, especially with men. I had to use my projections onto other people as the mirror for what I needed to accept within myself. They were the ugly, messy parts of myself that I didn't want to face.

1/13/03

I'm tired of laziness, I'm tired of cowardice, I'm tired of lies, I'm tired of deceit, I'm tired of manipulation, I'm tired of being alone, I'm tired of not living my dream, I'm tired of disappointment, I'm tired of cowardice, I'm tired of cowardice, I'm tired of cowardice.

I'm willing to release my need of being a coward. I'm tired of being a coward. What am I a coward about? Standing up for me, taking a chance, doing something different, finding me, living my dream, being respected.

Where's the pressure coming from? Whose standards am I trying to live up to? Raw nakedness fills the void. Shelter me from the storm. My soul stretches in unlimited directions.

Stop your fucking excuses for living. For not being able to let it all go.

1/18/03

I am angry about standing up for myself and not getting the results that I want. I hate it when people don't get it and I'm the one who gets hurt. I hate it when I try and try and nothing good seems to come of it. I hate it that I go unloved and unappreciated and am continually ignored and abused. See me damn it. I'm right here. Can't you see what's going on? The louder I am, the more I am ignored. Until I give up in despair. It doesn't do any good to stand up for myself. People don't listen anyway. People hate my neediness. They push me away.

I can't get my needs met. People don't care about my needs. I am easily dismissed. I am too nice.

Clouds hang over my head preventing me from seeing you. Gloomy Gus walking around afraid of her own shadow. Afraid of really giving in a relationship. Superficially giving. Keep it light Dusana. No one wants a woman with a ton of baggage. Just keep your mouth shut and you will never be known. Then you'll be safe for once. Keep everyone far, far away. You're not worth it anyway. They don't have time for you. No one wants to hear from you. Shut up already. No one cares, no one cares, no one cares. I'm too demanding, I'm too needy, I'm too much for others to handle. And I'm pissed about it and I attack others for it. I'm going to push you away before you can hurt me too. No one will get close enough to hurt me anymore.

I really fear hurting others. I think if I am honest and totally me, others will be hurt. I diminish myself in order to keep others coming back. I'm afraid to be myself honestly, completely. I fear I will be rejected so I play the game of being nice. This niceness is a theme. I'm afraid to hurt another person.

I'm in this needy feeling place and I feel stuck. It's gunky and gooey around my feet. I try to reach out but I fail. No one can get me out of this place. I try and try yet remain alone. I can't move. I feel happy because I have an excuse. I feel happy because I'm pathetic and can prove myself right about being unworthy. For once I am right about something. See it must be true, people are avoiding me.

I use my neediness to prove myself unworthy of a rewarding love life. See, no one wants a clingy, needy bitch. I'm not worth their time. See how right I am? See, see, see. And I can get attention by being unworthy. Feel sorry for me, feel sorry for me.

1/25/03

It's all their fault for not getting me and meeting my needs. It's their fault that I am where I am. It's their fault I can't find love. People are stupid, people don't understand, people are odd. If I try really, really hard and something fails it must be someone else's fault because I did everything that I could. I can prove I'm better by making your way wrong. I'm more evolved. I've grown more and I will throw it in your face at every possible moment. Of course you should love me, I am so great. Who wouldn't? I know what I'm doing and you don't. I will prove why you should love me and I will throw it in your face every chance I get. I need to be right. I need to be right at all costs. Even your self-dignity and respect. You are wrong and I will let you know it every step of the way. You are wrong, wrong, wrong, wrong, wrong. I know so much better than you. What, are you stupid or something? I will prove to you how great I am by always being right. I am great, I am great, I am great.

Am I sufficiently hiding how shitty I feel about myself? Am I hiding how unworthy I feel? Am I fooling you at all?

What if I've been wrong all these years?

What has always being right gotten me?

1/26/03

Life will get better if only I can keep my mouth shut. By being quiet I will finally make it all right and everything will turn out okay. Only if I keep my mouth shut will I get what I want in this world. I will keep trying to be better. I will try and try and try and try and then no more harm will come my way and everything will be okay. I've just got to keep my mouth shut. Be quiet Dusana, don't say a word, don't tell the truth. Be whomever everyone else wants you to be, not who you really are. Just shut up already and everything will be okay. Shut up, shut up, shut up. *Shut up and take it.** Who do you think you are to stand up for yourself? We will keep you down. We will all keep you down. Every time you want something bad enough be prepared to fail. It'll always be out of your reach. Don't even bother anymore. Life can be better

---

* It'll be another ten years before this subconscious belief plays itself out in my external life loud enough that I truly hear it and can't ignore it anymore.

but only if you keep your mouth shut. Standing up for yourself doesn't do any good.

Just keep your mouth shut and be a good girl then everyone will like you. No one wants to hear what you have to say anyway. No one cares, no one will help, there's no one around for you but me and I obviously don't care either. So don't even bother, don't even try. Just don't do anything and then people will like you.

2013: The following are answers to questions as part of a self-inventory but I didn't write the source or the questions down.

2/3/03

1. A few times when I was in doubt about what I should do I asked myself what would love do. How can I show him I love him by offering support? I gave him space, I offered to help with his son, I was willing to help his friends with their children, and I asked what I could do to make his life easier.

2. His actions don't match his words. His words are wonderful but his actions towards me don't support them. So why am I hanging on so tightly? Because I don't want to be alone anymore. I am ready for a meaningful relationship. I don't want to give it up and have to get back into the dating scene. Because I'm afraid there will be no one else for me. I don't want to have to start over with building a relationship. Though I do feel very positive about the experience overall.

3. I did need the positive experience and I enjoyed talking with him. I've learned so much about myself.

4. I do feel like I'm settling because he obviously doesn't want us as badly as I do. I do deserve someone willing to give me his time and energy. It is a deal breaker for me. I do deserve someone who is excited to be with me. I deserve someone who puts me first when appropriate. I deserve someone who loves and cares for me. I deserve someone who is there for me. I deserve a soft place to land.

5. I want our relationship to work out. I'm ready to be in a mutually fulfilling relationship. I'm not a quitter but I do need something to go on. I feel he didn't even give our relationship a chance. He wasn't fully in it.

What if it's me who has needed to accept and understand where I've come from? How does this change my relationships? What if I've needed to set up my relationships to verify that I am unworthy and unlovable? The standards regarding how others should be there for me fit into my self-destructive beliefs about myself. Whenever I start to feel good about myself I make sure someone else's behavior lets me know how much I am not worth it. I use their behaviors to fit my belief structure.

I don't confront or be real with another so as to avoid being told what I fear is true: they don't really care or love me.

2/16/03

I can be so mean to myself. I'm brutal on expectations and lack of appreciation for what I do. I don't stop to really see or hear me. It's time for love and tenderness in my life. I don't have to keep beating myself up for every little thing I do wrong. Every infraction where I don't measure up. I can stop and see what an amazing person I am. I have so many abilities.

Emotionally: my partner is my soft place to land. My partner and I agree that we have been hurt enough in the past and will check our behavior to ensure it doesn't happen anymore. My partner communicates his thoughts and feelings in an open, respectful and gentle manner. My partner and I trust our individual decisions to be the best both for ourselves and as a couple. My partner and I listen to accept, understand, and challenge each other to be the best person we can be. My partner holds me when I need it and allows me to just be. My partner stands with me every step of the way. My partner validates my existence and experience in life. My partner trusts me. My partner communicates his belief in me. This is what I am ready to accept in my life.

I was 17 when I knew I had to learn to love myself. What exactly am I waiting for?

3/6/03

Beauty and Love

I'm mad I didn't have better parents. I'm mad I wasn't loved unconditionally. I'm mad that other people screw up so much. I'm mad that I'm inconvenienced in life. I'm mad that I've put up with shit from others. I'm mad that I've had to disregard myself. I'm mad I had to put others first. I'm mad I'm alone. I'm mad it's not okay for me to express my anger.

9/15/03*

Love enters your life and throws the dogs a bone. Is it here or not? What do I feel? What do I want? My old life is waiting for me to pick up whenever I want. That is not the problem. I am finally liking my life here. I am finally feeling settled. Don't want to leave it. And what about where I am going physically? It's not like the next few years are going to be fun. Knowing the realty of my life and heading forward anyway.

You never understand the reasons I do what I do. I hate having to explain myself. I've done the best I could with what I've been given. I made the choices I thought were right. My heart hurts in a million little pieces. Will it ever mend? Why feel the pain? I used to know the reasons. I used to have a direction. I used to know what I wanted. Now it is endless suffering. What am I feeling? The sins of the world or my own? How ready am I for a new life?

My life as I've known and dreamt about it is coming to an end but I don't know what the new dreams are yet. Here I am in my little western state and I don't know where I end up or what I'll be doing next. All that I have worked for and I don't know if it's what I want to do anymore. A world you can't even imagine.

2013

On the days I feel like beating up on myself, I look at my recovery as something I didn't *do* right the first time. On the days I'm kinder to myself, I see my recovery as a deepening

---

* Starting to date yet again.

process. There's more about the issues that I need to learn. By going through this journey of healing wholeheartedly, I found a love deeper and more encompassing than I ever thought possible. Yet I know there is always more to discover. My love can surround the good, the bad and the ugly without condoning the behavior.

I had to move from an intellectual understanding of the effects of the abuse to experiencing the physical sensations I had from my thoughts and feelings. The burning, icy spears, knives, and the pressure on my heart so intense I thought I was having a heart attack. The screams stifled long ago coming through my tense muscles as they made their way to the surface. It has taken decades to get through it all as I was not allowed to process the effects of the abuse when I was a child. The process is like a pressure cooker letting off a little steam at a time so the whole thing doesn't explode.

I made my way through it by internally stating what I wanted and then the situations that healed my wounds were brought to me. I was able to challenge the untruths and learn to let new realities in a little at a time. I was able to gain trust of myself, the world and the process of recovery. I built on my successes and learned from my failures.

10/26/03

There is nothing better than being in the arms of a man who knows how to dance. I love to give up control and be totally taken care of for a while. Lord knows I spend enough of my life taking care of others. To be held by strong arms which have my best interest at heart and for a very short time, to stop thinking and let someone else do it. It is a true respite from the life of a woman. To me there is no better foreplay. It's an easy way for me to learn to trust the man I love and be able to hand it over to him in bed also.

11/15/03

I think dance is the most threatening art form. You are the art. There is no character to hide behind, no instrument that could be blamed for being out of tune and no canvas to be filled. You are the canvas. A friend of mine, who has danced professionally, asks her students to remember that the dance is not the person but I don't think you can separate the two. As you dance you put yourself out there for all the world to see. You are totally exposed and are allowing others to see your dedication, your beliefs about yourself, and the inner fire which stirs your longings in life.

I know I struggled when I first started to dance with feelings of total exposure. I used to imagine different people seeing me and immediately wanted to hide. But it was that spark that I was trying to hide from myself. Dance felt too big to me. I couldn't let the world see what was inside me. It was too risky, too much. I love that spark which defines who I am and is unique. I have let it come out and now you can be sure that when I dance I am certainly not the most technically accurate dancer but you will not be able to take your eyes off of me. It is because when I dance I am allowing you to see the real me.

1/4/04

I love children. I have been a child and an adult and childhood wins hands down. I love to enter their world. To challenge their perceptions and play with the reality they are trying to sort out. Who are they going to believe, me or themselves? I love to assist them with creating a world in which dreams don't die, beliefs aren't squished, and souls can fly free. Do I actually achieve this? God I hope so.

After many years of yearning to be a mother I am finally at the point where I can actually say I am grateful not to be a parent. I have an objectivity that parents don't in regards to their children. I guess I trust enough in the human spirit to know that adversity can be overcome.

1/16/04

I still hate having to start over. There is too much history for me to get into. Slow baby steps. I don't need to accomplish anything regarding men today. I've gotten myself back out there and that is enough.

2/10/04

What if I were to meet the relationship of my dreams today? It makes me cry to even think about it. I feel weary. I would have to say 'no' to it right now. I don't want to get involved with anyone. The risk of heartbreak is too much. He thought I raised the bar and I didn't think I even started. That's two people on different pages. I was too quiet. I didn't speak my mind, though friends would never believe such a thing were possible with me.

I walked on eggshells hoping he'd want to be in a relationship, hoping he'd stay. I sat back and watched and waited to see if he was finally someone I could build a future with. There were signs but I wanted the search to be over. I wanted to be settled but what I ended up doing was settling.

He drank too much, I even allowed him to drink in my car when I was driving. Like I needed to be pulled over and be caught with that. I let myself be treated so disrespectfully. It's so embarrassing. I did feel crappy about myself. I did want someone to like me, to accept me, to find me beautiful and alluring. He didn't do anything to me, I did. I've had enough heartache for one lifetime. He struck a nerve and maybe that was his only function in my world. It's time to move on to a relationship of mature love with reciprocal caring.

I never felt you were on my side. I felt like you sided with my family and their awful treatment of me. I felt you thought I deserved it. Or that it made sense to you that people who were suppose to love me treated me like shit. I hated your responses to what I shared with you. You weren't there for me. You blew me off. And I wanted to be loved so desperately that I hung on to the little scraps you flung me regarding how cool you thought I was. I thought you loved me. I guess I was wrong.

3/20/04

So how did the hometown girl part of me win out? I like the realness of the people in my redneck town. There's a genuine caring that I have experienced here that I have been in search of my entire life. I have certainly made it up in the past where it didn't belong. In people, schools, thought patterns and beliefs. I always tried so hard to fit in. I don't blame people for avoiding me. I don't fit in. I have been through too much in my life for that to ever occur. I like nice people and I am biased enough against the rich to feel they are genuinely nice. I'm sure there are some out there but the ones I grew up with had a holier than thou attitude that I had a hard time stomaching.

The one way I was always grateful for having arthritis is that I was certain that I would have turned into one of the rich stuck-up bitches without it. It made me human. It made me real. I feel lucky now to have lived with it for thirty years. It's been my spiritual teacher and guide. I can sit quietly for hours and be content with it all. I learned how to breathe through pain and there's nothing like pain to bring you back to the moment. Before I had my hips replaced I used to count the steps I took as though that would help with the feeling of someone shoving a knife into my socket with each step. I think I did it to take my mind off of where I was and how far the walk was to where I was going.

When the pain first started to become really bad I noticed that it became worse depending on my state of mind. The more negative my thoughts, the worse the pain got. I also became more withdrawn during this period as dealing with anyone other than my own state became tiresome. After a while I was unable to say which part affected the other part the most. Would my pain have been less, and the damage to the joint less severe, if I had been able to alter my thoughts? I really did try the spiritual healing but after a while my life had become so small that something had to be done. I wasn't able to let go of it all at that time and finally decided to have the surgery. It was either that or death and I wasn't sure I was done on the planet yet.

4/16/04

Dear Dusana,

I want you to live. I want you to be around for me. I need you here. I need you to finish my work. You aren't done yet. Don't give up. There are a lot of wonderful surprises awaiting you in this life. The best is yet to come. Please do not give up.

It is true that you have a lot of work left, but it will all be worth it someday. I love you very much. I wish that you would listen to me more. You are so damn stubborn.

You have an intelligence that is truly a gift from God. You need to learn to use it more wisely. You have a tendency to become impatient with others for not possessing the same gift that you have. It is something to be shared, not hoarded. You are to give it freely to others, not keep it to yourself. Share it with others and let the love blossom and grow from within. You possess everything you need to survive in the world. Embrace the love that surrounds you and allow others to bloom and grow as you do.

Now is the time to see the beauty that surrounds others. It is time to see the love that is around everyone. Now is the time to feel the breath of fresh air whenever you come into contact with others.

You have found what you need from within, now find it in others. Give them the same chance that you have given yourself. Everyone wants the love that you are finding. Give it freely to others. It is not yours to hold onto but yours to give to others as they come into contact with you.

Find the beauty in all those who meet you. Give them the same respect you give yourself. All that you want is attainable. It is within reach. You need to learn to intelligently grasp that which will benefit you the most. You know what it is, now you need to ask and find it. It is there but you need to get it. It is yours for the taking, but you need to ask. It can and it will come to you. You are love. Let it shine. You are pure joy. You are pure wisdom. Trust in all that ever was and shall be again. The knowledge comes from within. Use others as guides but the true source of your wisdom comes from within you. You already know it, now rediscover it. It is all there.

5/23/04

When I hung the picture up on the wall I couldn't believe that it could threaten me so much. I had read a feng shui book to help me figure out an old boyfriend but ended up seeing myself so much on the pages that I went out and bought pictures of couples dancing. None of my pictures had a man and a woman in them, only lone figures.

After the picture of the couple dancing on the beach, with their servants holding an umbrella, was up on the wall I felt sick to my stomach looking at it. I wanted to take it down but knew my reaction was not normal so I kept it up. As I became more comfortable with it I was able to add The Kiss by Kilmet and another picture of a man with a straight back and the woman he's dancing with leaning into him with trusting deference. They all challenge my sense of independence and dependence. I felt so vulnerable and exposed. Could I ever learn to rely upon a man and enjoy his attention the way the women in the pictures did?

2013 about June, 2004

I went home for my 20th high school reunion. During this trip I found a book my mom had, Marianne Williamson's *A Return to Love*. Within it was the poem* a former therapist had read to me and it became the basis of many of my writings about growing into my greatness and not diminishing myself to make others feel safe. As I read the book, it spoke to my vision of spirituality and subsequently led me to *A Course in Miracles*. I ordered a copy and read it cover to cover. It affirmed my belief that we are all here to do what Jesus did to become Christ and lays out the path he took to achieve this.

It also spoke to my experience with prayer and God through my healing journey. When I was able to hit rock-bottom with my

---

* It was the same poem which Nelson Mandela read during his inauguration speech.

pain and beg for it to be taken from me, these were the moments when relief would come. My desperate pleas that I couldn't take anymore and there must be a different way to live life were answered on the pages of *A Course in Miracles*. Everyday becomes another opportunity to find love and forgiveness. Years later I am still studying it and attempting to grasp how to do this in my life.

My relationship with God grew, changed and deepened through the years. I had my spiritual basis in Catholicism, studied Native American traditions, Buddhism, New Age and various other spiritual beliefs as part of my quest for inner peace. My communication with the above became a natural part of everyday life and my writings about my struggle with it lessened as my trust grew. I pray as needed, give thanks/appreciation when applicable, and listen to or heed guidance imperfectly. The integration of my spiritual essence and the flawed human being continues. I use the one to find the other.

10/18/04

My favorite therapy for the past seven years has been watching *Inside the Actor's Studio*. I look at therapists and directors as having the same job and the client and actor as being the same also. The director holds the larger vision for the actor and creates the context for what is within to come out and be expressed. There must be safety and trust, understanding and the belief that the actor/client is capable of being raw and vulnerable.

As a graduate student in a psychology program, I would watch the show to gain a greater understanding of what my job would be as a therapist. The main thing I learned whenever I watched the program was that humans were extremely complex animals and there wasn't one particular event in a lifetime that could define a person. It was a montage of events both great and small that shaped and directed and molded a person's character, or lack there of. The wholeness of life's experiences and responses were within us all and how we made meaning out of these experiences determined our actions in the present moment.

2013

In 2001 I started a childcare in my house in anticipation of being a mom and wanting to be able to stay home with my child. That child never came but I continued taking care of other people's children. I was able to love them then send them home at the end of the day. I also had the opportunity to re-parent different ages from my own past. I remember a huge one was working with three year old me. Situations had happened that made that a scary time as a child and that area of my life needed attention.

I learned more about boundaries including emotional and energetic ones. I would feel emotions that didn't have a belief attached to them that were applicable to my healing. I remember experiencing them and thinking, this isn't mine. Sometimes the emotions felt like they were coming from generations past and other times it felt like I had picked them up from people in my life.

From my understanding of Native American beliefs, what we do affects seven generations into the future. Added to this was my understanding of quantum physics. This can also go seven generations into the past. In order to heal the pattern of incest within my family, I felt the emotions as a hope to end it. I was okay doing this work because it felt like I was helping the whole of humanity.

As part of the enmeshment from my family dynamics and my training as a therapist, I was empathetic to others. I do believe in auras and mysticism based on situations that have occurred in my life. I have experienced energetic connections to people that needed to be cut like a cord. Other times, it has felt like I was helping one of my friends with her emotions. I was feeling things that did not resonate as being from my issues. I had to learn to put up an energetic boundary.

While running the childcare, one of the children's mother died when she was three. I had been watching Emily since she was a year old and I knew the mother archetype would naturally get shifted to me. I had been wanting to close it that summer but I kept the childcare open for another year and a few months as she grieved and went through anniversaries. While she continued to be raised by her father, I kept a close relationship with her and fulfilled a role of not quite mother but more than a good friend. We've all stumbled through the years as we tried to explain in a word how I'm connected to the family.

The below was written in response to things I actually heard while running the childcare or the covert messages of things said by parents.

2005

    Mama, why don't you tell me I'm special?
    I don't even like kids.
    Mama, why don't you tell me I'm special?

Quit asking me for stuff, I'm the adult.
Mama, why don't you tell me I'm special?
You didn't say hi to me this morning.
Mama, why don't you tell me I'm special?
You have been a brat all day long.
Mama, why don't you tell me I'm special?
You're bothering me again.
Mama, why don't you tell me I'm special?
Quit it, you're being a kid again.
Mama, why don't you tell me I'm special?
Why do I even bother, you just don't get it.
Mama, why don't you tell me I'm special?
Be more like your brother, he's the perfect one.
Mama, why don't you tell me I'm special?
You're the smart one, you never had kids.
Mama, why don't you tell me I'm special?
Taking care of kids, now that's the best birth control.
Mama, why don't you tell me I'm special?
Ohhhh, the mess.
Mama, why don't you tell me I'm special?
Kids destroy things.
Mama, why don't you tell me I'm special?
This kids needs medication.
Mama, why don't you tell me I'm special?

Childhood:
The world of rainbows and smiles,
Laughter and wonder,

Pretend and discovery,

Dreams and ice cream trucks,

Wide open plains and towering vistas,

Vulnerability and trust,

Silly songs and mud on the floor,

And words that cut like a knife and wounds that never heal.

Why do I think you're special my child? Because of the love you shower on me, the endless possibility you show me, your natural trust and your belief in the goodness of others. You keep on being a child as long as you can. Others will take it away from you soon enough.

HIDDEN AGAIN

6/18/05

A new journey. I love reading my old entries. So much passion and knowledge. Have the years chipped away at it too much? The journey of discovery that had so much brilliance to it. I am more there than I have ever been before. Yet the richness of the search seemed so much more alive than I am now.

I'm hiding and I've needed to hide and known that I'm hiding. Yet, I'm hiding still the same. I guess my new journey is to allow myself to come out of hiding and accept the life I was born to live.

The weeding through of what I want versus what I don't want. The enormity of my 'no' and the calmness of my 'yes'. I always thought I wanted to get married and have kids, yet the 'no' was discovered, hidden in the recess of my heart and soul. I'm fine having a husband, that isn't the problem. It's being someone's wife. Wife. An endless sentence of slavery to someone else's beck and call. Expectations and demands. Being stuck in a role with so many negative connotations associated with it and not being able to see a way to my ideals.

My 'no' keeps me on the outskirts of an institution whose ruling class is over. The divorce rate, the unhappiness of countless couples who don't know themselves enough to be able to reach out and truly connect with another. Are families truly what we are set on this planet to do? Stop and look at the beauty standing in front of you. Can you even see it and take the time to recognize it?

I let my family go. Dreams of a loving husband and children to tend and nurture their very beings. My struggle with being a better mother than my own. My selfishness at not ever wanting to be hated by another person, let alone my own child, as I have hated my own mother. I've finally reached a point in my life where the thought doesn't bring me to tears. I'm okay with the fact of the love-hate relationship I have with her and how difficult it is for me to continue a relationship with her.

I don't know why she treats Kevin so poorly. It's not a dismissal exactly, more a disregard. Disregarded, now that's a familiar pattern for me. Easily thrown away. That's what the members of our family are. Stay within the confines and don't make waves. No wonder I feel such a comfort being on the ocean, it is waves. Deep and unattainable but to the few who can stand the pressure.

I love seeing a horizon. After years in the mountains where the sun can set behind them by 3 p.m., it's a luxury for my eyes to stretch out and see flatness to a point indistinguishable by miles. It's just far. There's nothing to see but an expansive palate of blues and grays and the occasional whiteness as the wave turns over itself. Starting out as an oil painting and flattening out to oil pastels and then watercolor consistency. Nowhere to get to as any destination is imperceptible in the distance. If there is somewhere to get to, I cannot see it with my naked eye. I trust the captain knows where he is taking me.

I like that analogy for life. Riding along on a great cruise-liner where I need to take care of the minutiae of life but someone else is getting me to my destination.

2013: The following entry on 6/19 was my imaging or hoping what my brother Charlie might be thinking behind the mask he wears in life. I was still hoping there was some recognition of the work I had done and the person I'd become from it. It was an attempt for me to heal the repeating 'why' story in my head regarding the silence I experienced from my siblings. When we don't get the information we need from another, we make up a story.

I got to a point when I didn't feel the story I had been running in my head was of service to my healing. I had read or heard that it doesn't matter where a healing message comes from, real or imagined, the subconscious mind accepts it as being true. This was an experiment to see if the above theory worked. I wrote it to trick myself into feeling like my family cared and supported me; I was worth something. I didn't actually need it from my family of origin. It was just a message I needed to hear to recover another piece of myself. Like most of my issues, this one would spiral around a few more times in the years to come.

6/19/05

I don't know why my sister did it, or even how, but she broke free. She challenged the world created by our parents and their parents and all the subsequent children of that lineage. I've watched her go through it and cannot understand where she possibly gained the courage to risk losing us all and in fact, that is what happened. Or did we lose her? I guess both really. We've lost each other through the years.

That's not to say that I don't see her and attempt conversation but she's, I don't know, just so different now. And I'm so busy with my own life that, well, I don't think to call her. The betrayal of her by our family was too great that I can't face how I must have hurt her, how we all hurt her.

I thought the hurt would have stopped when our father quit raping her but all it did was become hidden away trying to eat its way into my consciousness fully but I keep it at bay. And if I don't see or talk to her, it'll be okay.

I walked in on it once with our older brother. God it was awful to see the anguish on her face. She was so scared and I wanted to help her so bad. But instead I got the beating of my life. My father let me know once again who was in charge. All I could do was to stare at her the next morning at breakfast. The three of us sitting there facing each other and the truth that could never be spoken about again. I was stunned and shocked as she chattered on and on. I'm not even sure what she was saying but I felt her letting me know she was okay and it would be all right. And somehow it has been for her. She's the one who came out of it ahead while I wrestled everyday with my helplessness and fury.

I couldn't help my baby sister. I couldn't help the sister I cherished the most. The one whose hand I held when she was afraid, the one who I wouldn't let back down from a challenge, the one who I would find when she hid from the beatings our mother gave her, the sibling I loved the most. When she has needed me the most, I have been unable to help her.

She's gone on to shine in life though. Somehow she didn't back down when we all sided with our father after the cancer was discovered. She didn't quit when we didn't call when the cancer finally took him. She stood her ground as the years went on and no one came to visit and the calls became less and less frequent until today, when we don't call at all. She essentially lost her whole extended family, yet when I saw her last, she looked radiant. She shines with a light that I wish I could explain.

I hated her for years for remaining friends with my ex-wife. That's when I first felt her leave me, when she sided with my ex. I didn't see it at the time but it was the love for my sons that made her do it. And they must have known it because they love her so now. She innately knows how to bring out the best in children. It's like she see their uniqueness and specialness and talks directly to that part of them. Come to think about it, she does that with everyone.

She certainly has been through enough hell; I guess I can't blame her for only seeing goodness and beauty now. Though I really wish she would have taken me along on her journey. I miss her.

Also written on 6/19. just a different version for myself:

I've often wondered what the effects the raping had on my sister. Night after night I heard them as my room was next to hers. Our older sister was away at college and she was stuck in the horrors of the empty room. During the day she acted as normal as ever and it was easy, or at least easier, to pretend it wasn't happening. And years later, when she came looking to us for support and affirmation it was just easier to think she had gone crazy. Or actually brainwashed, that was the way the rest of us—her whole family—referred to it. Wherever would she get such notions? Though I knew it then she was telling the truth. I knew it then. But I couldn't admit it, my own life was falling apart at the time and I couldn't face what she was facing.

She doesn't get into relationships, at least not too often. And when she does, they don't seem to last. Though I can't imagine why. My sister is beautiful. I swear she hasn't aged in the past ten years and even then she looked young. Again, she has a radiance that glows from within and she has a way of making everyone feel special to her. She works hard and is good at what she does. She's smart, more educated than I would ever aspire to, and just plain fun to be around. And while it's strange to admit this about my sister, the woman is just plain sexy. She has a confidence that is breathtaking to look at.

I can only imagine that she tires of men though. After me, our brother, father and grandfather, what must she think of men? I don't think I'll ever want to know the damage we caused in that department. I wish she'd find the man that she deserves. Though that quality must be rare to find. Her loneliness and sadness must fill her depths like the ocean she so loves. Strong and powerful, yet gentle and serene with depths the common man can't begin to fathom nor take the pressure to explore. That is how I see my sister.

As a fly on her wall, I wonder what I would find out about her. It's been so long since we talked, only the exchanges of niceties when she comes home to visit. But I still can't face her and I fail to know who she is anymore.

I just remembered, I did go to see her once after she moved. But her house was really a place to stay before I went skiing with my friends. She had to work the night I got in and though she offered, I didn't care to hang out with her and the people she cared for.

The next day she had off but my friends came to rescue me. I mean she lives in Colorado, am I expected not to ski? I haven't been back since. Our other brothers still go skiing there but even they don't call. One doesn't even let her know anymore when he's coming. I can't blame him at all. It's better to spare her the disappointment. And I fear we have all disappointed her vastly, and often.

7/1/05

I travel alone. It is one of my favorite things to do. The freedom of the open roads, roads I essentially haven't traveled before. Or even if I have, new ways to see the familiar and learn new things about myself.

I love people but I also feel crowded in by them. Living alone, I've always found it ironic my need to get away by myself in order to rejuvenate, to re-discover, to catch my breath and inhale.

When I travel alone I find I am friendlier when I do come in contact. The intake of breath has created an opening to stop and make contact with others. I was luckily born a social person and have learned the art of striking up conversations with others. Everyone has a story to tell and usually the threads of our lives cross in enough places that there is always something to say. The struggle of the human condition living on this planet. Love, loss, courage, it's all in there for each of us and it is the place where we all meet.

I am also lucky enough to feel safe wherever I go. I believe in the goodness of others and believe it will follow me wherever I go.

The young girl had just been abducted in Aruba before my last trip and the Caribbean was where I was headed. It's not that I want anything bad to happen to her, or anyone, but I figured something like that wouldn't happen again so soon. The law of probability and all.

When I returned home, my mom and I talked about the young woman. She made the comment, "they say it's not safe to go off alone." I was quiet on my end as I noticed this line didn't upset me anymore. I internally noted that this is what "they" would like women to do but it's not what I want to do. My 'no' to that statement declares that instead of women not being able to go off alone, men should learn to leave them alone. We have the right to be safe wherever we are and that is what I stand for.

11/7/05

Demons, will I ever fully purge them?

He's just not that interested in me. Is that supposed to make me feel better? I hate you for how unlovable you made me feel. How undesirable. How stupid it was for me to have needs regarding men and families. I don't deserve them. It's silly for me to want more. To think I could actually get them met and be happy. To think that someone could care about me. He's just not that into you. To think I thought I was special. I was someone worthy of a relationship? To think that someone could actually care for me? Stupid and foolish, that's what I am. I'm forever searching for someone to tell me I'm special, I'm unique, I'm worth it. That I actually have something to offer someone. That someone could be happy with me. That there wouldn't be someone better out there.

I'm so ready to believe any line that any man gives to me. I guess I am desperate. I don't like this part of me. I feel pathetic. I'm not willing to lay my heart out on the line again. It hurts too damn bad. This is where I am for now.

1/26/06

The old TV show *The Twilight Zone* influenced me during my childhood. I remember the episode in which the four characters had to put on masks that their wealthy, dying host had provided for them. Each character had to don these masks and was horrified with what the mask represented. The mask was so contrasted to the face they presented to the world everyday. But as life would persist, each mask accurately portrayed the inner thoughts, beliefs and feelings of the person. At the end of the episode when the characters were finally allowed to take off their masks, they found that their faces were forever fashioned to show their inner world.

From that moment on in the back of my mind I have thought about how my face may be portraying my inner world to everyone else. What I most wanted to hide was out there for all the world to see. What if that really happens everyday. What if what I thought was well hidden behind words and gestures was actually accurately read by everyone that I met on a day to day basis. How does this change what I do?

The Twilight Zone, the TV program that showed me a world different than what I had imagined. It challenged me to think outside the box of everyday perceptions. It was an intellectual spotlight of how one's world could play with you to find those inner beliefs and then challenge their very existence. With the vignettes Rod Serling brought to light how to face our humanness with compassion, fearlessness and honesty.

2/08/06

As the sun rises in the east,
I feel your presence beside me
Beckoning towards another day.
The questions and uncertainties that lay ahead;
Where will I find you?
When will you find me?
The unexpected moments in which we meet.
My sigh, my smile, let me know you're near.
The laugh in the next room.
The bum on the corner.
The many ways you present yourself.

I try not to question but I have my doubts.
Will I always be able to find you in another?
In the moment?
Do you end, do I?
What is the source of your beginning?

> Who allows you to shine forth?
> What can I do to beckon you?
> The same thing I do to beckon the sun.

3/18/06

Motherhood, the elusive dream always just past my fingertips. I've tried the past few years to be content with the daycare but my heart just isn't in it. It's not the same. And yet it's not a dream I want anymore. Can you have a child die without ever being a mom? That's what it feels like. I lost my child and my chance to be a mom forever. I don't want to go down that road again. I don't have the energy to get myself up and try again. I look at that path longingly yet know I don't have the strength to transverse it.

I feel the other path to my right beckoning. It feels all bright and happy and joyful. The motherhood path is gray and dreary. Yet I feel children on the other path. Children to love and play with but are not my own.

I turn and walk away.

6/20/06

Motherhood and my family. What is the role I play? What am I wanting to achieve? It was the love and inclusiveness that I never felt as a child. To be the center of someone's world. The adoration, the cherishing, the respect, the admiration, the wonder, the awe, to feel I really belonged to someone. That I was wanted. That I was loved. To be someone's world. To have a purpose. To be surrounded by support and love. For someone to care about me and put my best interest first for once. That's what motherhood means to me. A chance to be for another what was not given to me.

My heart burns as the icy spears melt in my heart. The body of my soul needs to speak and let its voice be heard.

The inspiration, the dream got me through some of the worst days of my life. At what point does one let go? Can I let go of my agenda? Poetic hills weaving their way through the tapestry of my life. How can he help me to love myself in spite of my family? The answer will come from within. It's just a matter of time. How do I trust and let go again? How do I join the stream of love? When will it be my turn?

GOING HOME

2013: The following entries were written as I prepared to go back home for my sister's wedding. I'd be seeing extended family members from both sides that I hadn't seen since my father's funeral 13 years prior. A couple of my friends flat out refused to go anywhere near my family. It took some urging but one friend and her husband attended and supported me. As hard as it is to read or hear about my life, I can guarantee it's harder to live it. I sometimes need to demand that my friends *suck it up* and be there for me.

I have had the experience many times where I share about my life and the other person can't handle hearing what I have to say. I am looking for support but end up taking care of the other person. I leave the interaction feeling more abandoned, isolated and alone.

I then work on changing my self-hatred for having needs and being dependent on another person. Intellectually I know it is part of being human, to be interdependent. The expectation I attach to others fulfilling my needs results in disappointment. I risk trusting another person in supporting me and s/he doesn't follow through. I feel my wound and needs are too much for others to handle so I end up relying only on myself. I have yet to move beyond this pattern. Am I displaying trust if I let the expectation of support go? Or am I putting my trust in the wrong people? Having to ask both questions leaves me feeling sad. I feel alone.

May, 2007

I am writing as therapy to help me cope with this family celebration. It's better than the guy I was paying $180.00 for a 45 minute session. "It's a reaching out from your sister; it's a time to talk with your brothers about what they did to you and how it's affected them; it's a great chance to become closer to your family and lessen the estrangement that's been going on for the past 15 years." Except for the fact that I have been reaching out for years now and what do I get back? Keep in line or we won't spend a couple of hours with you when you visit. Keep in line or we won't talk to you at all. Keep in line but we still won't call to see you when we come to Colorado. I'm sorry but I do this why?

My dress is different. My sister and all the other bridesmaids will be wearing long, halter dresses. Mine is a tea length, spaghetti strapped number. The perfect metaphor for the difference between us. Though I haven't met the groom's sisters-in-law, or the groom for that matter, and can't judge how they are. I like that mine will be sassy like me. Hot pink and sassy. I wonder if I can find some long silver gloves to match my silver jeweled strapped sandals. I have my own sisterhood backing me up. The sisterhood of women who aren't willing to lie down and take it anymore.

My sister doesn't call. Maybe she doesn't call from now until the wedding. Maybe she doesn't want to discuss the changes a woman single for 49 years goes through when she decides to get married. Maybe she is so busy at work. But why does it seem that she talks to the others? I don't care anymore. I just don't care. It is time to walk away.

I accept my relationships with my siblings as they are. I will not expect any more. We are not close and I don't feel the need to make more of an effort. I received a forwarded email from my sister today extolling the virtues of being there for another. The sisterhood of friends and women sticking together. I find this ironic coming from the sister who doesn't acknowledge the differences in how we perceive our father. She did stay with me in the boat last year when we were on the scavenger hunt. But the time at the shoe store felt so empty to me. I was trying on boots while out shopping with my mom and sister. I have a hard time putting on socks and had to switch the ones I was wearing for a pair of footies to try on the boots. Neither my mother nor sister helped. They figured the sales lady knew how to do this better than they did. It's putting a sock onto a foot. We've all been doing it for decades.

I was embarrassed that I needed the help and for them to go mindless on me hurt to the core. I felt left once again and dependent. The sales lady was so compassionate as we struggled to get my feet into the boots. The warmth crept up my face as I pulled at the boot and tried to make it easier for her to help. The loneliness and duration of their lack of awareness burrowed into my chest as I felt the weight of sadness settle into my heart and lungs. My lungs felt hollow as the exposure of my humiliation of how my family treats me was laid out for this total stranger to witness. Raw, the ever-present rawness was dug up once again for me to attempt to take a breath into. A hurt and shame so insidious to my life that at times I haven't been sure I would ever be able to bury it again in my day-to-day life of attempted happiness. But I breathe and cover the pain and try to pretend that it doesn't cut me to the core. I try to forget what I am missing in terms of love and acceptance and support.

May, 2007

I don't want to trust at all. My sister let me know that she will always be here for me. But I haven't had that experience with her for the past 15 years. I don't feel like starting now with just a promise. I would need acknowledgment of the ways she hasn't been there for me. I would need confirmation that she believes me about what dad did. That he wasn't such a great guy. How the family has totally abandoned me and understand the betrayal I felt. Three minute conversations with people I haven't seen in years does not constitute caring or being happy to see me. It equals years of neglect and dismissal. The family let me go with no problem at all. I do not feel like making an effort anymore. I am free from them. I am done.

What has brought all of these walking away fantasies and dramas over a dress, a dress mind you? My 49-year-old sister is getting married for the first time and I get the honor of being her maid. I get to go back to *dad was so wonderful camp* for the weekend. Ahhhhhhhh!

Though it's started already. Putting his name on the invitation? He's been dead for 13 years for Christ sake. Of course it's a Catholic ceremony. It's strange she's not having it at our childhood church but the church we went to during the summers we spent at the lake. Wouldn't that group love to know about our family secret? Wouldn't the world love to know the secret behind the outwardly successful family? People do love their peeks into other people's tragedgossip.[sic] "They portrayed themselves as so perfect but look what was lurking behind the masks." Brouhahahahahaha laughter spieling from behind our backs.

June, 2007

It's been a year since I dropped his stuff off at his house in a subtle way of letting him know it's over. I'm done with the waiting. I'm done with the not being listened to. I'm done with the harassment from the ex-girlfriend. I'm done being with a man who doesn't choose me for his dance partner.

Not all ballroom dance experiences end with the hero or heroine or school being in a dance competition and shining for the whole world to see. Sometimes ballroom dance classes end with the heroine deciding that group is mentally and emotionally incestuous and wants nothing to do with them anymore. Sure, I do shine and have found someone who does respect what I'm doing and is honored to dance with my challenges. But it came from being seen and acknowledged for what I contribute already, not something hidden inside of me. It's been there for the world to see all along. Pettiness and prima donnas need not apply. Being with me is a privilege and not a right.

June, 2007

I was just at the post office. I was looking for boxes to send out souvenirs from Italy when I noticed a man admiring me and I felt myself shrink momentarily. Instead of being in my *woman hear me roar* state, I shrunk. Stand in my power and beauty. There is a lot to be admired in me and I deserve the positive attention. I am feeling my fullness more and more. Why shouldn't I allow it to be seen and admired? That will surely bring a different type of guy. This is the person I'd like to be in a relationship. This person has a lot to give and receive.

June, 2007

Emails from your ex letting me know, that for all practical purposes, I had ruined her life. Strange coming from a woman who supposedly didn't love you. Would ridicule you not only to your face but around everyone. Had slept with someone else right before ending it with you two years before we starting going out. And what is the problem? "You're right; I am clueless why you haven't let this go yet. Thanks for pointing it out to me." You were such a poor soul; she would call and pretend you were still together. And you couldn't do anything to stop it.

You so easily became friends again once I was out of the picture. It's been a good year of me learning to keep that line much closer to me.

"I'm done."

July, 2007

I read our final emails last night. I can't believe I apologized for finally telling you the truth. To this day you don't get what I was trying to say. You didn't get me. I can't believe I put up with the neglect for as long as I did. It's another case of me not trusting my instinct.

I remember the respect I finally felt towards myself when I called you on what was happening. But you didn't see it then and I doubt you see it now. I really loved you but it was not meant to be.

I felt so alone with you. I remember how good it felt with Jacob to get some attention from a man and to have someone near. Someone who actually talked with me. And he called. A man who picked up the phone and called.

You told me I had a deep belief that a long-term relationship with a man would never work out because I would always end up disappointed. The trouble with us was that I started out disappointed with you and it never got any better.

You never got how hard it was on me the way Caroline reacted to us being together. Feeling like I was going insane before I realized it was my internal signal that I was being lied to. If I was going to go insane it would have been a long time ago. How I was sick for four months straight from the stress. How the disapproval ate away at me. How much I wanted to make it better for our growth and development. The highest and best good for all involved.

That was so stupid of me. I should have kicked you out on your ass after the first email from her. But I could empathize while she attacked. It wasn't that I couldn't believe someone actually cared for me. It was that I couldn't believe someone could treat me so bad. And the man who claimed to love me could allow it to happen. It was insulting the way you two treated me. I had to wonder how much I hated myself to allow it to happen. And then I acted.

September, 2007

You can never go home again. I went anyway. I went and I was and I left. I've left them all behind for sure this time. I'm sad that this is it. The empty relationships of home; never to be restored to what they were and never to carry on to a new level either. It is done and over with. It is time for me to carry on with my life. It is time for me to find the new family. It is time for me to let go of the dream that they'll ever be there for me. I don't even want them to try anymore. I am done with all that.

They could have done so much more but they didn't. They chose not to. They didn't choose me. All right, I can finally accept that is who they are. I'm sad they will never know who I've become and the beautiful and amazing person that I am. It is not for them to see. They can't and they won't. I've moved on completely without them. Never more, never more.

I am whole amongst the emptiness of souls, of desire. I fought and I came through on the other side. Not where I expected to be but still in a place of peace. I carried on in spite of my aloneness. I carried on in the face of adversity. I carried on beyond the doubts and the pain.

2013

It was the end of my belief that my siblings would ever be there for me and acknowledge what I had been through. I could finally start to get closure from this wound. When hoping for things to be different in my life continues to bring pain, I get to a place where I need to close that option off and learn to live with the new perspective of life.

After going home for the wedding I gave myself five years off for good behavior from having to do that again. Through the early 2000s I had been going back to see if the relationships could be repaired with my brothers and sister. Nothing was ever said between us and it always appeared to be business as usual for the family. Based on conversations with my mom, it seems they all continue to blame me for the estrangement.

I had grown to a place where I couldn't keep the front up anymore and they couldn't ask me to. Except for emails about the family business, I have not spoken to any of my siblings since 2007. I can't excuse their behavior of disregard towards me anymore. I love them, I understand how hard it is, I forgive them *and* I don't feel the need to put myself through the pain anymore.

I do talk with my mom. In her own way, she has been there for me and I honor the confines of our relationship. I see an effort from her though the relationship continues to be quite superficial. I get minor communication about my siblings through her. I have realistic expectations of what she can and cannot give to me. I have learned so much from our relationship about how to be in the world as a woman and what it means to support others. Most of it was from negative experiences but I learned the lessons nevertheless. And there is still more to learn from our interactions, I continue to recover pieces of myself.

I have been able to find substitute families in life and have many people who stand in as surrogates for those relationships. I take a little bit from this person and a little bit from that one to patch up the missing pieces. I can't live my life in the way I was raised but I can love my family from afar.

MAKING LEMONADE

1/28/08

The thing I find most damaging about incestuous sexual abuse is not the physical act itself but the mental and emotional climate that must be present for it to occur. It consists of keeping your head in the sand when there is so much evidence to the contrary. The slickness that the perpetrator is blatantly allowed to exhibit which perpetuates this crime throughout society. It's much easier to deem the victim crazy than to shed light on the true craziness.

I struggled for years with fully admitting what had been done to me because who would want to accuse another human being of such acts? But the healing only truly became effective when I was able to accept that people I had loved so deeply were capable of such manipulation of both my innocence and power. My immense love and kindness are my power. Even now when I do allow others to manipulate me, it is with clarity and awareness that I act or don't act. I clearly see what is occurring but sometimes choosing not to act is what brings me the most inner peace. I choose my fights. My faith and hope abound that the other person will also come to a place of clarity around their behavior and stop the games.

Again, as confusing and revolting as the physical act was, it was the audacious disregard of the act that made it so damaging. To this day as I look back on it all I am amazed with the questions of: How could you do this to me? What were you thinking? Who do you think you are? Who would do that to their daughter/ sister/granddaughter? How could you deny it? How could you blame me?

3/23/08

It's the long good-bye. Good-bye to what, I do not know. But I am melancholy these days. I forgot about the Stevie Wonder song, *Lately*. I must have been in high school when it was popular. It felt so real and sad to me. Another good-bye. The longing to change something that can't be changed. Watching someone go away and knowing there's nothing you can do about it. They are gone. They decided to leave. And you are left holding an empty plate that had once been full.

Did I experience this once because, for the life of me, I can't remember whom or when. All I know is you went away. And I wanted you to stay. Was it that other world I used to visit? I went and you weren't there. I never did try again. I left for good too. I only lived here from then on out. Did you tell me you were going to have to go? Then I met you again in dance class. I saw you so clearly.*

---

* When I was a young child I would go to another world while in, what I think of now as, a meditative state. There was someone very wise who would talk to me about life. I don't remember exact conversations, I can only recall that it was very deep. During a dance class, half of us were watching the other

273

5/16/08

The people I work with are shocked by how pervasive and complex the problems of incest and childhood sexual abuse are. I'm not for I lived it. Lived to tell the tale of a girl's struggle into womanhood. A woman proud to stare herself and others in the eye and say, "Who do you think you are? You are not entitled to my body. It is mine to share and it shall be cherished by the man worthy of its possession."

Contrary to popular beliefs about victims, I did not grow up cutting myself or masturbating uncontrollably in front of others. I was not anorexic or bulimic. I did not do drugs excessively, dropout of school or act in anyway which could be considered promiscuous. I was a good girl who played by the rules and successfully hid to the world what my dad did to me at night. With no one in my family acknowledging what they saw or heard, who was I to question or bring it up?

Once again I am reminded of the morning after my two brothers walked in on us. All I wanted was to let them know I was fine. I chatted away nervously at breakfast as they stared at me with shocked amazement as their worst fears were confirmed. I talked about who knows what, anything really, anything to get them to stop looking at me like that. Don't look at me like that, you scare me and then I don't know how I will go on. I don't want to go insane. I don't want this to affect me mentally. I don't know if I can come back if I lose it mentally.

---

students. As I watched I could see one change into a centaur and recognized her from that place. I was at least five years older than her and that was about the age I was when I stopped going to the other world.

After that morning, things went back to *normal* for our family. We resumed the act of the ordinary family who's happy on the outside but screaming on the inside. No one would ever know.

I'm your friend, your neighbor or your co-worker. You will meet me and have no clue what lies below the surface. Look around, I'm everywhere.

6/17/08

I stand at a crossroads. The path on the left I continue alone. The path on the right we continue together. I feel exposed having someone I know have the ability to read my profile.* It is so inner and personal, I don't want them to know. I don't want them to see. I don't want to share. I don't want them to know the real me. I know she's beautiful, I know she's amazing, I know she's a star. I know she is real.

Can I find love after all these years of near desert conditions in my heart? Dry and rough with a terrain that's so harsh that nothing can live here. It's so desolate I look around and wonder; why would anyone choose to live here? Yet it's where I've kept my heart all these years. The soul-quenching oasis of waterfalls and lush green vegetation seem foreign to me now.

6/28/08 *about a relationship in the fall of 2003. I was learning, again, to admit more of the inner causes to the outer effects that played out in relationships and situations in my life. I practiced accepting the lesson in front of me with love even when I was not feeling inner peace. I lived my way to the answers.*

---

* Attempting online dating yet again.

275

I became involved with him to fill my dread that no one would ever love me. The deep seeded belief that it would be a mistake to love me. It was a cruel time for me to find love. My dreams so newly dismissed forever. Too long had I held out for the love of my life to arrive. For the family I desired to sit down to dinner together and my heart to overfill with love. Too long.

It was cruel to meet someone now that I didn't want to. What life did I have to offer someone anyhow? Pain and suffering. Either in my mind or body depending on which one the year was serving on the platter of life. Half full cups, silver spoons, cutting edge of a knife and platters with either a succulent roast or a dead carcass. No wonder people were starving for attention.

Seeing all around the situation. Concerns about him being able to love. Not feeling a connection to him. Not being able to sleep. How comfortable am I with someone I can't sleep next to? Hidden dangers keep me from loving you. Or keep you from loving me.

Men just out of marriages or relationships. Available but not ready. Still safe for me not to have to get too involved with them. What is it about marriage that scares me so? Making the wrong decision. Getting stuck, no way out. Being unhappy. Quiet misery. Years upon years of quiet misery worming its way into my life. Eating out the very core of me. Struggling to survive it all. Men who don't want to get married again. Holding for me the part that's terrified of it all. They have a reason, what's my excuse?

What if I found someone and I was completely happy with him? How would I have to change my self-perception then? Who would I become? How would I act differently if I were ready for marriage? What would I do in relationships? How would I act differently if I were ready for a committed long-term relationship? How would every action be different? Not an in your face manner but as an intention.

What specifically does he take away from me by not being ready to move forward? Time, but it was time well spent. I am still engaged in the process of learning to love. Where am I not ready to move forward? Where am I stuck? Bring it on baby; I'm ready to learn.

The low, low place I was in the night we met. Having all those thoughts and feelings challenged. I am a different person now. The need to have my instincts tested. I do believe he loved me; he just couldn't go there. I hated the way he closed his eyes when we danced. There was no contact there. I did see his detachedness. I didn't want to hear that he might not be ready for a relationship. I was needing to be wanted and desired and to feel attractive again. I wanted someone to think I was the coolest thing on the face of the planet. I loved it when he said he wanted to just keep on driving with me. I needed to see that I do want a committed relationship with someone. I do want to get married at some point. I am worth someone's attention. I am worth someone pursuing.

I can see how my thoughts affect my relationship. I can see how my fears play themselves out in a relationship. I did have warnings. I just wanted to believe that my search was over. I give my all in relationships in an attempt to not have to try again. Let me be done with it. It was a relationship formed out of lower intentions.*

What was successful? I decided falling in love was worth the risk. I held in there when every part of me wanted to run. I gave him a chance and found out what I needed to know to really have an answer and not just my projections. I know I needed to be more vulnerable. I know I needed to trust more. I know I can trust my instinct.

So what do I need to trust? God. I need to ask for more of what I need. I need to confront more as needed. I need to stand up for myself.

10/15/08

The pounding of her flesh against the rails of mankind
split the ranks into those who would stay
and those who would leave.
The soul of the righteous,
the heart of a warrior.
Not the kind that killed anything really living,
just the demons that spent their days
tormenting its host.
The evil thoughts that made another act in a way
that was beyond their own comprehension.
Desires that don't get played out
because of these demons.
Years of torture
as one's dreams are kept ever at bay.

---

* Studying different beliefs about levels of consciousness, what we attract into our lives, and vibrational levels of thoughts and emotions.

12/26/08

Dear Sandra, Kevin, Steven and Charlie,

Our relationship ended long ago. Whether precipitated by me or you, it really doesn't matter anymore. Either way I view you as cowards. I did expect more from you. But it wasn't the level that was wrong; it was the people I was putting my faith in. You can't help but be the people you are. And I know it is possible to change and be there for others because I have stepped up to the plate for many people. I am a good friend. I am a good sister. I am a good person who does deserve the world. I don't see a reason to continue our relationships. When mom dies I anticipate that will be it.

I used to do it for your kids but the price was too high on me. Maybe someday you'll answer them with honesty about why I left but I doubt it. I can only hope they have more guts than you and come asking.

I did not tell lies. I did not deserve what happened to me and it was not my fault. I'm sorry you can't live with that but it's what I need right now. Good-bye.

Love always,
Dusana

2/22/09

Do you ever want to quit something so bad you can taste it? The bile in your mouth as the situation bitters by the moment. You hold on as tightly as you can knowing that your grip could loosen at any moment propelling you into a future of unknown means. You hope your fears end up not coming true when in your heart you see the end so clearly it's like it is happening right now.

3/22/09

Dear Incest,

I have hated you for a long time. For years I've wondered why you had to creep into my life and destroy it. You took everything I loved from me. My family, my sexuality, my dreams of marriage and having a family of my own. You took my confidence and dreams. You took my courage and my voice. You allowed others to push me around and bully me. You made me second-guess myself. You took the best years of my life and left me with just a shell of a person. You cruelly took my love and trust of men away.

I loved men and now I don't want to be around them. I don't feel good enough or worthy of their time or attention. I feel less than and unattractive. I feel stupid and dirty. I feel ugly and undesirable. I feel ineffective in the world.

What's my use to men? You made me feel that all I was good for was sex, to please others, to be used and left to fend for crumbs. You made me second-guess my perceptions and desires. You made me cowardly and a victim. You made me less than. You made me accept intolerable situations. You made me work harder than I needed to. You made me friendless and isolated. You made me unlovable. You made me what I am, alone in the world, struggling to survive another day.

I hate you for what you made of me. I hate what I had to go through. I hate the pain you bring the world. I hate what you stand for. I hate you for the destruction and havoc you wreak in people's lives. I hate that I am still having to clean up after you. I hate you for not being gone after all I have been through. I hate that you are still here. I hate that you exist at all. I hate the blindness you bring. I hate the excuses you bring. I hate the blame and guilt you bring. I hate the shame you bring. I hate you for existing. I hate that I can't make you go away. I hate how powerless you make me feel. I hate the entitlement you bring to men. I hate the sense of property you bring. I hate all that you stand for.

I hate your righteousness. I hate your face. I hate the excuses you bring to me and others. I hate how easy it is for you to exist. I hate that you are here. I hate what you've brought to my life. I hate the admiration. I hate the inspiration. I hate the greatness. I hate myself because of you. I hate that I exist. I hate what I've been through. I hate my family. I hate how alone I am. I hate having to admit about you. I hate having to talk about you. I hate how you make me feel. I hate, I hate, I hate, I hate, I hate.

I hate the men who've left me. I hate the men who may leave me. I hate how uncomfortable I am around men. I hate I've been alone all these years. I hate all that I do. I hate how happy others are together. I hate how easy it is for them. I hate my struggles. I hate how attractive others are. I hate how misunderstood I am. I hate how easy people think I have it. I hate how people don't know me. I hate all I'm expected to do. I hate that I'm the one who has to do it all. I hate that I have to step up to the plate. I hate that I have to lead. I hate that I don't get a day off. I hate how hard I have to work. I hate all that I have to do. I hate what you made of me. I hate being your slave. I hate answering to your whims. I hate what you made of me. I hate who I am because of you. I hate who I am. I hate myself. I hate, I hate, I hate.

I hate the love you took from me. I hate you. I hate you. I hate you. I hate you for expecting forgiveness. I hate having to forgive. I hate you to death. I hate you to death.

I will never forgive you. You were wrong and always will be wrong. Do not ask me for more.

Love,

Dusana

3/26/09

Dear Incest,

Thank you for listening to me the other night. I hadn't realized how much hatred and power I've been giving you. That was intense for me. But you are nothing in my life. You are just a concept and a very misunderstood one at that. You are a word. You signify my murderous thoughts. You are my lack of love in the world. You are a dream that's long gone. I don't have to be afraid of you.

Incest Cannot:
- Take my smile
- Claim my beauty
- Control my emotions
- Haunt me
- Make me uncomfortable around men
- Take my love
- Have my power
- Dominate my life
- Run my sexuality
- Make me less than
- Make fun of me

- Have my future
- Affect my present
- Live in the past without my permission

You are just a bad dream that happened to me a long time ago.

Love,
Dusana

Dear Dusana,

You are right, I cannot control you anymore. You have learned the lessons you came here to learn. You've done a brilliant job and you are free of me. I ruined enough of your life, be free to create the life you want. I see you in a beautiful fulfilling relationship with a man who doesn't care one lick for me. All he sees is you. Shine dear woman and bestow your gifts to the world. You have a lot to teach. Thank you for letting me visit your life but I am done with you now. Help others to let me go too. God is waiting.

Love,
Incest

2013

I have been jealous of the support people get from having cancer. Part of the above entry is my solution to that. I have seen the plaques for Cancer Cannot...and wanted one for incest. Though I can't imagine people buying one, putting it up in their homes or wearing it on a t-shirt. I laugh thinking of someone seeing a person walking down the street with their incest t-shirt on.

I want The Walk. I went to the end of a Susan G. Komen walk and saw the celebration for the survivors of breast cancer. I tried to take it in and imagine it being for me, for incest survivors. Just thinking about having that much vocal and demonstrative support makes me cry. There are no banners stating: Yeah, we survived incest. Our fight is terminal; it's here until the end.

5/17/09

The 'fuck you all' that I have felt for the past thirty years is burning a hole in my soul. It smolders under every thought, every interaction and every moment of every day. It is always there. Some people have brought it closer to the surface, while others have soothed the embers and prevented a flare-up.

The audacity of denial and neglect was always foreign to me. I didn't understand it and don't to this day. I felt like the lamb to the slaughter and a pawn. I was the expendable one in the family. I'd love to hear the justifications of why I don't go home. Does anyone else see they don't add up?

I sit here crying about my friends seeing me clearer than I see myself. All the good stuff, all my potential and all my beauty. Seriously, just rip out my heart and stomp on it. It's quicker and easier than dating. Why waste your time and energy when it's where you'll end up anyway.

2009

I am sad. I can find love. It is okay for me to love. I live a new reality for love and relationships from what my family taught me. I am lovable. I am desirable. I am loved completely. I am loved. I am loved. I am loved. I am loved. I am loved. I am loved. I am loved. I am loved. I am loved. I am loved. I am loved. I am loved. I am loved. I am loved. I am loved. I am loved. I am loved. It is safe for me to love. It is safe for me to love. It is safe for me to love. It is right for me to love. It is right for me to love. It is right for me to love. It is right for me to love.

11/15/09

There are so many stories out there about women who have lost themselves in marriage and motherhood. They finally leave their unhappy situation to find themselves and become more. They become the person they lost so many years ago. I think I got it backwards. I feel I am losing myself by being single. There's a part of me that has remained untouched and dead. Not that scary dead-in-the-eye look you see with some people. More just not fully living. I've been going through the motions by doing the house swap in England, traveling alone, living by my own terms and going to graduate school at an avant-garde school. But this has been its own type of being lost, its own type of hiding, its own version of a slow death.

I don't get overly involved with others so I don't have to be alive. Truly alive. I've been a free spirit but it can be a prison also. My life has been good because it's not messy. It's clean and quite predictable.

Stay and find out what happens. Get involved in another person's life. I am ready to be the woman in the picture. I'm quiet, I'm listening, I'm hearing. I am ready to not live my dreams alone. I am ready for the support that I deserve, desire and crave. I am ready to be abundantly supported in all my endeavors. I am ready for my life to begin. I am the heroine in control of her own life and destiny.

I've not wanted to get in a relationship because I've never wanted to share what a struggle life is for me. But I think the Johari window* joke has been on me and it's the square that both others and I see. Though maybe there are a few people who I've fooled and they don't know. To be seen in all my struggles of day-to-day living. To be honored and respected for it, now that would be love. Not the Lance Armstrong's of the world that get hailed because they had cancer but the souls whose physical lives are diminished decade after decade but they still manage to get up and face their day. Those are the unsung heroes in my life. There's a beauty to my life that the able-bodied will never get.

11/29/09

The respect issue of my life presenting itself once again. I remember in graduate school being asked as part of some class I was taking which was more important for me to have from a partner, love or respect. We were broken up into small groups at the time. My group consisted of myself and three or four other people, one of which was the instructor. I only remember his

---

*   See appendix

answer and my own. My memory recalls his stating love was more important to him. He would be crushed if his wife came to him one day and stated she didn't love him because she was the one person in the world that truly knew him. If knowing him as she did, she eventually sees him as unlovable; he just didn't know how he would cope.

I chose respect as being more important. Love without respect can just become too twisted in life. I have seen distain kill too many relationships not to believe this to my core. I don't believe respect without love is possible. There is a natural clarity to respect that can't be twisted by circumstances, beliefs or hormonal imbalances. Either you are acting with respect or you are not. You can have love without respect but it's harder to separate respect from love. Liking the other person might not always be there but the love and trust is.

3/30/10

I am still so embarrassed. I dread the day I have to tell him about my family. I've never figured out a way to tell others. I hate how alone I've been. I hate how I've settled into a life that's been so loveless. I hate how I don't even expect it anymore. It's been a dream that I let go. I let it go. It was easier than living with the disappointment. I've let the juices run dry. I used to have such dreams and hope for love. I had such a great vision. And I let it die.

5/18/10

My God I have lived through hell. The doubt and shame that were the essence of my being as I groveled and begged for any scraps that a man was able to throw me. The crap I have put up with from others in the name of love. What I thought love was. So desperate for any indication that I was okay, that it was okay. That I was not the scum of the earth. So many friends having no clue who I am. Who my dad was. What it was like night after night to live in terror and shame. The days of endless acting. Acting my way through life. Never telling the truth. Not allowing others to tell it either.

But I did it. I lived through the hell. I can have me back now. I can be me. I can tell my truth. And thank you for sharing yours. I know not to harm others. I know to challenge them. I do know what it takes to change. I do know the commitment. I do know the determination to survive. To get through.

I am pissed these days at the wasted chances as I see it. I'm mad because I know you aren't going to survive. We are giving you the chance and you are wasting it. You don't have the fire to change your circumstances and I am pissed at you. GET up and fight. That's the only way through. That's the only way to survive. Stop the bullshit and fight.

I am not afraid to be known anymore. I am free to be known now.

12/29/10

The first part has been years of darkness, denial and hard work to make a better life than I ever thought possible. Raw, tenacious fever of showing myself what I am made of. Diving to the depths of my soul to find love and happiness. Creating hope and love and inspiration beyond the odds. Not settling for what others gave me but forging into unknown territory until my world held a thing of beauty so wondrous that even the hardest heart melted from the kindness offered graciously on a daily basis.

Where does this story begin? I guess where all stories begin, with an event that changes you and your perception of life. Though it can't always be narrowed down to a single event and is often a culmination of several events and the perception of what they mean. Can the actual event be found in one's memory? Sometimes. More often it stays buried in the mind making its presence known through the passing of a shadow that when you turn to look at it, there is nothing there. Was its occurrence really that significant or just another moment in life similar to the one before or the one after? Endless moments that sometimes you grab and sometimes you let them go.

But still I start this journey as a means to find that moment. Is that what all the continued searching has always been about? My feeble attempt to find that moment that I have let define me for so many years? To finally stop the power which that moment has held over me for all these years?

I'm mad. I ask myself why am I mad? Why the tears? Why the frustration? Someone take care of me. Someone help out. Someone listen to me. The endless whining of a babe in arms. Will it ever shut up?

I had nothing to write for an X-mas letter. Nothing to share. Am I just so internal right now that it's hard for me to go out? Is my confidence so lacking?

Balance, I'm trying to find the balance of who I am right now. I have a new identity forming and the old one was so familiar.

Me as an expert. Me who knows what she's doing. Me who has to tell you what I perceive about you.

I get messages about other people. I see them clearly and what I see is not fun. I see the warts and all. And they ask me to help them. How do I help them? Do I have to tell them the ugly things about themselves? It hurts me to tell them. Can I get to the place where it doesn't hurt?

1/16/11

The ache in my heart once again. I feel so alone and do not feel like trying to change it. Can it just be okay? Can I not try to do anything? Is this really so bad? I feel so vulnerable. I don't want to risk rejection anymore. I'm done with it. Don't ask me to call, don't ask me to try, don't ask me to hope. It doesn't come when you're not looking, it doesn't drop out of the sky. It doesn't happen for me. It's been years of trying to fit in. Years, no decades of not having anyone to spend days with me. It's been decades of it not working. So how do I want to spend my time now?

I feel like shit. What does all this mean for me? It means I'm not wanted. It means I'm not loved. It means I'm not considered. It means I'm not worth it. Their time or energy or consideration. I'm not worth getting to know or spending time with. I'm not fun or enjoyable to be around. I'm not worth love. I'm despicable. I'm awful.

Unappreciated greatness. Someone who works her ass off and gets dissed and undermined and attacked. Assholes followed by excuses. It's just bull. I support people behaving badly. Hmmm,

I meant, I can't support people behaving badly. Silence is how I support people behaving badly.

Get up and put one foot in front of the other as I walk my way to feeling my strength. Where is my beauty this week? What will spring from these dredges of hell?

It's okay to make mistakes. People don't have to be assholes about it. The pressure to be perfect all the time is exhausting and unfair. We are human, it can't be done. It's cruel to be relentless on someone for being human.

1/22/11

When it comes to incest there are no easy answers. There isn't an "Incest for Dummies" manual to take you step by step through the minutiae of recovery from it. The intricacies of thoughts, feelings and beliefs that result from the betrayal, and in my case, utter lack of support from my family. The unending state of denial.

(From a dream I then analyzed) My dock is underwater, it's unconscious. It's under emotions. It's this vulnerability that I have spent years hiding so deep within that no one could touch it. I made sure no one could get to it, to me. It has made perfect sense, if you can't get to me, there's no chance you can hurt me.

GRIEF CATCHES UP WITH ME

1/23/11

Move on, but to what? I just don't know anymore. There's nothing else I want to do, to accomplish, to experience and to hope for change. The hole, the void I've been endlessly trying to fill. Trying to find the next best thing is empty as I know this too shall fade away into the mundaneness [sic] of life.

I want to go out but I don't want to feel alone amongst others. It makes being alone that much worse. I feel like there's a spotlight on me and everyone can see that I'm alone and judge me for it. I feel stoppable. I feel like I can't do it. And if I try, there'll be someone or something to stop me. I don't believe it'll happen for me. I don't see it. I can't hope for it anymore. It hurts too much.

Now to build my life with this option crossed out. What do I do now and how do I spend my time?

The rejection I feel. Bitter rejection and how to try again with relationships. I feel so rejected. Can I get to the place where I don't care what others do or don't do in regards to me? That I am okay no matter what disappointments face me? Kindness, I'm just looking for a little kindness, acceptance and belonging.

2011

I always thought there'd be time for marriage later. At least that was what I told myself in order not to face the fact that marriage terrified me. Who wanted to be stuck taking care of some guy who didn't listen to my soul sing? Couldn't even hear my soul sing because it would emphasize the deadness that permeated his skin, muscles and bones. Don't make him feel how every decision, every choice took him further away from the man he thought he could be, if only. If only what? He had married for love the first time? Felt love for anything at all? Experienced love anytime in the past twenty years?

What desperation was hidden below the surface that brought our two souls together to come forth months later in fear, longing and neglect? I would end up loving too much and he, not at all. The teeter-totter of love forever unbalanced by the sheer fact that one of us found love to be an adventure ride and the other a ride that he didn't have money to buy the tickets for. And no matter how much catching up he did, he'd never be able to lift my soul enough to give it the space that it needed to soar.

5/3/11

I am free from the judgments put upon me by others. It's always been more about them. It's not my fault. It's not my fault. It's not my fault. For once, it's not my fault.

It wasn't my fault and I refuse to hide behind it anymore. I don't need to make it okay for others. I needed to get out of the abusive, dishonest, soul-crushing family. I don't need to shrink from them either. I did need all the crap that has come my way these past 15 years so I'd know that it's not okay with me and I can live this fact. Right now it's the only fact I can live. There is a standard of how I expect to be treated by others and you can meet it or you don't get to be in my life. I feel strong and healthy. Live this. Be this. Have this.

2013

I repeat the issue of taking on the responsibility for the abuse and can see how it creeps into my life. I have to be aware of this pattern so as not to stumble back into it. I need to notice when other people are over-stepping boundaries or being outright bullies. I question my perception of what is happening. Am I blaming them or making excuses for my behavior? I hesitate standing up for myself out of not wanting to accuse someone of doing something they really aren't doing. I end up wondering how they find the victim in me and know they can treat me so badly. I could write a whole other book on my justifications for the bad behavior of others.

2011

There's a part of me that I let fall asleep. The hope and waiting had become too much for me to live with. The empty ache in my belly that signaled a life being wasted. A love unsung and unclaimed.

I feel it again now after many years of hibernation. Though the feeling isn't as empty now. It's coming alive again and needing to be expressed in my life. Manifested in my life. I feel ready and wild and passionate. My muscles are wanting to grab and push and stretch and embrace the newness of me. My breasts always felt saggy to me but as I looked in the mirror the other day, I saw that they were full. Not perky. They've never been perky but womanly and aged and oh-so-real. I feel more grounded than I have in a long time. My 'what' is quieter. It's open and willing and here.

I have been alive. I have taken risks. I've gotten to the place where I am not afraid to make a total and complete fool of myself. There are just some things in life that I am done with. I'm done keeping friendships where the effort isn't reciprocated. I am done with friendships where I am being lied to. I am done with friendships where pettiness exists. I am done with friendships that aren't vibrant and alive. I am done.

6/11/11

Not following orders can get you killed. Not following orders can get you banished. Not following orders can get you outlawed. The order of command must be obeyed and the command is to: don't talk, don't see, don't believe and for God's sake, don't question. Please don't show us what cowards we are. Please don't show us where we failed you. Please don't show who we really are to the rest of the world. It would be bad for business.

6/28/11

Do you need to destroy in order to create? Room does have to be made in order to create something new. Tear down, break down, clean out, get rid of, give away, rearrange, rip apart, tear asunder. There's a satisfaction with moving that energy within oneself. A completion that cannot occur in any other way. How do you assist another with moving that energy in a safe way?

Will I ever be able to really help others with all that I have learned? Will I ever get the chance to help others in that deep way? The wealth of information I am gaining. Will I be able to leave it for the world? Does it matter? Is it needed? Will it be heeded?

It seems a shame to let it go to waste. How can I convey it in a way that is accessible yet profound? Does it need to be? Does it need to be profound? What is my need for my work to be profound? To know I was here. To know that my daily struggles mattered. To know that my being born made a difference in the life of another. I want my Frank Capra, George Bailey ending.

The words float up from below. Coming to me from the great unknown. Dreams long since forgotten. The things I wanted. The things forgotten. The things stolen. The things denied. The reasons why I do what I do. To help, to serve, to care. I just wanted to care. I just wanted someone to care. To fight for the underdog. The righteous.

7/3/11

The endless days of summer that take one to the melting point again and again. The heat beating down from above in the persistent pursuit of salvation. Is there a correct way to spend a holiday? Do I have to Bar-B-Q? Do I have to spend it with others? Do I have to watch the fireworks? What if there just isn't anyone to do these things with? What are your options then? Do you spend it alone or do you force yourself on others celebration or do you go but alone?

They all have their advantages and disadvantages. Yes I would love to have people to do things with but is that really the point? How is it that I want to spend my day? Space in which to do the things that I love. Time to do the things that I love. Energy to do the things that I love.

To dance, to write, to tend to my flowers, create beauty, to talk with friends, to sleep, to not be productive for a little while, to clean, to make room, to organize, to laugh, and to help others lead a better life.

9/16/11

I don't talk about it much anymore though there was a time when it seemed it was all I could talk about. I relived it every waking moment of the day. The terror, the confusion, the sheer pain of it all. How could my family treat me so badly? How could a father do that to a daughter? How could a mother ignore it? How could my brothers and sister deny what our childhood had been about? To this day my friends still don't want anything to do with my family. They always say, "no thank you" when I invite them out. And I still don't have the answers to the above questions. I have learned to live with that too.

9/24/11

I don't know why I survived my childhood. As I studied Psychology through the years I learned that I should be massively fucked up. Surely I have contained myself, but as I look back at my life, I can now see that I have always been okay. I also know I want to protect my family and so I haven't told my story. But I also feel that I am keeping myself limited and I'm not okay with the expense of it anymore.

The heartbreak of my life has been unbearable at times. I'm not sure how I did it except for the fact, the very driving force, that I wanted a better life for my children. I did not want to pass the family legacy onto another generation. It was this dream of mine that kept me going when the pain crippled me. The searing pain of grief for the life I was not allowed has almost done me in many times. But at some level I always knew that it was just some part of me that was wanting and needing to die. I always have to be careful when driving because the desire to swerve my car into a pylon or something is very intense when I'm grieving. Just to end it, let it be done once and for all. One of the main reasons I never act on this desire is because I'm more afraid that I will fail.

I know that there isn't anything anyone else can do for me and being in a psych ward is not going to help. Plus my family would finally get the proof that I am indeed insane. I'm sure it would be a comfort for them to know all my insane notions about who did what to me as a child would finally have an answer. They could finally rest the guilt for not being there for me and could surmise the answer with a simple, I knew she was making it up all the time. The threat for them having to look at everything I have lived through would be gone forever in one swoop.

10/1/11

I am alone. I am so alone. I wrongly think that love happens so easily for everyone else but me. I feel so unwanted. No one will ever love me. No one will ever want to be with me.

I just can't concentrate on men. I hate breaking up with someone. It totally sucks. I feel so ugly and foolish. Like who would ever want me. Why did I ever think someone would be interested in me? Why did I ever think someone would love me? I'm obviously totally unlovable. I so wanted to believe that someone could love me, be interested in me.

10/17/11

I am so sad. Will the sadness ever finally leave? Oh my God, it is years of the same old crap. Can I finally let it go? How many times have I asked that damn question?

I've often wondered if my life would be more tolerable if I was watching it as a movie. Is it an important story to tell? The heartbreak of it has left me unwilling to risk another one at this time. Maybe telling it will help me to put a different spin on it. The one my friends see when they look at me. Lord knows my latest attempt at an intimate relationship with a man ended in part because I was unwilling to let him see me. My career decisions have also been the result of not wanting to really see me, show me.

10/29/11

This time I am really heartbroken. I've been heartbroken before by men, my family or the actions of others. But this time is ten times worse because it is me who has done the heartbreaking. I thought I was something. I thought I was someone who mattered. I was going to change the world. I was going to make a blaze and set the world on fire. I was going to stand for truth and not let anything or anyone get in the way of my message.

Twenty years and countless disappointments later, I am not sure who I am anymore or even what I want. Why dream? The world is just going to come and shit all over them anyway. The Course is right, there is no hope in this world. No matter what you do, the next disappointment is waiting around the corner ready to smash the hope you are holding to bits. This world holds nothing that I want or value. All the glitter glue in the world can't make it shiny again Dorothy.

So I sit in my apartment day after day. Oh, don't get me wrong, I still go out. I hold down a job. Many people even think I am happy all the time. But I've been an expert at fooling others for years. It's not even that their perception is wrong. They are right, I am a happy person. It's just that at the core of it all, I am sad.

One of my students recently commented that I just looked so sad. The mask was down, I was raw and it showed. How many people would be surprised to know that this is what is at the heart of me every day of my life? It's always there. It never goes away. As is said, you never get over trauma, you just learn to live with it. And right now it is wanting its time to be out in the sun for all the world to see.

Even that isn't entirely true. When I go out later to get my haircut, I will be pleasant, possibly even amusing. I guess I have lost my truth. The container of my being is needing to expand to incorporate all the new truths that have come my way over these past twenty years.

12/07/11

I wanted to die so bad this year but I didn't. I am still here. I have to start over. I have to get up and try again. I have to move on with my life. I have moved back to Denver and it's time to show the world what I have to offer. It's time to stop playing small. When did I let this happen? When did I start to cover it all up again? What has the cost been to myself and the world? My lungs burn. My whole body burns, how ironic I had an inflammatory disease.

2013

What is depression versus grieving and sadness? I had to wonder about this through the years. After not being allowed to experience my devastating emotions regarding the abuse as a child, I was finally safe enough in adulthood to feel them. There was so much sadness to get through about the different losses associated with incest. I once read a book about the aftermath of divorce. I realized it was the same experience I went through as I separated from my family. I *divorced* both of my parents, my four siblings, and two of my brother's wives as I chose to heal. I lost my real family and my ideal family. I lost my childhood, again real and ideal. I lost my spirit. I lost my capability. I lost my frame of reference. I lost everything I had believed in. It was all gone and all of it needed to be grieved. All of it.

Monica, my youngest brother's wife, was a Godsend to me as their marriage broke up during the 90s. She was the outside perspective of our inner family that I needed desperately. I used to call her and seriously ask, "am I insane or are they?" I did not know the answer to that question. She assured me over and over that they were. Through this I was able to trust my perspective that their beliefs and how we treated each other was beyond not normal. For obvious reasons, my relationship with that brother was never the same after I wrote a deposition cautioning against their sons being able to be around my family. They eventually were able to spend time with my family after a period of supervised visits. From what I know, none of my brothers have ever abused children. It has been a fear of mine through the years. What if my not speaking out resulted in a child being hurt? I don't know how I'd live with that. Hopefully I don't have to find out.

I had so much mental and emotional work to do to heal. That I could ever get through it all did feel hopeless. It felt insurmountable at times. It felt unfair. I can't think of how to explain how hard it is. My writings repeatedly used the phrase 'a million pieces' and that is what it felt like. You have to put together a one million pieces puzzle and there's no picture to follow. Unless you have been through it, you have no way to know how hard it is.

What could have looked like depression to others, to me felt like the outward experience of what had been buried for years. *For myself,* depression was a cover for the feelings that needed to be felt. It acted as a pressure gage to ensure I didn't get flooded.

There was a reason for it. There was that much to grieve. I wanted to feel all the yucky emotions in order to get through them. I had spent years repressing them; it was time to express them.

As a child my energy had to go into surviving day to day and repressing what haunted me at night. Through these means I was able to function. As an adult, I finally had the strength and coping skills to feel the long denied feelings. It was painful and messy and it was what I needed to accept to stop the demons from ruling my life. Now when the demons arise, I am able to let the mess be there and clean up the meaning I adopted that was never actually accurate.

My sadness and hopelessness were never debilitating in that I was able to hold down a job and have some semblance of a life. Early on in my recovery there were days when getting out of bed and getting the dishes done was considered a major accomplishment. I always celebrated these relatively small tasks no matter how inconsequential they may seem to someone on the outside of my experience. For part of the time, there would be days that I spent part of it in bed feeling the pain but they never turned into multiple days or weeks.

I was able to put the feelings below the surface enough to get up and face the task at hand. I was able to go through the day doing two things at once. I would be feeling the underlying pain and taking care of business as usual. It's an incredible teacher of patience, acceptance and understanding towards others. I doubt the people around me even knew that underneath the surface it felt like knives were stabbing me and ripping me apart. Compartmentalization was a needed coping skill as a child of incest and a wonderful ability to have as an adult. It comes in handy quite often.

The pain would be so intense at times that I did want to die. I wanted it to stop. I wished I had never started on this path. The gains weren't worth the sacrifices. But there was no taking it back. There was no way to undo what I now knew. The only way was to go forward and keep feeling the pain. When I did wish to die so intensely, at some point I realized it was part of the grief process. There was some part of me needing to die as I learned new ways to be in life. There was an ideal or fantasy of *life as it should be* that needed to die. Reality was calling and it wasn't always pretty. I didn't exactly know what was coming next but it was time to move on to something new. This was an incredible teacher in learning to leap into the unknown. Go ahead and jump, the net does appear.

Through all of this I learned to be extremely gentle with myself. It's okay to be a little weird or different. Not everyone is going to understand and it's self-defeating to expect them to. It's okay to take as long as I need to heal. It's not up to me to do my healing in a way that makes others happy. It's okay to put a time limit on how long I feel the pain during the day before I put it away and return to life. The pain will still be there another day to pick it up again and feel it. I don't have to get it right on the first try. When I do something I perceive as wrong, I tell myself 'I love you'. I cut off the negative self-talk trying to come through.

One technique I learned during a meditation class in graduate school was to label thoughts as *thinking*. Sounds simple but it helped me to gain control of my thoughts. They were like clouds floating by. There would be another one coming soon enough. Through this practice I was able to give importance to the thoughts of my choosing. 'I'm stupid and will never succeed' could be replaced with 'this is the first time I'm doing this, it's normal not to do it perfectly'. I could still feel the insecurity behind the thought but could replace the negativity with a gentler version of support towards myself.

Another important lesson I learned was to keep a balance between the good of my childhood versus the bad. I had to integrate the two into an accurate assessment of all the moments of my life. The bad was horrendous, I cannot deny that. But there were many, many good memories too. One does not cancel out the other and I needed to come to terms with that. I put this in perspective for myself by thinking of the abuse in terms of minutes instead of number of incidents. The actual number of minutes in which the abuse was occurring was much less than the number of minutes of my life in which it wasn't. Which led me to the question of *why I was allowing this tiny portion of my life to rule it*? I could choose a more favorable meaning for my life and what I deserved. I could see it another way.

MY LIFE IS CALLING

7/1/12

It's always been harder to miss the dad I didn't have, then the one that I did. I guess the same could be said about my family too.

Doug is dying and I feel my chance at a family is dying all over again too. Not with Doug per se but with Emily. She's fine without me and however much I feel she's like a daughter to me, she isn't. She's not my family. She has her own. And how do I fit into it? I don't really. I do and I don't. I'm that friend that it's good to have but is not really included. Do I even know how anymore?

Fathers and families and love are in my face. My New Year's intention to love and be loved more. This is different. The former theme was to learn to love and be loved. I do feel I've accomplished that. Now to love and be loved more. To be it, not necessarily doing anything in particular. I am in a new place and open to learning new ways to be in a family. And I am loved. I am so loved. I am loved and I am seen. Can I love a family and not expect anything in return?

I am giving Doug's family a huge gift right now. Let's give Emily a good gift this time with Doug's passing. Let's get it right. I did help her to get to this place. I love her so much and just want her to be okay. She's had so much to deal with and I want to do what I can to give her the best childhood as can be expected. She is so loved. She is so cherished.

Let's keep her protected. I want to keep her protected. I don't want one hair on her head to be harmed. I want to give her what wasn't given to me. I don't want anything to happen to her. I don't. There are so many bad people out there and someone has to protect her. I want her to know she's loved and cherished. I want her to know it's okay to be loved. I want a man to treat her with love and respect. I want a man to know how truly beautiful and special she is and she deserves all the goodness and kindness in the world.

I don't want anymore harm or hurt to come her way. I want it to be okay for her. I want to know my love has protected her. I want to know my love has saved her. I want to know my love has made a difference. I want her to feel my love has made a difference in her life.

I want to know I have saved at least one little girl from the misery we lived Gwen.* I hope my love has been enough to save Emily from the crap we had to live. I want one little girl to not spend years torturing herself with what a worthless piece of shit she thinks she is. I want one little girl to be saved from the torture that were our lives. I don't want Emily to live like we did. I want Emily to be okay. I want Emily to have a freedom we never did. I want Emily to thrive where we only survived. I want Emily to live the life she was meant to live and not one scripted from years

* Emily's mom is the one who passed away in 2005.

of abuse. I want to save Emily where I couldn't save you. I want to save me too.

10/12/12

I stop and look down. My chin falls to my chest. The sorrow of the years having to be felt and shared with someone else. I don't feel alone here. No one's near me just yet but I know they're around. They'll not believe that anyone could live such a life. It's a foreign land to them. And one I never have to return to again.

It's over, it's truly over.

10/28/12

I was awakened last night by dreams of changes I'm being asked to make. I'm scared, truly, truly scared. I have to be seen. I have to be heard. I need to move on from the hell that has been my life. There is no way to explain to another the depths of pain that have encompassed it. Day after day of hiding from others. Not letting another in to know how deeply I was hurt. It's time to let some happiness into my life. It's time to stop denying myself what I so truly deserve. I did nothing wrong. I was a happy child going on with my life when my dad came in and tore that out of me. What he left was an empty shell that has been getting by as best she could with what was left.

I deserve the most incredible man alive. I deserve an incredible career. I deserve to give back to the world all that I have been able to learn in a clear manner. I feel freedom and hope today as the vapors of possibility leave the confines of my soul. It's over, once again I have the feeling that it is time to move on and the latest struggle is over. I don't have to put up with good enough anymore. As my friend Linda said, you are the best at making lemonade. It made me cry to hear that. It's okay to stop putting on the happy face and accept a happy soul. Something that comes from deep within me to be shared with the world.

I sure do like that. Sharing with the world. I've always felt a deep sense of need to give back because I did make it out alive. The sticky, messy jungle that I have fought my way out of to embrace the changes needed to survive. The damaging relationships and friendships that I have walked away from as I learned to accept real love into my life. And discovering how to love in the most amazing places. Falling in love over and over with the people who have crossed my path. Some come for the season, the reason, or the lifetime.

I willingly accept what God wants for me into my life.

11/9/12

Rape occurs everyday. Rape occurs at every moment of the day. If you aren't mad, you're not paying attention. What does rape accomplish? What does it bring to life? Why is it okay, why is it protected? Why is incest and sexual violence the last taboo?

It started so young for me. Grandfather, neighborhood boys, brothers, and father. How many of those boys ended up molesting other children? Their own children? Relatives? Or was I the only lucky one? A friend recently asked me "why you" when it hadn't happened to my sister. At least with our father it didn't. The expression on my face quickly changed her question to an, "or not". The mask had fallen down again. I'm not sure what my face revealed but I felt lost. I felt horrifyingly lost. It's a mystery whose only acceptable answer has been, it's my fault.

Why is it okay to take what doesn't belong to us? What gives you the right? Who put you in charge?

11/17/12

I've finally learned I deserve more. As a friend said, you know there's a best. But there is a better greater than that. That is the coming year for me. To learn more about what is even better than the best I could ever have imagined. To accept into my life all the goodness that God wills for me. With no limit or constraints from the previous life I'd known or imagined before.

I feel my heart start to beat faster as I think of my new life. The possibilities and the unknowns of the road before me. What I will do has yet to be revealed in the bends and rises. What will the new destination look like?

12/5/12

What would I have to do? What would I have to change? What would I have to admit that I deserve? What would I have to allow into my life? What would I need to ask for help with? What would I need to ask for from others? What would I have to see for myself, within myself? How much goodness can I let into my life? And what am I so afraid of? That it'll be taken away? That it won't be true? That it will be true? That it'll all be a lie?

A solid man with the clearest blue eyes that sees me nakedly to the core. I feel there is nothing I can hide from him. I feel my brain skew in my head as he speaks to me. I don't know what he is talking about because it is so foreign to how I have arranged my life. It just doesn't fit. But it speaks to a want so deep inside that some part of me recognizes the gift he brings. I know we have set this meeting up a long time ago and it is spiritual in nature. He is one of the many angels that will visit upon me during my life.

Some are seen and others unseen. The seen ones call to a memory from long ago and speak of a truth that has been long forgotten. They challenge me to change and remember. To remember an agreement of what I am called upon to fulfill. This fulfillment comes into my life as a yearning. Other times it's disillusionment to the ideals I have held for too long. Still other times it's a call for something more, the missing piece of my current situation. Will its discovery bring joy at last?

It's the unseen ones that scare me. They hold a deeper truth that I am unable to admit to myself. I know they see all and have the answers to my deepest questions and desires. I see their flashes out of the corner of my eye and I know I don't really want to see them. I don't want to admit how I have failed myself. I don't want to admit how I have allowed others to manipulate me. I don't want to have to admit the cruelty and anguish we heap upon each other daily. All my defenses are ripped to shreds in their eyes. All I have built my world upon crumbles in their light. The world I have built is shattered in a million pieces and I don't have it within me to pick each one up and make my vase whole again. I don't know of a glue strong enough to make it right. It will never be the same and it scares me to death. The endless desire to have the world be as we thought it once was. Pure and simple and uncomplicated by deceit. A world in which intentions were honest and direct. You could take the other person at their word.

12/12/12

I have looked at it and looked at it. Why is it knocking on my door for attention now? I smashed the crystal vase. I picked up each piece and looked at it. I took each piece and put that vase back together. It was never as beautiful as it once was but it was functional. It could hold water. Maybe not forever but for a day or two. I have felt the emotions. I have challenged the thoughts. I have become a woman willing to search for the truth and fight the battles needed for myself and others. Why is it calling me back from the grave? Doesn't it know I buried it? Doesn't it know I am done? Doesn't it know I have moved on over and over again?

What is the safety I have discovered in my life that propels me forward to look at it once again? Where will it take me this time and what more does it have to teach me? What part of me was left behind? I want to go back and take that little girl who sat cross-legged on the floor dipping the champagne cork into the flute, sucking it of the strange delicious liquid. I want to go back and bottle up her happiness. I want to go back and protect her innocence. I want to go back and cherish her dreams. I want to go back and get her out before it is too late. Before it is all destroyed. Before she gets thrown away like some old forgotten bike wheel left out in the rain to rust. Not useful to anyone. Passed up time and again as something not worthy of attention or care. I am so sorry for what the next few years will bring you. Little did you know how your life and its very existence would forever be altered by the act of a man possessed by fear and madness.

12/15/12

I don't write this to cause harm. I don't write this to get revenge. I don't write this to get even. I write it because my very soul depends on it. I am screaming to be heard in a silent world. The eyes and ears of the passersby don't really want to know what happened.

It's too risky to get involved. It's too risky to ask. It's too risky to help. What if I can't do anything for the child? What if what I do is not enough? What if I have to see the horrors that one person can inflict on another? What if I can't stop it? What if it happens to me? Will I ever be happy again?

I did not know when I started this journey how hard it would be. Days when I could only get through them by getting up and putting one foot in front of the other until the time when I could crawl back in bed. The fetal position became my favorite pose for the raw emotions pushing through me as an unanswered plea for death. The tomb of my hopes and dreams crushing down on me as I see my attempts to change my life are thwarted. Take it away, oh God please take it away. I can't bear anymore. There has got to be another way to live.

The endless sadness that I covered over to get through the day. No one around me knowing the chasm of emptiness left by cruelty and neglect. Friends are always surprised to learn what I have lived through. The ones I felt safe enough to share with in my life so few and far between I often wondered if I would ever be truly known by another.

I did not know how long it would last. I did not know how often it would present itself in my life. If anyone had been able to tell me I wonder what I would have done. Would I have gone forth in healing? Would I have believed them? I doubt I would have thought it would be the same for me. I'm sure I would have thought that I was different. I was more capable of weathering the path set before me.

12/17/12

Damaged goods. Seriously, who came up with that term? Because I am human and have had different experiences than most people? I am not like this forever. It's a term signifying forever. Can't be changed. It is the ultimate in hopelessness. And goods? Am I for sale? A mere trinket to be traded?

What was traded? The soul and beliefs of one person over another. A belief that I was the property of another person. My beliefs and perceptions to be traded from health to something skewed and dismissed.

Was my heart something that could be ripped out of my body and stomped on? The jagged edges of a knife serrated in my chest. Sharp and gritty interactions which pass for intimacy. Words that leave an aftertaste in my mouth.

The love denied in reaction to protection of my family. How do you explain this love to others who prefer to view them as monsters? No matter what they've done to me over the years, I don't want to hurt them. Their behavior towards me doesn't excuse my potential to hurt them. I know how the world would view them and I love them enough not to put them through it. I don't want to hurt them. My whole life has been in response to this. What I say and don't say to others.

The love I have denied myself. I sit here totally terrified of your love. The love and clarity I see within your eyes to the depths of my soul. You see me and accept me as I am. Stripped of all my defenses. You read my mind and respond to the unasked questions I long to ask. The longing of decades float up in wonder of this time being answered. Am I safe? Will I be seen? Will the ripping tears through the visage of my soul start to mend with your love? Can I be known in all my wounds? Can I show you how hurt I have been? How much I have been shit upon?

I walk around with a vulnerability so raw it's amazing I can propel myself forward at all. I wasn't cared for enough to be loved. For the rape to stop. I wasn't worth anyone's time or value to be saved. And I am so afraid of having to show this to you.

Do I have to admit this to another person when it's been my most cherished secret? I have fought it and hid it and ignored it and shut it up. I never needed anyone else to shut me up because I've been doing such a fine job of it myself. How can I ever trust a man with all I've been through? I can't risk being that vulnerable again. What if I'm hurt that badly again? What if I'm cut to the core again? You're solid. You're accepting. You have firm boundaries. I don't want to hurt myself anymore with bad choices. Or in this case, foolish choices. Fantasies I make up. I will look at this and see what role you play in my healing. I will feel the fear and hope the appropriate man will someday appear.

I want a man to see how beautiful and incredible I am. I want a man to treat me with the respect I deserve. I want a man to cherish me and value me through and through. I want to learn to trust and accept help. I say yes to a relationship that allows all this to be so. I say yes.

12/26/12

After talking with my mom last night, I again waiver on writing about my experiences. I don't want to hurt her. She does mean well and loves me to the best of her ability. But what do you do when that isn't enough? It feels like such an insult to her. I love her and don't want to hurt her in the same way I've been hurt. But I also know I want rape and incest to be obliterated in my lifetime. How do I help accomplish that by being quiet?

It is because survivors don't speak out that it can continue. One reason I decided to heal was to explore how this can happen in a family let alone society. It has been difficult to do without fellow family members to talk about their experiences. Why do people stay silent? How does group mentality become the norm? How can one safely disrupt the status quo for the benefit of all? Or is the only option to join the martyr archetype and be crucified for standing up for one's beliefs?

How can incest become such a thing of beauty that it never happens again? How can light be shined upon it in such a way that it is understood and therefore becomes an option nevermore? Can humanity evolve to such a degree that rape or harm to another person is no longer tolerable? Idealistic notions, maybe, but I don't want to live any other way. That is intolerable to me.

12/31/12

I so love New Years. It is my time to look back and look forward. I look back at my past intention to love more and be loved more. It has been a year to test that.

I consider Doug the man I never dated. After his wife died, it was a possibility that we would date. I knew him and his daughter very well. Many people, myself included, thought it was a logical conclusion considering the relationship I had with Emily. I loved her and she loved me. It would be natural for me to become her stepmother. Though the fact that I was an nth degree of his wife and he couldn't handle her was a deterrent in my mind. I couldn't foresee a future of diminishing myself in order to make someone else happy.

Though I didn't know it at the time, he was within a month of dying. He told me he loved me and I hated it. I shrank away. He was in love with me and I knew there was no future with this relationship. Yet I was threatened by it. I didn't want it. Love was such an unknown to me that I couldn't conceive of it. Love had led to my greatest deception. My greatest despair. My greatest fear. I wasn't ready to face it.

So now he is gone. No longer a threat. Yet he beckons me from the other side to continue with my quest to love more and be loved. He can see all that I am and all that I struggle with and he challenges me to reach beyond my self-contained limits. You help me to see me more clearly and accept the beauty that lies within.

It is my intention for 2013: To willingly accept into my life all the goodness that God wills for me. In relation to love and work. It is time to accept my worth. And so it is.

2013

I saw a news program last night that showed a woman who had been sexually abused as a child by her mother and stepfather. As I watched it I said to myself, we're not all like that. We don't all become promiscuous or alcoholics or child abusers ourselves. Some of us get through it. Some of us do heal. Some of us do lead very productive lives. Some of us get to the point where we get to define ourselves as more than a forever damaged, to be pitied, pathetic, unloved whore who doesn't deserve to be loved and respected.

Some of us have relationships that are healthy and fulfilling. Some of us do know how to be in the world without lying and cheating. Some of us do have a great enough sense of self that we know not only who we are but what we have to share with the world.

Yes, I was abused but that act does not define who I am. I am more than that and I will not let the worst moments of my life define who I am. Those weren't my actions but the actions of someone else. I was manipulated for love. I had nothing to be ashamed of. I have gone on to live the best life I could. I have strived to grow and heal and to become a better person. It's my edge and my compassion. It's my knowledge of the horrors of humanity and my knowledge of what we, as individuals, can achieve with hope.

It is from this hope that I am changing my life. I quit my job without another one lined up. Crazy, maybe, but it's what I need to do for myself. I have been in recovery for 20 years now but it never goes away. I thought it would. I thought I would be done with it all at a certain point. I thought I could go back to normal. But a normal shall never be found again. I can never be the person I was before. I can never have the happy childhood back. Every year it's about integrating all the things I learn about myself into a new version of me.

2013

I pray silently with only God as my witness. I've never understood those who need to do a production for everyone to see. The closing of the eyes and the clasping of the hands. This might work for them but mine has always been quieter. I can pray without anyone around me even knowing it is taking place. I can only think this started as an early practice for me as I prayed to God to stop the rape. It was my way of escaping without my father knowing where I was going.

Through the years I have learned to listen to the quiet voice that comes through as guidance from above. It is quiet. There is no great demonstration of what is happening below the surface. It reminds me to remember little things like car keys or to speak to others. I usually don't understand the message. When I don't listen to the voice, it repeats itself. If I still don't listen, a gentle nudging occurs and I finally speak whatever is coming through in my mind. I give up what happens next. My only job is to speak it. Whether it is received or not is out of my control and frankly, none of my business.

Through the years when I have been at the ends of my wits, I would finally surrender my pain to something greater above. I knew I couldn't go on another moment with what had been assigned to me. I didn't have the strength to fight the reality that I saw. I was able to change my prayer from a wish for things to be different to an allowance for it to be taken from me. Desperation allowed the prayer to become a willingness for change. I was finally willing to see the situation or myself differently.

Every time I was able to surrender to this low, low point, a lightness was able to permeate my being that allowed the situation to be tolerated once more. The burden was lifted in a way never obtained by fighting it. It always occurred when I was able to bring the darkness of my feelings and pain to my full acknowledgment. I fully accepted what I was feeling or believing and knew into the depths of my heart and soul there had to be another way of seeing the situation. This wasn't the truth of who I really am.

I couldn't continue on in the same way, there had to be another way. This has been the most healing prayer that has ever come my way.

2013

My heart bursts open as I learn to take love in. I feel so much appreciation for myself and the grace of God. All the crap I have gone through to get me to this place of peace. How long it will last this time, only the years will tell. I appreciate my tenacity, my fight, my humor and my dedication.

Years of changing negative thoughts about myself by stopping them and saying, "I love you".

2/14/13

My mom sent me a Valentine's Day present. Once again I feel awful. I feel like an ungrateful daughter. I feel like the worst daughter in the world. How can I be writing this book for all the world to see? How do I explain the love I still feel for her? The part of me that still screams inside, I want my mom. How do I explain how I don't want to hurt her or my family? And I need to tell my story.

Will this end us for good? Will she stop caring for me? Buying gifts for me? Though it's never been what I most wanted, I do know it is how she knows to show love. I've accepted this for all these years but at what cost?

Once again I grieve for the mother I wanted but never got. And see another exercise in forgiving the mother I had and loving her through her flaws. I also have another opportunity to bring back a piece of the child that had needs and who wanted her life to be different. Who desperately wanted to be saved from the terror and confusion. I have another chance to let her know it wasn't her fault.

2013

I can now see that there was always a part of me that knew the abuse was wrong and it was this part that drove my career and education choices as I found another way of being in the world. One that didn't involve hurting others. I learned this through human history and historical figures. I knew the human behaviors that weren't fully acknowledged would get repeated in life. I can see the paths my life took that helped secure me enough as a person to cope with what life was bringing me.

In psychology it's referred to as your core self. I had strong enough of a core self established that I was able to get through the abuse with repression as one of my coping skills. I didn't need to spilt myself into totally different personalities like the survivors who use Dissociative Identity Disorder (formerly Multiple Personality Disorder) to cope. The feelings, thoughts and beliefs about the abuse and my life became different aspects of the core me. As I healed, I still needed to integrate these different aspects into the adult person I am now and they are different facets of my personality as is normal for all adults. Who I am at work is different than who I am while relaxing with friends.

I only went to a support group for a very short time at the beginning of my healing. I was in the emergency state as described in *The Courage to Heal*. It was soon apparent that I needed more intense help. I went to a therapy group for about a year. I chose a group at the time to help me be open, honest and vulnerable with others. A lot of my healing has been to choose a personal goal to work on and then find the situation in my life to assist me with reaching it. By doing this I learned to trust step-by-step.

As I would be thinking, feeling and doing certain things throughout the years, I would stop and ask myself how old I felt in the moment. When I figured the age out, I would then think, "three year old me needs this" or "five year old me wants that". While writing this book I have been craving and making homemade buttermilk pancakes quite frequently and I'm generally more of an egg breakfast person. After being curious about this, I realized the pancakes were making twelve year old me happy. I loved pancakes and french toast as a child. It's the little ways I continue to nurture and re-parent me throughout all my ages.

A lot of my recovery has been realizing and accepting that, for all intents and purposes, I'm generally just a normal person. Some insecurities and wounds are amplified but otherwise I have been living my life as others do. The general themes of my life are universal struggles. There have been times when I had to admit to myself that incest was just a fantastic and handy excuse for not doing something. Who could blame me for not succeeding when I was *an incest survivor?* Other times I've had to discover when the excuses were really areas where my development had become stunted and I needed to continue on with my growth.

It takes some getting to know me—or so I like to think—to see where the abuse still plays out in my life. With time people may notice I don't visit or talk about my family. When I do I keep it quite general. I have been a late-bloomer in my career as I gained confidence that I wasn't too screwed up to help another person. I will suddenly act quite contrary to how people usually experience me, others not understanding that I've been triggered by something. Comments or interactions that I would normally let roll off my back suddenly hurt me to the core. The wound is hit. I have my physical challenges. And for the most part, I don't date.

Examining my life, I have been able to identify certain conditions that helped me make it through with my core-self intact:

- I was a wanted pregnancy
- I was a girl after three boys
- The first year of my life was secure and my needs were met
- My mom did intervene with the abuse from the neighborhood boys and my one brother by telling me to stay away from them
- Mr. Roger's Neighborhood: He let me know there were adults, somewhere in the world, who understood a child's vulnerable emotions
- The kindness and understanding of my kindergarten teacher when I was crying because I didn't want to eat all my cake-sounds silly but its stayed with me all these years
- The stability of attending the same school for grades 1-8
- The more conscious parents of my schoolmates
- One of the summers before the rape started I would get up earlier than everyone else and I went to a neighbors house and we would sit on the couch while she listened to me
- The year the rape started, I was the teacher's pet at school
- I put the stress of the abuse into my physical body
- Enough interest, kindness and nurturing from various adults in my life as I grew up

- The rest of my childhood was stable enough. All my safety needs were more than taken care of and there was enough love, nurturance, acceptance and understanding. Maybe not my ideal version but something was there. I'm thinking of the joke: Other than that Mrs. Lincoln, how did you enjoy the play?

- Enough attitude, stubbornness and a dark sense of humor

As an adult starting the healing process, I vowed to myself that they had my childhood but I get my adulthood. I couldn't change anything that had happened in the past but I could go through the pain to live my life the way I wanted in the future. Especially in my 20s, I lived by the conviction of *no excuses*. If there was something in my life that I didn't like and it was within my capabilities to change the circumstances, I either made the change or shut up about it. Sometimes I had to live my *not yet*. There would be something I wanted to change but wasn't ready. By allowing myself the *not yet*, I had the time to work through my resistance and move forward when the time was right.

2013

Over the years I have had to wonder, when are the ruminations healing and when is it just picking at an old scab? Is this pain I haven't felt to completion or just an old sweater I put on as an excuse to avoid the world?

I look at Susan Lordi's sculpture of the adult holding the young child in an embrace that communicates; I am here for you, I've got you through your pain. I cry looking at it. It's pain that needs to be felt more. The twelve year old me is still in need of being heard, of being understood, of being loved. There is still more.

2013

Being part of the human race, I have a constant commentary running in my head regarding what is happening to me, around me and to others. They are only my perceptions of how I make sense of my world. As much as I'd like to think they are the right way to view the world, there are over 7 billion people on the planet also thinking they hold the one truly right version too.

I love the picture from the Indian fable involving the six blind men all feeling a different part of an elephant.* One has the trunk, the second the ear, the third the tusk, the fourth leg, the fifth side, and the last has the tail. They can all describe the elephant as they experience it but only the part they are holding. In our lives we must be able to know both the detail and the whole picture. And be willing to listen to another person's perspective from their viewpoint.

Healing and changing my perceptions through the years has allowed me to learn about *how* I think. Coming from an alcoholic and incestuous family, distorting my thinking is part of my survival skills. It takes a constant vigilance to find the distortions, challenge their accuracy and live in the present moment.

Depending which source you use, there are 8-15 or so distortions people commonly use when thinking.** I have been

---

* See appendix

** See appendix

guilty of them all. Learning them, recognizing them in myself and finding a new perception has led me to the conclusion that I don't need anyone else to be an asshole towards me. I can take care of that one on my own. My writing shows my struggle through them, sometimes from one day to the next.

They can also be thought of as projections. I am putting my filter of the world over my situation. I know one of them is running through my head when I am internally ranting and raving over something repeatedly. My interpretation happened and I can't let go of it. I need to hear the meaning I associated with the event. This is a great lesson in discernment.

Gaining control over them would be a big part of my definition of empowerment. My thinking affects my emotions which affects my thinking which affects my emotions, ad nauseam. Being willing to see a situation in a new way brings an acceptance and peace for myself.

Depending on the situation, I may need to accept the world as it is and not how I want it to be. I may need to stand up for myself. I may need to practice a new interpersonal skill. I may need to leave the situation. I may need to be more positive or take off my rose colored glasses. I may need to give someone else their responsibility back. I can ask the question of myself, what action or non-action will decrease the drama?

It was easier to see the distortions other people were running than it was to see my own. Through painful trial and error, I found it was best to clean up my own mess rather than pointing out another's mess. No one likes it when their mess is thrown back in their face while they are in the middle of it. At some point, in different situations, I was able to wonder what I needed to learn from my latest mess. I looked at it through the context of love. I love you, I love me and I love our mess as we work through it. By realizing I am projecting onto others or the situation, I can take the appropriate action needed to find my peace once again. This usually takes a matter of time and calming down enough to listen to what I am saying to myself. This step is enough; I can let go of the outcome. Whatever it is will be perfect for the healing of our souls.

2013

I have written it down. I have looked at it again. I have felt the feelings that never go away. I have let them come to the surface once again. I have listened to the voice that's been calling me through the years to write a book, to tell my story. The perfect storm of years of being silenced and diminished came together with the hormonal changes of mid-life and Emily hitting the ages I was when being raped. The emotions were coming more intensely and frequently. I wanted to look at them with hope that needing to recreate parallel situations from the messages of my family of origin would finally leave.

My external life mirroring the situations for the *shut up and take it* to scream in my face to the point where I could finally declare, NO! There are questions that will never be answered. This never will go away. I will have to look at it over and over again as all the pieces of my soul are recovered. The sadness will always accompany me. Sometimes deeply hidden away and other times begging for attention. Though it is less now, the sorrow of what was once done to a precious child will never fully heal. I will learn over and over how to live with it as the different stages of my life offer a new perspective. I will have another layer of the onion to chop.

After more than twenty years I finally know that. I have found a greater love and appreciation for myself and what I have been through by completing this task that's been niggling at me for years. Once again, I tell myself I have lived through hell and it is okay.

One day towards the end of the 1990s I was talking with a family friend who didn't know about the abuse. He told me my father had once made the comment, Dusana has her shit together, she just doesn't know it yet. I remember being surprised my dad had such insight into me.

As I look forward at the rest of my life and the path of recovery, I wonder if I will ever know it.

AFTERWORD

2013

As I healed through the 1990s, incest and childhood sexual abuse were becoming more open and prevalent in the media and societal consciousness. I didn't believe they were new issues and in fact had been around for centuries, if not millennium. As society attempted to heal different injustices, survivors were coming forward to express the effects the abuse has had on their lives. They were trying to find support and compensation for all the pain that was wrought through the actions of others.

As I watched this process, while going through my own, I was figuring out how I wanted to proceed with my healing. In the beginning I felt like a champion, a trailblazer. I was out for the cause and making changes. As I saw and heard the reactions from others, being so vocal became less safe for me.

It affected the way I chose to go through my recovery. Through the years I was hesitant to use my counselors and therapists for the retrieval of memories because of the platform regarding false memories. I admit that's a much nicer concept to believe in. I only used a counselor to walk me through speaking aloud the one memory in which I knew there was a chance I'd go insane retrieving it. The memory was coming up and being released from where it was stored in my body. I knew what it was before I even walked through the door of her office but it was such a disturbing memory I needed a witness to support me through fully admitting it to myself. Other than that time, I have been able to allow the memories to come into my consciousness on my own. Throughout all the years of my healing, I have spent less than 3 ½ years in therapy for this issue. Even during the two consecutive years in which I had the most intense therapy, my therapist once commented that what I mostly did was come into her office and recount the healing I had done on my own from the situations of my life. How I went through my healing and recovery is by no means the only way or the right way. It was what I knew how to do at the time. Every survivor needs to find his or her own path for healing and recovery.

I never wanted to be hospitalized as I dealt with the pain and confusion. Part of this decision was the stigma associated with mental illness and the other reason was I didn't want to give my family that out. I knew it would be easier for them to dismiss what I was saying if they could attribute it to a mental condition. They were already doing that and I felt an actual stay in a psychiatric hospital would give them proof that I was insane.

The feelings and mental confusion I was experiencing needed nurturance and care. I wished there was a place that was like what I dreamed a convalescent home would be. Somewhere I could stay and deal with emotions while someone else took care of cooking and cleaning. A place where someone was there to witness, validate and support me through the mess. As recently as this past fall I still wished for such a place. But I can only find that place within, it is not outside of me.

I dealt with the emotions at home after work and on the weekends. I took the opportunity at work to let a little bit of the emotions out in the bathroom while on break. From years of experience with healing, I can be feeling the emotions quite intensely one second and then shut them off, pull myself together and other people would never know I had just been crying.

I worked in the human services field and a part of it was learning about healthy interactions and teaching them to our clients. They were mostly new concepts for me too and I was able to see them in action as I adopted them into my repertoire. During professional developments I learned about: boundaries, assertive communication skills, active listening, alternatives to defenses, self-care and other important healing and recovery techniques.

As I used these practices with others I was also re-parenting the wounded child within myself. Giving to others has been the easy part for me as I'm more of a caretaker in life. It has been much harder for me to understand that I also deserved healthy interactions and treatment in my own life. I luckily have never gotten into an extremely abusive relationship. What I have had to work through mostly was learning and accepting the good treatment I deserved for no other reason than I am a human being. I sabotage relationships and situations when I am too happy. I was happy as a child and look where that got me. I certainly don't want to do that again so I will just move along.

Being treated poorly has been such a given for me that I don't recognize it when it first starts in relationships or work situations. When I do start to question the behavior, I will bring it up to the other person. They deny what I am seeing and I fail to recognize that I am repeating a relationship dynamic. I then question my perception of the interplay between us so as not to make the other person bad or wrong, I don't want to accuse them of doing something they aren't really doing. I assume I'm making too much of an issue or I am seeing the present through the filter of the past. I conclude I deserve it because of something I've done or believe. Until it happens again and again and again.

Early in my recovery, I had been given the *Autobiography in Five Chapters* by Portia Nelson. It has always stuck in my head and has been helpful for learning how to take responsibility for my life. My process was rarely that I learned about the other street and went directly there. The other street was my destination but my journey took me through the hole. I had to fall into it many times and in many different situations in order to learn the patterns that kept me walking down the same street over and over again. I had to find the meaning and belief I had adopted to make sense of the insanity in my life. The beliefs had become such dear friends to me that it took time to see the harm they were causing me and finally let them go. I've had to experience the hurt behind the belief and not jump ahead to the rainbows, unicorns and bunnies.

I've needed all these reenactments of the abuse dynamics in order to find my nugget of truth within the emotion. I hadn't found my truth in earlier reenactments for the issue to be complete. It always amazed me when I was able to get to the point of recognizing what was happening in my outer life as a reflection of what happened during my childhood and the meaning I had attributed to it in my inner life. The internal story of my life needed to be seen, heard and honored. Only after this could I let it go to find new experiences that met my standards for life. I've accepted that I will continue to need to do this as recovery lasts a lifetime. I've had the thought many times as I go through the process, *incest, the gift that keeps on giving*. I recently heard Dr. Drew also say this and it reassured me I wasn't just being dark and demented. It is the truth about this path of recovery.

This book is one sided. I'm sure the different members of my family would have their own version. I'm sure they would disagree with some of the perceptions I wrote about. I'm sure they would flat-out deny others.

Society vilifies pedophiles *and* these are still people I love. I choose not to spend time with them because I have found it's not a healthy environment for me to be in. The denial is too strong and my behavior towards myself becomes unhealthy. I've had to weigh what my brothers did as single acts or signs of monsterous behavior to come. I've had to weigh being present to be a protector for children and taking care of myself. I was vocal until the lack of support became too painful to tolerate and I became silent once more. I showed up until I could no longer play the game.

For years I wished we could acknowledge and talk about it. I wished we could understand it. I wished we could forgive each other for being in such an awful situation together and move on to new interactions. I wished there was a way to heal this horrendous epidemic and rid the planet of it forever.

I've had to grow older and become the age of my adult perpetrators. I've had to have a child in my life close enough to be a daughter. I've had to have the opportunity to really see the age I was when the rapes started. I've had the opportunity to utilize my peri-menopausal hormones to amplify the emotions that accompanied the thoughts of: How could a father do that to his daughter? How could someone do that to someone they loved? And I don't get it.

I have studied it. I have looked at it. I have felt it. I still don't understand it. I am grateful I don't. I am grateful I have the boundaries and can't imagine crossing them. I'm grateful I learned to love, to care and to forgive.

Is this finally the millionth piece? Is this finally it? I no longer think so. Pieces of the puzzle fall on the floor. They pop out of their place. There's another layer of the onion. The recipe calls for minced onions not chopped. The vase falls over and cracks. There will always be more to learn, to heal and to grow.

APPENDIX

JOHARI WINDOW	KNOWN BY SELF ↓	UNKNOWN BY SELF ↓
KNOWN BY OTHERS→	Part of the personality that both the self and other people are conscious of	Part of the personality that is known to others but the self is unconscious of
UNKNOWN BY OTHERS→	Part of the personality that the self knows but others are unaware of	Part of the personality that is unknown to both the self and others

Common Cognitive Distortions

Cognitive Distortions are the unconscious lies we tell ourselves about the world around us. They can also be called negative thinking, stinkin' thinkin', drama, Downer Debby, wetblanket, exaggerations, etc. They become so automatic we don't even realize they are running through our minds and distorting how we view life and therefore, our emotions. Aaron Beck first came up with the theory of cognitive distortions and then more recently, David Burns made it more mainstream by attaching names to the different types of distortions. Some have about one degree of separation between them.

1. **Filtering**: Removing all the positive aspects and concentrating on the negative. What you focus on grows so the negative becomes larger than life.

2. **Polarized Thinking** (Black and White): Shades of gray are not allowed. It's an all or nothing view of the world. Everything is great or everything is horrendous.

3. **Over-generalization**: Bumps in the road become mountains. The expectation for dismal outcomes clouds potential new situations.

4. **Jumping to conclusions**: We are all-knowing regarding how others think and feel, particularly towards us. Our information comes from their behavior and the under-lying meaning we attach to it.

5. **Catastrophizing**: Doom and gloom to the maximum. We are hyper-vigilant to the next disaster to befall us. Everything that happens in the world is going to come after us next.

6. **Personalization**: We are the center of the world and everything happening around us is somehow caused by

us. This can include comparing ourselves to others to see how we measure up.

7. **Control Fallacies**: Our loci of control is from the outside in. We see the world around us as causing our actions. (Powerless) The other option is to have the loci of control from the inside out. We are the cause of others state of being. (Guilty)

8. **Fallacy of fairness**: Good things should happen to good people and bad things should happen to bad people. We all have an inner gauge of what is fair and when others don't match it, our world is disrupted.

9. **Blaming**: It's your fault I feel or think this way. If only you'd change, then I would.…

10. **Shoulds**: You just need to listen to your internal monologue to learn your shoulds. It's the way life should be if everything and everyone were perfect. You'll never reach that bar.

11. **Emotional reasoning:** Our feelings are the ironclad truth. It's best to ignore the thoughts associated with the feelings or you run the risk of having to challenge the script you have of life.

12. **Fallacy of change**: Our inner salesman works to get the other person to change in whatever way best suits our needs for happiness. If only she'd.… I wish he'd.… When life.… then I'd be happy.

13. **Global labeling**: This takes #3 (over-generalizing) to the nth degree. All, every or always are common words associated with this distortion. You take one incident and

make a negative judgment about yourself, another, groups or events.

14. **Always being right**: Let's repeat after Dr. Phil. "Do you want to be right or do you want to be happy?" Last word, prove your point, see it my way, hear me out, etc.

15. **Heaven's reward fallacy**: God is watching over every single thing we do with *His* scorecard in hand waiting and determining how worthy we are to receive. What goes around, comes around. Bitterness takes over when the rewards don't arrive on our schedule.

Grohol, J. (2009). 15 Common Cognitive Distortions. *Psych Central*. Retrieved on April 11, 2013 from http://psychcentral. com/lib/2009/15-common-cognitive-distortions/

The Elephant and The Blind Men

This story is found in various spiritual traditions. Below is my re-telling of it as it relates to my use of it in the book.

Long ago, six blind men lived in a village. One day an elephant wandered into the village. The blind men had never experienced an elephant before and decided to use their hands to learn about it. Each blind man felt a different part of the elephant.

The first blind man held the leg of the elephant. He declared, "Ah, now I know. An elephant is like a pillar."

The second blind man clasped the tail. He stated, "You are mistaken my friend. The elephant is like a rope."

The third blind man touched the trunk. He laughed, "Fools. The elephant is like a tree branch swinging in the wind."

The fourth blind man felt the breeze around him as he moved with the ear. He concluded, "An elephant cools the air like a giant fan."

The fifth blind man pushed against the side of the elephant and knew, "The elephant is strong like a wall."

The sixth blind man clutched the tusk. He said, "You are all wrong. An elephant is like a pipe."

The six men held their ground as they shouted at each other their version of the elephant. How could their fellow men be so stupid? The more they shouted, the more distressed they became. Finally the village wise man walked by the scene. He noted what was happening and inquired, "why are you so upset?" They replied they could not agree on what an elephant is like. Each man told his version of the elephant to the wise man. After each had said his peace, the wise man let them know, "you are all right and you are all wrong. You are each touching a different part of the elephant. An elephant is made up of all that you described."

To know the elephant, you need to be able to accept there is more information than just the piece you are holding. Everyone has a different piece and some people can even see the whole elephant.

Retrieved on April 17. 2013 from www.**jainworld.com/ literature/story25.htm**

Disclaimer: This is the story of one survivor's experience and does not constitute the path other survivors need to take to heal or recover. The scope of this book is for the author to share her journey through life as an incest survivor. An appropriate use is for educational or reflective purposes. It is *not* to be used in place of necessary services provided by professionals trained in trauma.

If you have been the victim of incest, sexual abuse, sexual assault or other traumas; it is your responsibility to seek out professional help as needed for evaluation. Neither the author nor the publisher is responsible for the use of this book beyond the stated scope above.

BIBLIOGRAPHY

A Course in Miracles. Foundation for Inner Peace, Mill Valley, 1992.

Alter, Robert M. with Alter, Jane, *The Transformative Power of Crisis.* ReganBooks,New York, 2000.

Bass, Ellen and Davis, Laura, *The Courage to Heal.* Harper & Row, New York, 1988.

Cox, Fran and Cox, Louis, PhD., *A Conscious Life.* Conari Press, Berkeley, 1996.

Davis, Laura, *I Never Thought We'd Speak Again.* HarperCollins, New York, 2002.

Davis, Laura, *The Courage to Heal Workbook.* HarperCollins, New York, 1990.

De Angelis, Barbara, *How Did I Get Here.* St. Martin's Press, New York, 2005.

Graber, Ken, *Ghosts in the Bedroom.* Health Communications, Deerfield Beach, 1991.

Goldner, Diane, *Infinite Grace.* Hampton Roads, Charlottesville, 1999.

Hastings, Ann Stirling PhD., *Discovering Sexuality that Will Satisfy You Both.* The Printed Voice, Tiburon, 1993.

Johnson, Robert A., *He: Understanding Male Psychology*. Mills House, Berkeley, 1989.

Johson, Robert A., *She: Understanding Feminine Psychology*. Mills House, Berkeley, 1989.

Johnson, Robert A., *We: Understanding the Psychology of Romantic Love*. HarperCollins, New York, 1983.

Landolphi, Suzi, *The Best Love The Best Sex*. G.P. Putman's Son, New York, 1996.

Lee, Victoria, *Soulful Sex*. Conari Press, Berkeley, 1996.

Longaker, Chrintine, *Facinig Death and Finding Hope*. Doubleday, New York, 1997.

Remen, Rachel Naomi, *My Grandfather's Blessings*. Riverhead Books, New York, 2000.

Somé, Malidoma Patrice, *Ritual*. Swan Raven & Co. Portland, 1993.

Terr, Lenore, M.D., *Unchained Memories*. Basic Books, New York, 1994.

Welwood, John, *Love and Awakening*. HarperCollins, New York, 1996.

Williamson, Marianne, *A Return to Love*. HarperCollins, New York, 1992.

Wilson, Robert Anton, *Prometheus Rising*. Falcon Press, Phoenix, 1990.

READER'S GUIDE

What types of language signify that Dusana thought of the child within her as an object? What language signifies she is becoming a human being?

Which specific entries sound like a young child wrote them?

Do you believe in the theory of repressed memories? False memories?

How does the one-step forward, two-steps back show up in the process of recovery? How does it parallel your own process of personal development?

What are specific examples of the different cognitive distortions? Are some more common throughout the book? Is there a theme?

What are some of the universal themes in this book that don't only apply to incest survivors?

How is the struggle between the human being with earthly problems and the spiritual being who can transcend it all repeated throughout the book? Does it get resolved?

Do you think incest is an earthly problem or a spiritual journey? Is there anything this relationship dynamic could be teaching us for evolutionary growth?

Do you have safety nets in your life? What do you imagine would happen if you cut them?

Is there a specific poem that speaks to your own healing journey? How?

In what ways would you make different choices regarding Dusana's family?

What do you imagine would have to happen for incest to stop?

How do the internalized beliefs regarding why Dusana thinks the abuse happened play out in her life? What are the long-term effects of the abuse for Dusana?

Besides the title, Chopping the Onion, what other metaphors are used for healing?

Is there anyone in your life who you have wondered if they might be a survivor of incest?

What would you do if a sibling came to you and told of getting memories of childhood incest?

Is Dusana insane? A victim? A survivor? A heroine? An idealist? How?

ABOUT THE AUTHOR

Dusana Michaels has spent over 20 years in the process of recovering from childhood incest. In addition to her personal experience, she has a M.A. in counseling and has interwoven her professional experience throughout her journey. She draws upon her sense of humor and spiritual connections to find the next step on her path. Dusana lives in Denver, CO and looks to the mountains for inspiration and gratitude.